Teen Mental Health in an Online World

of related interest

The Mental Health and Wellbeing Workout for Teens
Skills and Exercises from ACT and CBT for Healthy Thinking
Paula Nagel
Illustrated by Gary Bainbridge
ISBN 978 1 78592 394 4
eISBN 978 1 78450 753 4

Teen Yoga For Yoga Therapists
A Guide to Development, Mental Health and
Working with Common Teen Issues
Charlotta Martinus
Foreword by Sir Anthony Seldon
ISBN 978 1 84819 399 4
eISBN 978 0 85701 355 2

A Multidisciplinary Handbook of Child and Adolescent
Mental Health for Front-line Professionals, Third Edition
Nisha Dogra, Andrew Parkin, Fiona Warner-Gale and Clay Frake
ISBN 978 1 78592 052 3
eISBN 978 1 78450 309 3

Cyberbullying and E-safety
What Educators and Other Professionals Need to Know
Adrienne Katz
ISBN 978 1 84905 276 4
eISBN 978 0 85700 575 5

Digital Kids
How to Balance Screen Time, and Why it Matters
Martin L. Kutscher, MD
ISBN 978 1 78592 712 6
eISBN 978 1 78450 296 6

Cyberbullying
Activities to Help Children and Teens to Stay Safe in a
Texting, Twittering, Social Networking World
Vanessa Rogers
ISBN 978 1 84905 105 7
eISBN 978 0 85700 228 0

Working with Anger and Young People
Nick Luxmoore
ISBN 978 1 84310 466 7
eISBN 978 1 84642 538 7

Teen Mental Health in an Online World

Supporting Young People around their Use of
Social Media, Apps, Gaming, Texting and the Rest

Victoria Betton and **James Woollard**

Jessica Kingsley *Publishers*
London and Philadelphia

First published in 2019
by Jessica Kingsley Publishers
73 Collier Street
London N1 9BE, UK
and
400 Market Street, Suite 400
Philadelphia, PA 19106, USA

www.jkp.com

Library of Congress Cataloging in Publication Data
Names: Betton, Victoria, author. | Woollard, James, author.
Title: Teen mental health in an online world : supporting young people around
    their use of social media, apps, gaming, texting and the rest / Victoria
    Betton and James Woollard.
Description: London ; Philadelphia : Jessica Kingsley Publishers, 2019. |
    Includes bibliographical references and index.
Identifiers: LCCN 2018020750 | ISBN 9781785924682 (alk. paper)
Subjects: LCSH: Social work with teenagers. | Mentally ill
    teenagers--Services for. | Internet and teenagers--Psychological aspects.
    | Teenagers--Mental health.
Classification: LCC HV1421 .B48 2019 | DDC 362.20835--dc23
LC record available at https://lccn.loc.gov/2018020750

British Library Cataloguing in Publication Data
A CIP catalogue record for this book is available from the British Library

ISBN 978 1 78592 468 2
eISBN 978 1 78450 852 4

Printed and bound in Great Britain

Contents

Acknowledgements

Victoria would like to thank her teenagers Molly, Ruby and Asa who have put up with many questions and conversations about their use of digital technologies over the course of writing this book.

A note about terminology

In this book we use a number of terms that we explain here.

This book is aimed primarily at anyone working with teenagers who have mental health problems. You may be working in health, education, social work, the criminal justice system, or elsewhere. We use the word **practitioner** as a general term to cover these sorts of roles. This book is not specifically intended for mental health practitioners, although many of our case studies and interviews are with professionals who have expert knowledge and experience in this field.

Whilst this book is not specifically orientated towards **parents** and **carers**, we hope that it will be of interest to any adults who look after or who are connected informally with young people who have mental health problems.

Throughout the book we refer to a number of different terms to describe aspects of the internet. We use the term **digital tools** or **technologies** to refer to mobile applications (apps) that sit on smart devices. We use the term **social media** to describe platforms whereby people create and exchange content online. We use the phrase **internet of things** to refer to sensors and wearables that connect to the internet. When we use the term **internet** we are using it as a catch-all for online information and interactions.

We understand that terms used to describe mental distress are problematic and often contested. In this book we have avoided focusing on specific diagnoses or medicalised language except where relevant to the point we are making. We use the phrase **mental health problems** as a general term which we hope will be meaningful to practitioners who work in a range of settings beyond health care. We sometimes use the phrase **vulnerable teens** because the Children's Commissioner has included experience of mental health problems as an aspect of vulnerability amongst children and young people (Bright, 2017).

We challenge the notion that young people are **digital natives** – a term commonly employed to describe those who have grown up with the internet. Like a number of academics in the field, we believe this is not a useful way to think about young people's use of the internet (Jenkins, Ito and Boyd, 2017; Livingstone, 2014). The phrase tends to obfuscate the nuances and subtleties as well as the diversity of online behaviours we have found. It also assumes that adults, as supposed **digital immigrants**, have nothing to offer their counterpart natives. We do not believe this to be the case and find it an oversimplification which does not help adults feel resourceful in helping young people in respect of their engagement with the internet. We believe it is critical that practitioners helping young people with mental health problems take responsibility for understanding how they use the internet. This can only be achieved through an inquiring orientation rather than a passive mindset.

Chapter 1

Introduction

What if we approached the internet as a resource to be deployed rather than solely as a problem to be solved (Jenkins *et al.,* 2017)? What if we shifted our focus from the deficits of young people's online lives to an asset-orientated approach which seeks to identify young people's strengths and how we can enhance them? And what would this mean for practitioners working with young people who have mental health problems? Perhaps there are ways to make sense of young people's connected lives that enable us to be better and more effective practitioners. Perhaps we can focus our efforts on creating a society in which young people can thrive online and develop better mental health and wellbeing as a result. In this book we combine the voices and lived experiences of young people with what the evidence tells us about this important topic. Young people's points of view often get drowned out in the melee of popular media commentary about digital media and so we have endeavoured to put them at the centre of this book – generating insights into their attitudes, motivations and concerns.

As digital technologies increasingly permeate our everyday lives, it is imperative that practitioners seek to understand what this means for vulnerable teens. This imperative is born out of a significant shift in teen behaviours whereby young people imperceptibly blend and weave together their online and offline existence. Digital media provide an emerging context for growing up that is unfamiliar to Generation X (who were born between the early sixties and early eighties). If as practitioners we fail to grasp this emergent digital sphere, we will be less equipped to offer effective support; we may say and do things that have a negative impact on the very young people we are there to help. Rather than seeking to avoid that which we do not fully understand, as practitioners we should embrace a courageous vulnerability by stepping into the reality of young people's connected lives and seeking to understand it from their point of view.

Much existing research focuses on the risks posed by digital media to young people and practitioners alike. Popular discourse is often characterised by a moral panic in which the internet is conceptualised as essentially harmful and needing to be contained and controlled (Common Sense, 2016; Gabriel, 2014). Adult views about young people's online behaviours, typically characterised by concerns about risk and antisocial behaviours, dominate public debate and crowd out the lived experience of teens (Third *et al.*, 2014). Adolescent years are a time of expanded internet use along with developmental traits such as increased propensity for risk-taking, impulsivity, sensation-seeking and sexual interest. It is for this reason that we believe a focus on the connected lives of vulnerable adolescents is an important subject for practitioners to explore and understand.

In this book we focus specifically on the connected lives of teens and we investigate how practitioners can leverage digital technologies to promote resilience and wellbeing in young people, whilst understanding and managing associated risks. In doing so, we draw on both empirical evidence and firsthand accounts from our conversations with young people. A global research project into children's digital rights (Third *et al.*, 2014) found that young people overwhelmingly experience the internet as a powerful and positive influence in their day-to-day lives:

> Children see digital media as crucial to their rights to information, education and participation. By engaging with digital media, they learn new skills and develop their talents; they become informed citizens of the world who can contribute meaningfully to their communities; and they foster friendships, family ties and a sense of community and belonging. These things are important to their resilience and wellbeing. (Third *et al.*, 2014, p.12)

Through interviews and case studies, we show how teens are using social media, digital technologies and the internet in creative and imaginative ways to manage their mental health and improve their wellbeing. We illuminate nuanced and diverse online practices which challenge what can be an oversimplified dichotomous narrative of good versus bad. As Professor Simon Wesley, previous president of the Royal College of Psychiatrists, asserts:

> I am sure that social media plays a role in unhappiness, but it has as many benefits as it does negatives. We need to teach children how to cope with all aspects of social media – good and bad – to prepare them for an increasingly digitised world. There is real danger in blaming the medium for the message. (quoted in Campbell, 2017)

If a practitioner's task is to help young people become more self-aware and resilient, then what is it we need to consider in respect of the internet (Barth, 2015)? Teens who have grown up with the internet are mostly focused on what it means to enter the social and adult world, developing and sustaining relationships with their peers. For them, technology is in the background and is a given (Boyd, 2014). Indeed, when teens talk about their conversations it often doesn't even occur to them to refer to the medium for that exchange whether it be face to face, on Instagram or via Snapchat (Coleman *et al.,* 2017). In contrast, adults have more freedom, and experience in, engaging with a range of public environments and so are more likely to have technology at the forefront of their minds (Boyd, 2014). There is perhaps a subtle but significant difference in emphasis between that which is a concern to teens' connected lives and that which is a primary concern to adults.

Both young people and adults hold parts of the digital jigsaw between them and both have something to offer in making sense of the emerging digital public sphere. It seems amazing to think that Facebook was launched just thirteen years ago and now has 2.06 billion monthly active users worldwide. Massive tech giants such as Google, Facebook and Amazon are relatively new companies but hold massive sway over our everyday lives and in many ways they mediate our everyday realities. Recent revelations about how the British firm Cambridge Analytica harvested Facebook data for political campaigns shone a light on shady practices and raised widespread public concern about how our data is being used and what this means for civil society and democracy. We will return to these themes throughout the book.

The term 'digital natives' is often used to describe those who have grown up with the internet. However, this is not necessarily the most helpful way of thinking about this subject, insofar as it assumes that young people are essentially knowledgeable and older people are essentially ignorant about the internet – as we shall see, the reality is more nuanced and complicated than that. This is a present and a future to be understood, negotiated and navigated – a shared endeavour for both teens and adults alike. Whilst social media platforms may come and go, we focus on underlying principles and approaches that we believe are constant. We have approached the writing of this book in the spirit of cooperative inquiry; we do not have all the answers, but we are curious and we are eager to help practitioners who wish to support teens to develop digital resilience in their connected lives.

A mixed methods study of mental health practitioners found that many are enthusiastic about the role of the internet in supporting people for whom they care. However, they also identified a wide range of barriers, such as worries about privacy and risk, poor infrastructure and draconian organisational policies (Schueller, Washborn and Price, 2016). Our intention is to promote a curious mindset on the part of practitioners, which will better equip you to understand this emerging landscape and enable you to offer effective and informed care and support to young people. We hope this book makes a small contribution to supporting a workforce with the right mix of skills, competencies and experience to help young people with mental health problems in an increasingly digital world.

The book comprises a review of evidence alongside in-depth interviews with teens and focus groups. Young people's lived experience is at the heart of this book. One focus group was undertaken with teens who are members of the Future in Mind group, which works mental health commissioners in Leeds. Another focus group took place with Black, Asian and minority ethnic teens who are volunteers at Speaker's Corner in Bradford. All our participants were between 14 and 18 years of age and comprised a broad ethnic and gender mix. Almost all the young people we spoke with had personal experience of mental health problems. We also draw on participatory design work that mHabitat has undertaken with children's mental health services alongside experience of mental health practitioners.[1] We are grateful to everyone who took the time to share their views and expertise.

Why teens, digital and mental health?

One in ten children has a mental health problem for which they need support or treatment. The prevalence of mental health problems has increased over the last decade and there is increased demand on mental health services (Grist, Porter and Stallard, 2017). The 2015–2016 Childline annual report states that mental health issues are the main reason why young people contact the charity, with one in three counselling sessions focused on this topic. The charity is experiencing increases in the most serious mental health

---

1   www.wearemhabitat.com

problems, with 19,000 counselling sessions being delivered to young people thinking about or planning suicide during 2015–2016 (Childline, 2016).

Only half of the young people who would benefit from specialised mental health treatment actually receive these services (Ye *et al.*, 2014) and for some the relative anonymity of the internet along with its always-on availability is a more acceptable way to find out information than via a health professional (Gray *et al.*, 2005). Mariam, one of our interviewees, exemplifies this point when she describes the value of the internet from her point of view:

> I feel like, by using the internet, making apps for people, that can talk about their problems, or using websites where people can talk about their problems. I think that's important, because a lot of people suffer in silence, which leads to horrible things.

Mental health problems can range from depression or anxiety through to more long-lasting and severe experiences which can be highly disruptive and frightening for young people and families. Mental health problems can result in young people doing less well at school and are also associated with behaviours that pose a risk to health, such as smoking, drug and alcohol abuse and risky sexual behaviour (NHS England, 2015). The particular vulnerabilities of children and young people with mental health problems require that careful thought is given to the possibilities and the challenges associated with digital technologies.

There is evidence that the internet can have negative effects for young people's mental health and wellbeing in a number of domains. One study identified three specific areas in which young people aged 10–15 report lower life satisfaction as a result of their use of internet: the negative impact of making social comparisons with others through the posting of selective and idealised images; 'finite resources', in other words feeling like you are wasting time on the internet over other activities which may afford more enjoyment; and the inability to escape from bullying when it takes place online as a result of the 'always-on' nature of online social networks (McDool *et al.*, 2016). If it is for this reason that there is a role for practitioners to help guide young people into thinking critically and resourcefully about how they use the internet as well as the amount of they spend time online balanced with other activities. In Chapter 8 we focus on how practitioners can have helpful conversations with young people that enable them to make mindful choices about their connected lives.

The book will focus on the interplay between child developmental factors and the impact of external factors in influencing young people's use of the internet. We also take a rights-based approach to considering the digital skills and confidence we need to help teens develop in order to navigate their online lives successfully. We make the case that young people's relationship to the internet is as much an issue of technology as a manifestation of issues of contemporary life such as social and parental pressures (Boyd, 2014). We believe that practitioners have a vital role to help young people develop resilience in respect of their internet use and that this can only be achieved through an inquiring and nurturing approach.

Our review of the evidence in relation to teenagers' use of the internet shows a mixed and emergent picture in which both positive and negative effects can be found.

What is clear is that the internet is an increasingly a core part of teenagers' lives and this creates an imperative for parents and practitioners to keep themselves up-to-date and informed. As Rafla and colleagues argue:

> Professionals are at risk of being out of touch with their patients and missing online behaviours that may exacerbate pre-existing vulnerabilities and psychiatric diagnoses. They also risk breaching professionalism standards if not informed about how to incorporate technology into practice. The Internet and digital technology play an essential role in the knowledge, skills and attitudes of the twenty-first century mental health professional working with adolescents. (Rafla, Carson and DeJong, 2014, p.8)

An introduction to book chapters

We begin our exploration of the connected lives of teens with mental health problems by exploring online social networks. In Chapter 2 we introduce popular social media platforms, explore recent research about teens and the internet, and focus on more specific research related to young people with mental health problems. We interweave this evidence with insights and reflections from young people with whom we have had conversations. We set out common themes that young people shared with us about their experiences of social media. We go on to examine the evidence about the potentially positive, negative or neutral effects of online social networks on young people's mental health, which are mixed and sometimes contradictory. We conclude with a summary of common parent and carer responses to teens' use of the internet.

In Chapter 3 we consider online creative and civic participation as a means of developing self-esteem and self-efficacy. We suggest how practitioners may help people harness the opportunities that digital media present to help young people develop resilience. We investigate the role of vlogging and YouTubers in exploring mental health issues, and the role of digital media as a tool for distraction from troubling emotions. We consider how practitioners can help young people make use of their smart devices to access convenient and discrete materials which they can use as a tool for distraction, as part of their care and support.

We then explore what the evidence has to say in relation to digital mental health technologies (such as apps and websites) which are seen by many as a way of providing scalable tools to widen access and meet demand for care and support. We explore professional and peer-to-peer online support platforms and what the evidence tells us about their effectiveness and we go on to consider emerging technologies such as artificial intelligence and virtual reality.

In Chapter 4 we investigate social media, digital technologies and the internet through the lens of bio-psycho-social child development. We explore how the internet provides an important context for the normal stages of teen development, characterised by conflict, transgression and change, to be played out. We look at the evidence in order to understand what may be helpful and harmful, along with the sorts of issues that practitioners ought to be addressing when supporting teens with mental health problems. We present a typology of child development, internet behaviours and risk as a useful tool for practitioners to understand what they may need to look out for when supporting teens at different stages of adolescence.

We go on to address two core aspects of child development and the implications for internet use. The first is the drive towards autonomy, in which digital media can both facilitate and constrain independence, depending on how it is employed by teens and their caregivers. The second is the importance of self presentation and identity, in which young people are increasingly influenced and affected by social comparison with peers.

In Chapter 6 we explore a range of adverse experiences that teens may encounter online. They include exposure to pornography, bullying, unwanted contact from strangers, troubling content and sharing of sexually explicit images. They also include either witnessing or engaging in self-harming behaviours and sharing suicidal thoughts online. Each topic area has a substantial literature related to it and this chapter aims to simply provide practitioners with an overview and key insights into the evidence with regard to adverse effects. As with the rest of the book, we approach the theme of adverse effects by seeking a balanced understanding of the risks alongside the benefits of digital media in young people's lives.

We set out a number of conceptual frameworks for understanding the types of risks young people face online, alongside the factors which may make some young people more vulnerable than others. We also explore the protective factors which help young people manage those risks and find that, perhaps rather counterintuitively, those who are *less* exposed to both opportunities and risks tend to be more negatively affected when they do have adverse experiences online (Third *et al.*, 2014). We provide examples of how some young people are harnessing online social networks to find information, engage in peer support, and challenge negative stereotypes through their own campaigns. We consider how practitioners can help teens anticipate, minimise and manage adverse experiences online.

In Chapter 5 we investigate digital literacy and eHealth literacy, and explore how digital skills and confidence are key to participation in contemporary life and an important facet of managing mental health problems. We examine issues of access to digital media along with differentiated usage of the internet which is influenced by a number of demographic characteristics. Along with insights from our conversations with young people, we consider how young people access information and discuss mental health online. We introduce a number of conceptual frameworks which help illuminate the factors associated with eHealth literacy, including the importance of being able to evaluate information and the role of practitioners in encouraging critical thinking.

In Chapter 7 we investigate the theme of young people's digital rights and introduce a number of frameworks which aim to promote resilience online. We believe that a rights-based approach to thinking about young people's online practices is a helpful one – this orientation recognises that adults, and their perspectives, often dominate public debates about digital rights and responsibilities which affect young people. A rights-based approach not only includes the right for young people to express their views about digital technologies and the internet, but also the right to form those views in ways which are not dominated by adult discourse. We explore how practitioners can harness a rights-based approach to the internet which promotes positive mental health in teens and which fosters resilience for young people affected by mental health difficulties.

We explore the role of parents and practitioners in role modelling good digital citizenship and investigate the impact of over-sharing or *sharenting* by parents and the implications for young people. We go on to consider the ways in which data produced through activities such as online searches are used by digital media providers and what the implications are for teens searching for mental health information and using wearable devices and sensors. These issues raise questions and concerns for our privacy as citizens and for civil society that we need to engage with as citizens. The ways in which we inadvertently generate data, and how they are used by companies, is a facet of digital literacy that we should endeavour to equip ourselves with both as practitioners and as citizens. It is only by developing the knowledge ourselves that we can gently guide young people towards making active and responsible choices regarding their data as a component of their connected lives.

In Chapter 8 we move on to exploring how practitioners can have helpful conversations with young people about their connected lives using a simple three-step model. We think about how practitioners can take a holistic approach to teens' use of digital media and promote a peer-based approach to teens making sense of how they can exploit the positives of the internet whilst navigating the downsides. We promote an approach to the internet whereby parents are encouraged to role model positive online behaviours and we suggest that practitioners should aim to do the same. We go on to propose an approach for harnessing the civic and creative opportunities that the internet affords and which can build resilience and positive mental health and wellbeing amongst young people. We employ a conceptual framework associated with self-determination to set out how practitioners can help young people develop intrinsically motivated self-regulation in their use of the internet, along with a range of practical strategies for working constructively and helpfully with young people in respect of their connected lives. Finally we examine how practitioners can support young people to hone their critical skills in searching for and appraising information online; we provide practitioners with simple guidance to appraise digital tools and services for mental health.

In Chapter 9 we move on from a focus on practitioners to consider the implications of digital media for services and organisations. Many services are struggling to work out how they can leverage digital technologies to better meet the needs of young people they aim to help. We believe that there is currently a massive disconnect between the blended on/offline lives of young people and their mostly analogue contact with services. Whilst this is changing, it is still the case that even texting, the most ubiquitous of technologies, is not routinely used as a communication tool in many services.

We explore how services and organisations can set the conditions to help young people develop digital skills and resilience; to support practitioners to develop digital capabilities; to deploy digital tools that facilitate communication with young people; to design new services or redesign existing services with digital as a key enabler; and to ensure an informative and relatable internet presence that increases access and acceptability of services to young people. We conclude by considering issues for commissioners and policy makers.

Conclusion

Throughout the book we combine evidence from the field with lived experience elicited through firsthand accounts from teens. We draw on our experience in practice and our conversations with practitioners. There are limitations to this book – it is a small-scale, qualitative study that endeavours to generate insights from teens about their experiences of the internet and does not claim to be a more substantial research study. Whilst we do touch on inequalities throughout the book, there is substantially more work to be done in order to understand the lived experience of teens who face discrimination due to their backgrounds, such as Black, Asian and minority ethnic young people. This is a highly emergent field, and there is much more work to be done to understand the implications of the internet for young people, parents and carers, practitioners, and wider civil society. We hope this book makes a small contribution to the literature through the lens of digital technologies and mental health.

Chapter 2

Social media, digital technologies and the internet

Introducing teens' connected realities

Introduction

In this chapter we provide an introduction to online social networks along with insights into the connected lives of teens. We review evidence about teens and the internet, along with more specific research related to young people with mental health problems. We interweave the evidence with insights from young people with whom we had conversations whilst researching this book. We found much of what they told us resonated with the available evidence, and that occasionally they shared experiences which we had not come across before. We therefore hope that, in this chapter, we add to the emerging knowledge base of teens' connected lives, through the voices of young people themselves.

Whilst writing this chapter we have kept in mind those practitioners who are less familiar with platforms that are popular amongst teens, such as (at the time of writing) Instagram and Snapchat. Throughout the chapter we highlight particular facets of the internet, which can be experienced as both positive and problematic by teens with mental health problems. We introduce the reader to ways in which young people typically blend their online and offline lives in a mode of communication sometimes referred to as *connected presence* – characterised by a sense of perpetual contact with friends and family (Licoppe, 2004). As Matt, who is 19 and has lived with anorexia throughout his teens, simply puts it:

> Being able to just talk to a mate by tapping a few buttons, just helps you to feel more connected.

What does connected presence mean for young people and their families? We believe that there is a need to move away from dichotomous thinking about online and *real life* insofar as this simply doesn't reflect young people's lived experience. The notion that social media are distinct to the material conditions of everyday reality is one that is deeply embedded in our thinking – particularly for those of us who were not brought up with the internet (Van Doorn, 2011). It is not uncommon for parents to bemoan that, by virtue of being continually attached to their phones, teens are somehow detached from real life. Matt, like many of his peers, rejects this notion and wishes his parents would be less concerned about when and how he uses the internet. Whilst his parents just see his phone, Matt sees beyond the device to the wide range of activities it enables him to perform:

> My parents, they often seem worried about how much I use my phone and stuff. Dad's like, 'You've got a phone addiction'. [But] I guess it depends on what you're doing on your phone, because if it is just mindlessly scrolling through Facebook all the time,

then obviously I reckon that would have some bad effects on you. If you're talking to mates, there's that view that it should be a supplement and not a replacement, but talking to mates is kind of helpful, and researching things and Googling things that are interesting to know. I can't see why that would have any bad effects on you.

The urban acronym IRL (in real life) suggests that what takes place online is somehow not properly real and, by extension, less significant than that which takes place offline. However, as we will illustrate in this chapter, social media provide a meaningful public sphere in which teens congregate and through which they engage in many and varied activities; just as rife with social norms and conventions as the physical haunts of the bus stop or school playground. For young people, chatting on social media is just as much real life as having a conversation with a friend in the school canteen. Two friends may start their morning chatting on FaceTime whilst getting ready for school, meet in person at break, and message each other on WhatsApp on the way home – blended connectedness throughout the day.

It is for all the reasons above that, for those of you who are instinctively sceptical about digital media, there is a need to suspend judgement and step into the everyday reality of teens, in order to better understand how they seamlessly weave their online and offline existence. We hope this chapter will help you develop further insights and bring critical perspectives to this ever-shifting online public sphere. It is through deepening our understanding and critical reflection that practitioners can seek to optimise our effectiveness when offering help and support to vulnerable teens. The borders between online and offline are porous; teens told us throughout our conversations with them that *social media matter*, and if they matter to teens, they must matter to practitioners too.

Introducing online social networks

Online social networks, sometimes called social media, are websites and applications that enable users to create and share content and to communicate with each other. The distinction between social media and other types of digital media is increasingly blurred; for example, many video gaming sites are now internet-based and incorporate social networking elements (Frith, 2017). Social media are constantly evolving, with once dominant platforms such as MySpace fading away to be replaced by Facebook which in turn is losing a younger audience to Snapchat. Whilst Facebook remains a ubiquitous social networking platform, its popularity is decreasing amongst teens – 52 per cent of 12- to 15-year-olds are still most likely to consider Facebook their main social media profile but this has fallen considerably since 2013, when 87 per cent of 12- to 15-year-olds considered Facebook their main site (Ofcom, 2016b). Social media are characterised by fluidity and emergence both in terms of platforms and practices. Many social media platforms allow multiple activities that span private and public communication practices – from private messaging and video calling through to posting to a public profile and livestreaming video.

A report from the OECD found that participating in social networks is the most popular online leisure activity for teens, followed by chatting online (OECD, 2015). Around three-quarters of 12- to 15-year-olds in the UK have a social media profile, with just under a third saying they access their main social media account more than ten times a day. Below is a brief description of some of the most popular social networking platforms used by teens at the time of writing. The following sites and descriptions are taken from NSPCC's NetAware website[1] and are just a selected few of the 39 social media platforms they describe:

---

1   www.net-aware.org.uk

- **Facebook and Facebook Messenger** – Facebook is a social network which lets you create a page about yourself. You can add friends, write on people's pages, share photos and videos including live videos. Facebook Messenger allows you to instant message in group chats or one to one. Facebook allows livestreaming.

- **ASKfm** – a social networking site where you can ask other people questions. You can choose to ask the question anonymously.

- **Instagram** – a picture and video sharing app. Users can post content and use hashtags to share experiences, thoughts or memories with an online community. You can follow your friends, family, celebrities and even companies on Instagram. Instagram allows livestreaming.

- **Kik** – an instant messaging app. It lets you create your own username and message others without using your mobile number. You can share photos, organise events, share games, news and anything of interest to you from the internet.

- **Snapchat** – an app that lets you send a photo, short video or message to your contacts. The 'snap' appears on screen for up to 10 seconds before disappearing, although it can be screenshotted (a photograph taken of the image on the screen). There's also a feature called Snapchat Story that lets you share snaps in a sequence for up to 24 hours.

- **YouTube** – allows you to watch, create and comment on videos. You can create your own YouTube account, create a music playlist, and even create your own channel, which means you will have a public profile. YouTube allows livestreaming.

- **Twitter** – a messaging service that lets you post public messages called tweets. These can be up to 280 characters long. As well as tweets, you can send private messages and post pictures/videos. Brands, companies and celebrities can also have Twitter accounts and Twitter can be used as a source of news and information.

- **WhatsApp** – an instant messaging app which lets you send messages, images and videos to friends. You can have one-to-one and group conversations.

- **Tumblr** – a social networking site that lets you share text, photos, quotes, links, audio clips, slideshows and videos. You can customise your page and share other people's posts. You can also send private messages. Tumblr allows livestreaming.

- **Musical.ly** – allows you to create, share and discover short videos. You can share videos with friends or with other Musical.ly users.

There is a wide range of gaming platforms that are popular with teens. Here are just a few, as highlighted by the NSPCC NetAware website:

- **Pokémon GO** – allows you to find Pokémon characters and catch them to add to your collection. The map is based on where you are standing (in real life).

- **FIFA Mobile** – a gaming app where you can build and manage your own football team.

- **Clash of Clans** – a combat game where players build their own armies (clans) and battle against other armies from around the world. You can join forces with other armies or battle against others on your own.

- **Fortnite** – an online game with up four players who cooperate on missions on randomly-generated maps to collect resources, build fortifications that help fight storms and protect survivors. Players gain rewards through missions to improve their hero characters, support teams and take on more difficult missions.

Whilst each social media platform shapes how users participate in subtly different ways, there are some shared facets across all of them which are qualitatively different to physical public spaces where teens come together. In particular, four characteristics of social media have been described by Danah Boyd, an American researcher into teens' use of social media:

- **Persistence** – the durability of online expressions and content.

- **Visibility** – the potential audience who can bear witness.

- **Spreadability** – the ease which which content can be shared.

- **Searchability** – the ability to search for and find content (Boyd, 2014).

These four characteristics shape three dynamics which inform how people interact on social media:

- **Invisible audiences** – we can see who is in earshot in offline environments but when we are online our audiences may be invisible to us and we do not know what point of view they have.

- **Context collisions** – social media can collapse contexts that we can more easily keep separate offline (for example, our friends and our parents).

- **Public and private convergence** – in our offline lives our homes might be considered private and everything else public. We can be in the privacy of our homes whilst participating in public through social media. On the internet privacy is mostly about what we are able to control (Rheingold, 2012).

Each of these characteristics and dynamics carries opportunities and challenges which young people negotiate in their day-to-day lives. When considering teens with mental health difficulties, there are specific affordances of the internet that can have both positive and adverse effects. We go on to consider these in the remainder of this chapter.

How and where are teens accessing the internet?

With the rise of mobile devices and smartphones, teens are increasingly likely to access the internet privately, away from the gaze of adults. The average age for a child in the UK to get their first smartphone is 12 years old (Frith, 2017) with 83 per cent of 12- to 15-year-olds owning a smartphone (Ofcom, 2017) and just over half owning a tablet. Twelve- to 15-year-olds say they spend on average 21 hours per week online and that their mobile phone is the device they would miss the most (Ofcom, 2017). It is clear that smartphones and social media are a pervasive facet of the connected lives of teens.

Young people routinely use digital media as tools to facilitate their face-to-face interactions with friends – finding out where people are, where they can meet, who is available and organising activities (Third *et al.*, 2014). In an ethnographic study of 13- to14-year-olds in one London school, researchers found that teens routinely used social media to supplement their friendships when they were not able to meet in person and to have private time with them away from prying adult eyes:

> The young people tried to protect their personal autonomy by seeking out unsupervised places or times in their day (the walk home from school, their bedroom, certain online sites). Their friendships were conducted face-to-face when possible, as this – still – optimizes flexibility, authenticity, and reciprocity. Insofar as friendships were also conducted online, doing so already represented a response to adult control over their physical freedom of movement. (Livingstone and Sefton-Green, 2016)

Young people who spend more than six hours online outside of school are more likely to report they are not satisfied with their life or they feel lonely, which suggests that the ability to balance internet use with other interests and activities is salient to positive mental health and wellbeing (OECD, 2017). However, a common theme that we shall see throughout the book is that positive or negative effects associated with time spent online have limited value in the absence of an understanding of context, practices and meanings. For example, participating in a supportive online forum is qualitatively different to browsing Instagram's timeline for celebrity updates. Engagement with social media can be both passive and active; life-affirming or depleting; enjoyable or destructive; and anywhere in between. In Chapter 8 we propose a more nuanced and holistic approach to considering teens' wellbeing in respect of their internet use.

There is a trend towards teens using instant messaging in preference to posting on public profiles, whereby their communication is contained to a smaller, defined group and is less publicly visible (Frith, 2017). Group chat has emerged as a popular form of online conversation amongst teenagers. Platforms such as WhatsApp provide a semi-private space online, where young people can socialise with relatively large groups, without having to broadcast messages to their entire list of online contacts. In their qualitative longitudinal study, Ofcom found that:

This is normally a space relatively free from adult scrutiny, fulfilling a range of functions, such as chatting, gossiping, swapping homework or arranging to meet. Most of our respondents were members of multiple group chats, spanning several platforms, each with a slightly different function and membership. (Ofcom, 2016a, p.40)

Privacy emerged as a strong theme with all of the teens we spent time with and we explore this topic in detail in Chapter 7. For example, Zahid was enthusiastic about the functionality within Snapchat that makes a photograph disappear after it has been opened, and an individual's *story* only last for 24 hours before also expiring:

Bringing it back to Snapchat, I really like the fact that it disappears after 24 hours. The main reason I deleted my Instagram and my Facebook was that I could see embarrassing things popping up all the time. I was like, 'Oh, yes, I remember I did this', and then I had to delete it… It deletes itself so I don't really have to do the effort… Out of sight, out of mind.

Despite the rise in mobile devices, home is still the main location for children and young people to use the internet. Older teens tend to use the internet in their own bedroom rather than in communal spaces. The privacy of personal devices means that parents and carers are less likely to be able to observe teenagers' online activities than they might have been able to with a laptop or computer (Mascheroni and Ólafsson, 2014). This can cause consternation for caregivers who often have many concerns about social media, which are routinely stoked by alarmist articles in mainstream media. We consider parental responses to social media in the penultimate section of this chapter.

An emerging trend is for the internet to be accessed via a wide range of everyday smart devices which are otherwise known as the *internet of things*. Devices such as games consoles, fitness trackers and household items can be fitted with an IP address that allows them to receive, process and transmit data via the internet. Personal assistants such as Amazon's Alexa and Google's Home enable the internet to be searched via voice command.

What teens told us about mental health and social media

Teens tend to view social media as a positive influence and value its social benefits as well as the ability to develop their social skills and access information, advice and emotional support (Frith, 2017). Robby, a 19-year-old who participated in one of our focus groups, describes the positive effects he experiences from creating and sharing content online:

> [Twitter is] an excellent tool to broadcast a simple message to a very wide audience, and so you have this sense of empowerment on Twitter as well which can contribute very well to your mental health and wellbeing.

As teens grow older, so does their dependence on anytime and anywhere mobile communication, with almost constant access to their peer group (Mascheroni and Ólafsson, 2014). For some, the sense of always being contactable can be positive, as expressed by Ava:

> It's very instant and you feel more connected because most [Snapchat] messages are sent through pictures, so you do feel quite connected to who you're talking to.

However, connected presence is not always welcome; constant contact can feel overwhelming to some, even though teen social norms appear to demand it. As Ella explains:

> Just even knowing that I'm contactable makes me feel quite suffocated. So it does help me just cutting off in that sense from the internet and whatever. But at the same time, it's hard to do that in this world, it is quite tricky.

Martha describes similar pressure arising from almost constant contact:

> I know it's a bit exaggerating, but it's almost come to the point where you can't be a functioning member of society without being present online or on social media.

Despite this necessity to be connected, some young people are able to manage these tensions and set personal boundaries. For example, Mariam told us how she takes active steps to remove herself from social media when they begin to negatively affect her mood:

> Like, sometimes obviously I switch off my phone, sometimes I just log out of social media. Sometimes I distract myself with other things, and just talk to people about it, who will understand.

There are gender differences in the types of social networking that girls and boys engage in, with boys more likely to play interactive online games, and girls more likely to participate in other forms of social networking, such as Snapchat (Frith, 2017). Girls are more likely than boys to share photos online and are also more likely to edit photos using, for example, filters (UK Safer Internet Centre, 2017). We found a similar pattern emerging in our interviews. Zoe, aged 14, describes gender differences as she sees them:

> I find that Snapchat, girls use it more for selfies and stuff like that, posting with friends. Guys just tend to use it when they're bored. I don't know if that's just because of the people I follow but that's what tends to happen. Boys kind of use it more to film each other for funny things, whereas the girls tend to post selfies and what not. I don't know if that's just because I follow more girls, but that's what I've found when I'm on Snapchat.

Whilst there may be some gender differences in social media use, chatting online is popular amongst both girls and boys (OECD, 2017). For Martha, having friends available online when she needs them reduces feelings of loneliness:

> Having friends there all the time is good because when you're not around them physically, you can still text them and it makes you feel less alone.

Emojis are an important visual communication tool on social media and messaging apps; one survey found that that young people find it easier to share emotions using emojis than words (UK Safer Internet Centre, 2017). Zoe reflects on how her friends share emotions on social media through a variety of multimedia:

> I find that quite a lot of people hide behind a screen. Same when they talk to you about, I don't know, something mean or if they're really mardy, they'll definitely express it on a video or Snapchat or through text with emojis [rather] than face to face.

It may be that the use of emojis and Gifs provide handy shortcuts to having to explain complex emotions and reduce the barriers to expressing one's emotions. Rose described to us how she uses emojis to communicate emotions to her friends in code – with a pizza slice emoji, for example, showing that she is in a good mood.

A number of social networking sites, including Facebook, Instagram and YouTube, allow users to broadcast from their smart device in real time. Livestreaming is an emerging trend with a third of respondents to one study saying they had livestreamed, of which 1 in 10 had done so in the last day; there are no gender or age trends in respect of livestreaming. Another survey indicated that a third of young people have used the livestreaming function of a social networking site, which again suggests this is becoming an increasingly embedded aspect of social networking (Frith, 2017). This was not a topic area that arose in the conversations that we had with young people but is worth practitioners being attuned to it.

All of our interviewees and focus group participants were keen to describe how their use of the internet can affect their mental health, and how having a mental health problem affects their use of the internet. For example, Ava, who is 15 and has an anxiety disorder, describes how this impacts on her use of social media:

> [Having an anxiety disorder makes it] harder to broach issues online…because you always think that people are watching you…you get really self-conscious about what you're saying or are posting.

Zoe, who is 14 and has been accessing CAMHS (Child and Adolescent Mental Health Services) for multiple issues over a number of years, highlights the pressures she feels to conform and articulates a belief that if she uses social media to talk about her mental health problems, it will have a negative effect on herself and others:

> My online life can be great. There are loads of pros and cons to it, but there's a lot of pressure to be perfect and be Pinterest goals. Social media goals, like you see celebrities to be. I feel that online life is good but there's a lot of stress on having to be on media. If you're not on media then you're not cool or you miss out on social events because they'll all text rather than organise it in person. I'd probably say that it is stressful. There is a lot of force on it. At the same time, it's also great to hang out with friends and to see long distance family or something post a good experience. So I feel like it depends on how you use the media. If you use it to just tell all your depressing thoughts or angry thoughts or something, then obviously it's going to have a negative influence and you're going to use it negatively, which will affect others negatively because you're just raining on their parade.

Despite Zoe's reluctance to talk about the more difficult aspects of her life, the ability to talk about sensitive topics more openly than may be possible face to face, is one of the positive implications of the *online disinhibition effect* whereby anonymity or distance can enable people to talk more openly, or search for information they may be embarrassed to ask for. In contrast, that same anonymity might embolden people to engage in antisocial or harmful behaviours (Bell, 2014). Robby explains how he uses social media to express himself without the necessity of talking about problems to one person specifically:

> I think one of the great things about social media, YouTube and Facebook and Twitter and all that, is it's a great [way] to express yourself and get any feelings out without having to actually say to someone, you are saying it to someone, but you're not, you're kind of just saying it to everyone.

Mariam also describes how she values the distance created through social media that allows her to compose what she wants to say in difficult situations:

> I think it happens to everyone; it has happened to me, and it's the fact that you… Because you're behind, essentially behind, you're not face to face, the confrontation is a lot different. And you might feel more confident about confronting that person over social media, because you might have time to think about what you're going to say to them.

Teens increasingly combine the use of a variety of social networking platforms, choosing whichever platforms best suit the particular context and relationship(s) (Mascheroni and Ólafsson, 2014). For example, Ruth, who is studying at university, describes how she uses a closed Facebook Messenger group for mutual support:

> I use social media as a support group with my friends, so if one of us have like a mental health crisis then we can all support each other, which is great considering we're all at uni in different cities. So it's helping you keep supported, but without being physical.

Mariam told us how she and her friends sometimes share photos that reflect their mood as a means of reaching out and offering help and support:

> Sometimes they don't know how to express it, so they might download a photo that tells someone how they're feeling, and [their friend realises] 'Okay, she's not okay. I'll message her and talk to her about it.'

Ava has a similar bond with her close friends which is facilitated and extended through social media:

> They can tell just by conversations online if you're feeling down or something, they're like, 'Are you alright? You don't seem so chatty', or things like that.

Martha finds that knowing her friends are available to her even when they are not physically with her is reassuring: 'it makes you feel less alone'. Social media enable teens to be with their friends and support each other even when they are not physically together. This is a particular aspect of social media that young people told us can be an important facet of managing their mental health. The ability to connect with friends and help each other out is one of the big benefits of social media for many teens, particularly those with mental health difficulties.

As well as enhancing friendships, the internet enables teens to search for and engage with communities of people who have similar experiences. Sally describes how she follows Twitter accounts and websites that facilitate sharing of mental health stories. In particular she refers to The Mighty which is a website where individuals can read and share personal stories, create an account, set up a personalised newsfeed and subscribe to an online newsletter. The Mighty creates peer communities around specific health conditions and enables people to connect with each other through the site:

> Millions of people are facing serious health conditions – including many of us at The Mighty. It's so easy to feel like we are facing these challenges alone. The truth is, we are all facing disability, disease and mental illness together. But when we look online for help, all we often find is medical information. We want a community, too. That's what The Mighty is building. We publish real stories by real people facing real challenges. We are building a brand and a community around them. Having a disability or disease doesn't have to be isolating. That's why The Mighty exists. We're creating a safe platform for our community to tell their stories, connect with others and raise support for the causes they believe in. We are stronger when we face adversity together, and we know it.[2]

A number of our focus group participants and interviewees told us about how they seek out mental health content on websites and through social media accounts and hashtags.

It can be tempting for parents and practitioners to underestimate the conscious and strategic practices undertaken by teens to curate positive self-impressions online. Indeed, self-presentation no longer needs to be constructed in real time or even be fully tied to reality. Teens can and do craft and edit their public personas with great care as part of their desire for self-expression (Cooper *et al.*, 2016). Even the cultural practices of teens and people in their early twenties can differ significantly, as described in this article by a 24-year-old:

---

2   https://themighty.com

Teens, either because they're better at it or because they're more aware of online safety and of the consequences of fucking up, seem to post less, post better, and delete posts more often. They have more rigid rules attached to their social media use, and more social consequences if they stray. (Eloise, 2017)

Aliya is a popular 18-year-old with a close circle of female friends. Her main priority whilst abroad on holiday with her family is to identify the best locations to create images that can be shared on Instagram. She has pre-planned her outfits for these selfies and, once taken, she shares various versions featuring different filters with her friends before posting the preferred image online at the optimum time of day for maximum likes. Like many others, she will take on average at least 12 selfies before choosing one to post online (UK Safer Internet Centre, 2017). She is fully prepared to take down the image if she does not get sufficient likes from her followers. Teens report that, on average, they need to receive 48 likes on a photo before they are happy. Her parents regard these activities with disdain, but for Aliya this is the everyday currency of her social group, with a mutual understanding of the artifice that underpins it.

However, for more vulnerable young people, such heavily curated presentations can feed into detrimental self-comparison. Tom told us how he often feels when reading status updates from his peers:

If you're feeling particularly depressed and your Facebook live feed is just full of, 'Just bought a new car…' It can actually make you feel worse, because it's someone else saying, 'I'm so positive'. And you're like, 'Oh, I'm not.'

Despite a similar reaction, Matt indicates that he is nevertheless aware of and attuned to the artifice behind such posting:

I guess that when you see other people putting themselves out there on social media, showing themselves having a good time, making you feel bad, you just have to think, 'They're putting the best of themselves out there, but they're not showing any of the problems in their life.' So you see them and think, 'Aw, look at their perfect life', and all that, but you have to think in your head that, actually, their life isn't perfect, they've got all sorts of problems going on, haven't they?

Like it or otherwise, it is important that adults are at least aware that subtle, nuanced and opaque teen cultural practices may have a new context, but in other ways may not be so dissimilar to those practised in previous times. Practitioners cannot necessarily keep up with these ever shifting micro-rules and practices, but having an appreciation of their salience to teen identity is nevertheless important. In Chapter 4, as we explore self-presentation and comparison in adolescent development, we highlight how researchers have coined the phrase 'quantified social endorsement' to describe the unambiguous nature of the number of likes on social media as an indicator of support from peers and how this may directly impact on brain activity.

There are a wide range of social media platforms available to teens, and we came across some in our research that we had not heard of before. For example, several of our focus groups participants spoke enthusiastically about Amino, which is a social network of micro-communities who connect around specific interests. Zahid described Amino as follows:

> I don't know, obviously you will get the odd people who just want to abuse that kind of thing, but generally it's quite a nice com-munity spirit and it's, like, communities within communities, and it's nice to see people from across the world come together for common interests and a common focus group.

Such communities can enable teens to develop new interests and to connect with others who share them. This leads us onto the opportunities related to online creative and civic participation.

Social media and mental health – good, bad or indifferent?

In this section we summarise what the evidence tells us about social media and their impact on the mental health and wellbeing of teens. Unsurprisingly, given that teen online behaviours are largely unobservable and often a mystery to parents and practitioners, there is significant concern about the damaging effects to their mental health and wellbeing. But are we right to be worried?

The evidence about the potentially positive, negative or neutral effects of online social networks on young people's mental health is mixed and sometimes contradictory (Barth, 2015; Seabrook, Kern and Rickard, 2016; Berry *et al.*, 2017). One systematic review found that, contrary to growing academic and public concern, the majority of empirical research finds either mixed or no effects of social media on adolescent wellbeing (Best, Manktelow and Taylor, 2014). A more recent systematic review of the literature relating to social media, depression and anxiety, similarly found a mixed picture (Seabrook *et al.*, 2016). The authors identify that use of social media is associated with protective factors such as lower levels of loneliness, greater feelings of belonging and greater access to social support. However, social media interactions can increase exposure to problematic social interactions which can in turn have a negative impact on mental health and accentuate differences between people who are doing well and people who are less well. In an Ofcom survey, one in eight young people reported that they feel pressure to look popular all the time (Ofcom, 2017). This theme is exemplified by a comment from Tom:

> There's something about how everybody seems to have a really good life, they're out and about and they're doing stuff and it's all exciting and all that kind of stuff, and you see that quite obviously, but then when it comes to that kind of wellbeing of feeling down, you see less of that.

Many studies are limited by the an overly simplistic focus on the impact of self-reported frequency of going online rather than seeking to understand and distinguish between different types of activities (Valkenburg and Peter, 2011, p.126). For example, watching YouTube videos to learn coding for Minecraft® is likely to be qualitatively different to posting selfies on Instagram. This reminds us of the need to have a holistic and context-driven understanding of how young people are using the internet if we are to help teens leverage the positives whilst mitigating the negatives.

A global participatory research study with teens found that young people did not necessarily conceptualise how they use the internet in respect of their mental health. However, they did make frequent references to ways in which social media helps them connect with friends, family and wider communities in ways which they found positive and which have proven benefits for mental health and wellbeing (Third *et al.*, 2014). Given that communicating with friends is the most common use of social media, it is noteworthy that friendships are of significant importance to the psycho-social development of young people along with their overall wellbeing (Wood, Bukoswki and Lis, 2015). As Matt told us in his interview:

> If you talk to people online a lot, it's…you have to imagine that 20 to 30 years ago people would never be able to do that kind of thing. So then, being able to just talk to a mate by tapping a few buttons just helps you to feel more connected.

However, Matt's parents are concerned that he is prioritising online communication over seeing his friends in person, an example perhaps of the dichotomous thinking that we described in the opening section of this chapter:

> Yeah, so my mum and dad talk about social media a lot. Especially Dad, he's really focused on, 'Is it bad for us?' So we came up with an analogy, on food supplements. You know, like vitamin

tablets and stuff, where it says on them 'These should be used as a supplement to a healthy diet.' So that's what we were saying about texting and Messenger, it shouldn't be used as a replacement for talking to people face to face.

Young people who communicate with friends on the internet feel closer to their existing friends (Valkenburg and Peter, 2007). Researchers demonstrated through a longitudinal study that instant messaging increases the quality of relationships between adolescent friends due to intimate self-disclosure (Valkenburg and Peter, 2009) and as a result of being able to release emotions that might otherwise remain pent up (Wood *et al.*, 2015).

We had many examples from our interviewees about how they actively and consciously make use of social media to improve their mental health. Ronan illustrated how he uses social media for social connection and also to raise awareness of mental health:

Sometimes I try to be funny, not always successfully, but I try to make jokes or have a laugh, and then sometimes it's like the complete other side of it where I'm trying to highlight an issue. There are often times…I do often have people either screenshot my story and put it on theirs, or someone replies and says, 'I feel the same', or some form of reciprocation, something to show that they resonate with what I'm putting up on my story.

In contrast, Zoe, who has been accessing CAMHS for over seven years, describes her irritation when people in her peer group post about negative emotions. She feels annoyed that peers who do not have mental health problems, can post status updates that she regards as attention seeking:

One of my pet peeves definitely is when people put really depressing quotes on. They're like, 'Had such a bad day', and then you ask them if they're okay and they won't tell you.

I'm like, 'Well, don't show everybody that you're sad and then not tell everybody.' I think people jump to conclusions about mental health and wellbeing quite a lot because quite a lot of people are like, 'Yes, I suffer from depression', but then they don't really understand what it is. They kind of abuse the label of having it. I'm like, if you really have it, you'll know that it's not fun.

A survey of 790 American teens aged 13–17 found that just under 80 per cent say engaging with social media makes them closer to friends, 50 per cent closer to family, and just under 50 per cent say it helps them feel more informed. There were some gender differences, with girls more likely to say they felt they always need to show the best version of themselves and boys more likely to say it makes them feel overloaded with information (Lenhart *et al.*, 2016).

Zoe talks about the pressure to perform a perfect representation of one's life on Instagram, despite the fact that it is insincere and whilst knowing that others are doing the same:

Obviously, I'm not going to lie, I'm very fake on social media. Quite often, I post things and I'm like, 'Oh, yes, we're having so much fun', but quite often I don't really feel like that on social media… They're [peers] probably doing the same thing I did; fake your amazing life. I mean, I do have an amazing life but on Instagram, fake all of this, 'I'm happy all the time.'

In conclusion, research relating to mental health and social media is in its infancy and the results are mixed. Teens tend to broadly be positive about social media and, in particular, the ability to maintain contact with friends. However, as we shall explore in more detail in Chapter 6, where there are offline vulnerabilities, it is likely that they will also manifest themselves online. In Chapter 8 we consider how parents and practitioners can help young people navigate the more problematic aspects of social media in order to promote resilience and positive mental health.

Parent and carer responses to teens' use of social media

It is striking that seven in ten parents of 12- to 15-year-olds say that their child knows more about the internet than they do and one in six feel they don't know enough to help their child manage online risks (Ofcom, 2016b). Many parents do not feel confident helping their children navigate their connected lives; this is hardly surprising since teenage years are developmentally a time during which young people endeavour to separate from parents and orientate towards friends. We explore aspects of child development in Chapter 3. One of our interviewees, Zahid, gives both a damning assessment of both his parents' knowledge and their response to this deficit:

> I feel particularly my family and friends, at least that I know, the only reason that they impose and they're really strict on social media is because they don't understand it enough to have a proper opinion, so they say, 'I'm just going to say no. It solves me having to go into the effort and trying to find out all about it because I can't be bothered to find a report, so I'll just say right, that's it, we're not having it, end of.'

Mariam is similarly pessimistic about adult understanding of young people's use of the internet:

> But I just think, there's a lot more to social media than what they might see, and how young people use it, than they might use it. Because I feel like a lot of young people use it to make themselves feel better, and it might give young people more confidence. But they might not see that, and they might think that they use it for totally different reasons, or something.

Parents have a range of concerns about children's online lives which includes the amount of time they spend online and giving out details to inappropriate people. More than one in four are concerned about their child seeing content online that encourages them to harm themselves (Ofcom, 2016a). A recent survey of parents in Ireland found that 75 per cent of parents believe using the internet is important for their child's education, but only just over a quarter (29%) believe that the benefits of the internet outweigh any risks for their teen (Farrugia, Grehan and O'Neill, 2017). Zoe describes her family attitudes towards social media:

> Well, I've talked to people like my grandma and people. They have Facebook but they never go on it, but they only have it for family and stuff. My mum, she enjoys texting and stuff, but to be honest, even though she has Facebook she never uses it at all. She's like, 'I don't really see the point of social media.' I suppose they all kind of think it's almost frustrating and that they don't really understand… Again, YouTube none of my family really understand, apart from my cousin Sam, who is 12, and get the point of it. They kind of think it's a bit boring and a bit of a waste of time.

Five common parental responses to children and young people's use of the internet are described below:

- **Collaboration and co-use** – parents actively co-using the internet with their children and helping them mediate their online activities as a shared endeavour.

- **Active mediation** – parents talking to their children about online safety, giving advice and helping them address problematic experiences as they arise.

- **Restrictive mediation** – parents setting rules to restrict use of the internet either in respect of activities they can undertake online or the amount of time they spend online (or both).

- **Monitoring** – parents monitoring children's use of the internet, for example through sharing passwords.

- **Technical restrictions** – parents using software to filter, restrict and monitor their children's use of the internet (Mascheroni and Ólafsson, 2014).

More restrictive parental responses to children's use of the internet are associated with reduced chances of children benefiting from the positive aspects of internet use. Martha is judgemental about parents who enforce limits through restriction:

> I've heard lots of stories of parents forcibly confiscating their children's phones and going through them and finding out things that are personal between them and their friends. There is a line… If someone invades your privacy, it makes you more of a private person, doesn't it? Then it makes them form negative habits like lying and things like that.

There are increasing numbers of digital surveillance and restrictive tools that adults can employ to impose technical restrictions. Ava describes mixed feelings about her father's use of a mobile app which monitors her use of the internet and restricts access after an agreed time:

> You download it onto the phone you want to control, and then you also have it on your phone and you can set a daily limit. You can choose what apps are included in the daily limit and things like that. You can also see how much time they're spending on each app. You can't actually physically see what they're doing, but you can see what apps they're using and when.

Whilst she told us that she didn't want to have her time restricted in this way, she can see the benefits:

I didn't like it at first at all, but I've gotten used to it now and it does help, yes.

A strong theme in our interviews and focus groups was frustration with lack of understanding from adults about how young people use the internet as a way to cope with difficult emotions and as a distraction from mental distress.

What I've seen is particular family members don't seem to realise that different people cope with mental health in different ways. …my first thing to jump to is the internet, you know, whether it's to go on social media, watch videos on YouTube, play video games with people online, something like that… It's a bit annoying, because if it's your only form of escapism and then someone is telling you to throw it away, it's basically throwing away one of your only coping mechanisms.

Young people felt that parents and carers saw the behaviour on a superficial level but did not take time to understand the motivation lying behind that behaviour. This was a common source of frustration to the teens we had conversations with. Matt's account of a family negotiation about use of smartphones at the dinner table is illuminating:

Essentially we're not allowed to use phones for anything during dinner, or in the living room if we're sitting down and watching TV together. It's not necessarily a time constraint but a restriction.

That's brought up loads of different arguments and conversations, because what we used to do is have our phones at the table, and if we got a message or something, we'd just have a look, and Dad was like 'What? No, we're all eating together.' So then it was just a complete ban on phones at the table.

What we then discovered is that we might be having a conversation about something and we don't know something, and we'll think, 'I'll Google it', but Dad will be like, 'No phones at the table' and we're like, 'But that is having a detrimental effect on the conversation, because we now can't continue with the conversation we're having.' Still, he'll insist on no phones at the table.

In contrast, Rose's family does allow phones at the table but expects the primary focus of everyone to be in the room with the family. This approach has worked for their family by minimising friction and means that if someone wants to share a photo from their phone or check out some information on the internet, there is the flexibility to do so. However, there is always the tension that the phone may take precedence over family conversation at the table and achieving balance is not always as straightforward as it may seem. Mariam wants parents to strike a balance between showing an interest whilst not being intrusive:

> I feel like a lot of the time, either parents or adults are too strict on these guidelines. But then sometimes I feel like they don't really care. I feel like there needs to be that moderate gap, where parents are trying to see what's going on, but then not pry too much into it. Otherwise, young people will start to rebel, or something like that.

In Chapter 8 we focus in more detail on how parents and practitioners can develop an authoritative but supportive voice when helping teens navigate their connected realities. Mariam is open to her parents knowing more about her online life but she is concerned about what this may lead to:

> I think, within reason, they are allowed to know a lot. It's just how they deal with what they know. Like, my parents had never even heard of Snapchat before. And when they did, they found the concept of Snapchat really strange.

Internet filters are commonly promoted to parents as a means of limiting young people's access to adverse experiences online and are used in many schools and other institutions, such as libraries. However, such filters can and do block legitimate as well as illicit content and may disproportionately affect vulnerable teens who could benefit from access to information in relation to, for example, their sexual orientation or mental distress. One study found that the use of filters was not associated with reduced exposure to adverse experiences and the authors questioned the assumption by adults and institutions that they are a sufficient or effective means of protecting children (Przybylski and Nash, 2017). Enabling teens to avoid exposure to content that may cause harm whilst respecting their right to access information and express themselves is a challenge for parents, carers and practitioners alike.

Received wisdom dictates that good parenting consists of monitoring what young people are doing online (Jenkins *et al.*, 2017). Paradoxically, it is this very surveillance that exposes adults to teen behaviours that they would not have previously witnessed in a pre-internet era when a visible trail was less likely to be left behind. Teens have always engaged in risky behaviour as part of their development; but with the internet it has become visible and can be taken out of the context in which it was intended. The panicked response of a concerned parent can result in the imposition of restrictions which in turn may limit opportunities, undermine trust and have unintended consequences (Jenkins *et al.*, 2017). Parents, carers and practitioners have to strike a balance that keeps the door ajar for conversation, whilst setting clear helpful boundaries. We do not believe this is a straightforward thing to do and we offer thoughts on how to go about it in Chapter 8.

Conclusion

> **Rod:** That it [the internet]means more than what it looks like. Because it can be quite a big thing in someone's life, if they don't get texts often, or if they're not getting as many likes on a picture or status, because it makes them feel like they're not really cared for, like they don't have anyone looking out for them. And when people go, 'Oh, just ignore it, it's only the internet', it's more than that, because you find people younger and younger getting into it, and then that's becoming a key part of how they connect with people, how they make friends, how they find career paths.

In this chapter we have introduced social media and digital technologies and presented an overview of what the evidence tells us about teens' connected lives. We have gone on to review the evidence in respect of social media, digital technologies and teen mental health from two vantage points – first, how teen online practices impact their mental health; second, how experiencing a mental health problem has an impact on teen online practices. Throughout the chapter we have offered insights from our conversations with teens who are affected by mental health problems.

In conclusion, we set out key takeaways from the chapter which we believe are salient for practitioners supporting teens who have mental health problems.

The expansion of real life

The boundaries between the material and online world are increasingly blurred and a dichotomous conceptualisation of online and offline does not reflect young people's everyday reality. It is critical that practitioners appreciate teens' connected realities and incorporate this awareness into their practice.

What makes social media different to offline public spaces

Social media have specific qualities which make them qualitatively different to physical online spaces. These include the persistence of online content, the visibility and spreadability as well as the ability to search for and find content. Social media dynamics mean that when we post online our audiences can be invisible to us, the contexts we keep separate offline can more easily collide, and the public and private aspects of our lives can converge. Appreciating the nuances of social media is increasingly a critical skill for practitioners.

Navigating the benefits and the downsides

Social media and chatting with friends are important leisure and social activities for teens. Both can be a source of support as well as promote resilience for vulnerable teens. However, peer pressures associated with self-presentation and social comparison can negatively affect teens who are already vulnerable, along with the pressure to be continually connected. It is helpful for practitioners to consider how they can help young people recognise and take advantage of the benefits, whilst navigating the more problematic aspects, of connected lives.

The value of distance

For some vulnerable teens, the ability to search for information anonymously online and take productive risks with identity, such as joining forums discussing mental health, can be beneficial and mitigate stigma. Practitioners have a valuable role in helping young people take advantage of this facet of the internet.

Parent and carer responses

Many caregivers lack confidence about helping young people navigate their connected realities. This can result in beliefs and actions which are less helpful to young people, particularly those who are vulnerable and have more to lose by not being able to make use of the positive benefits of the internet. Chapter 7 sets out in detail how practitioners can help parents and carers make sense of this terrain and have helpful conversations with teens.

Chapter 3

Getting creative

The affordances of digital for good mental health

Introduction

In worrying about the harms of the internet to young people, we can overlook what it offers for creative expression and participation in public life. For young people with mental health problems, the internet can offer a window into any number of activities that can help them to build resilience and a sense of identity, as well as reduce stress.

In this chapter we explore the ways in which young people are using social media, digital technologies and the internet to improve their mental health and wellbeing. We consider the developing sphere of digital mental health therapeutic tools, along with online peer and professional support. Lastly, we investigate emerging technologies and their application to the mental health sphere.

Creativity and civic participation

The internet offers the potential for any number of creative and civic activities that are, at least in principle, accessible to any young person to engage with. An awareness of the creative potential of the internet enables practitioners to turn their focus towards how young people can be positively stimulated and engaged in self-directed learning activities. Creative affordances of digital media include, but are not limited to:

- digital media such as animation, filmmaking, music production graphic design and photography

- social and online such as social networking, campaigning and online gaming

- hardware and electronics making activities such as makey makey,[1] sewn circuits (connecting a circuit through conductive thread), scribble bots (a robot that colours on its own), modular electronics, programming and robotics

- 3D and virtual reality such as 3D graphics, 3D printing, 3D game design, 3D augmented reality and virtual reality.

A Northern Ireland survey of youth workers who support vulnerable young people showed that social and digital media were rated as 'highly effective' or 'effective' by the majority of respondents in terms of supporting citizenship, life skills and thinking skills, and participation and advocacy (Harvey, 2016, p.13). The results of an Ofcom survey of 12- to 15-year-olds found that almost half report choosing content to watch online that helps them learn about or find out about new things; over seven in ten choose content that

---

1   https://makeymakey.com

makes them laugh, closely followed by content that relaxes them or gives them something to talk about with their friends (Ofcom, 2017).

Tom describes how playing video games is not only a distraction from his mental distress but bolsters his sense of self-efficacy:

> It's basically a way of forgetting that we actually have this problem by doing something that we're not only good at, but we enjoy. And then, they have a go at us for going at it for so long. But at the same time, it's just our way of coping with something that we have that makes life difficult for us.

Rose, aged 14, is from a middle-class white British family in the West of England. Many of Rose's friends are from Muslim backgrounds and her family context means she sometimes feels out of kilter with her friendship group. Rose strengthens her shared identity with her friends by teaching herself Arabic through YouTube tutorials. In this way she feels closer to her friends and their families which whom she spends lots of time. Rose is developing valuable skills in self-directed learning outside of a formal teaching context based on intrinsic motivations. However, this remains hidden from her family and her teachers as she fears they may disapprove of her interest in Muslim culture. There is a missed opportunity to support Rose's inquiring mind and to help her bridge her new skills into other aspects of her life. Matt, who is 17 and has anorexia, similarly exploits the internet to find new opportunities related to his interests:

> I'm always looking for my acting, and performance opportunities. Like, I found a short film competition the other day that I put towards one of my friends who is writing for film and television: I thought it might be good for us to work together.

Tom is an ardent player of Minecraft® and routinely watches YouTube tutorials made by children of a similar age in order to learn new coding skills to increase his enjoyment of this creative game.

When James, co-author of this book, found one of his inpatients was a keen Minecrafter, he conducted a therapy session with the teenage boy whilst they played the game together. Not only did this make the boy feel more comfortable as they were able to talk whilst both focused on a screen, he was also able to take more control of the therapy session, with James as his supportive wingman. Bringing digital technologies into the therapy settings or encouraging young people to develop their self-efficacy through creative production are both ways in which practitioners can use the internet to help vulnerable teens. There is an opportunity for practitioners to engage our own creativity by harnessing digital media to enhance how we support young people.

Despite adult's often dismissive views about young people wasting time online, a 2016 Ofcom survey found that nearly a third of teens have engaged in civic activity online. Just under a third of 12- to 15-year-olds who go online say they have signed petitions, shared news stories on social media, written comments or talked online about the news.

It is not just participation in civic and democratic life that is important. It is also the ability to understand and navigate networks, which are increasingly becoming an organising principle in society (Davies, Wilcox and Farrow, 2012). Whereas hierarchies and bureaucracies remain the norm, it is also networks that influence our behaviour and can make a difference to the life opportunities we are able to grasp. Evidence shows that some young people are acting as creators as well as consumers of online content. Photos, videos and avatars are the most popular online creative activities. Two-thirds of online 5- to 15-year-olds (67%) have used their digital devices for creative activities, with making pictures, editing photos, making videos and creating avatars the most popular. One in five 12- to 15-year-olds have made their own digital music and one in six have made their own animation. The children in Ofcom's qualitative research reported using digital technology to support offline creativity, with the internet, and particularly YouTube, providing a source of inspiration, information or instruction for their offline creative hobbies (2016b, p.8). Zoe, a dancer, describes how she uses her favourite social media platform, YouTube, to learn new skills which she can then apply in her dance practice:

> This sounds really weird, but I watch a lot of fitness videos and stretching videos to help with my dance and stamina and stuff so I can work on my dance and improve and help to do jumps and turns and stuff. Obviously, I'm very passionate about dance and drama, so I like to do my research.

For Martha, Instagram is more appealing as a means of curating memories than it is for connecting with friends:

> In Instagram they're taking two different functions and putting them together and one of them is taking photos and sharing them and storing your memories, which is hugely important to me because I love photography. If you've seen my Instagram, the main function of it for me is having beautiful photos that help me to have memories of things. They've taken that and combined it with talking to other people having interactions with other people. So there's one function that I don't necessarily need or want or enjoy and there's another function that I really love and I think makes my life better.

However, we should be hesitant about a simplistic analysis of networks in creating an equal playing field for young people to engage in creative activities. In their ethnography of a class of 13- to 14-year-olds in a London school, Livingstone and Sefton-Green found a somewhat more mundane reality:

> Young people could use the internet to get to know almost anyone, but they stick to their own kind. They could explore esoteric forms of knowledge, but they stick to the top-ten Google

hits, and their favorite sites include Amazon and eBay. They could create and remix their own content and become 'producers' but they actually consume stuff made by others. (Livingstone and Sefton-Green, 2016)

They argue that the narrative of connected networks, as an enabler for self-motivated entrepreneurial individuals to succeed, is a populist vision of an ideal society that belies the reality for many of an 'insecure, exploitative and precarious labour market where risks are borne individually not collectively' (Livingstone and Sefton-Green, 2016). It is also the case that the social media platforms where young people spend most of their time, Instagram and Snapchat, heavily mediate and constrain the creative expression of the people who use them (Fuchs, 2017, p.68). We suspect that this evaluation of vulnerable teens in the UK will most resonate with the day-to-day experience of practitioners reading this book.

Even though not all young people are exploiting the internet for its creative potential, it does seem that they are sharing images online in order to have a positive effect with their friends. In one survey of a representative sample of 1500 12- to 17-year-olds, respondents said that they shared images to cheer up a friend (40%), share something interesting (38%) and inspire people to do something positive (17%; UK Safer Internet Centre, 2017, p.19). These themes were repeated in our conversations with teens. For example, Zoe describes how she uses social media to connect with and engage in peer support with her best friend and close family members:

[name of best friend] sends me a lot of funny videos. She always makes me feel better. She'll just send me loads of memes. So that definitely helps, having people like that who are very supportive definitely gives you a reality check in a way, but a good one, that you shouldn't care about that, life is too short… Even if then I thought it was bad, I'm like, 'Thank you, you pulled me out of that', if you get what I mean.

This quote from Zoe provides a touching insight into how young people can and do use digital technologies to offer support and extend friendship when it counts. However, this is not without its challenges; Zoe describes the pressure that can be associated with supporting friends who are also experiencing mental health problems:

> I have a friend that also suffers with mental health. She has depression. When she was having a breakdown, she would write really distressing notes to me and she'd say really distressing things that would really freak me out.

Whilst peer support can be powerfully positive, as Zoe's story illustrates, it can also put pressure on people who are themselves already vulnerable.

Even though our interviewees were not typically making their own creative content, they were going to some length to access other people's content to support their studies as well as their mental health and wellbeing. Connor described how he uses YouTube videos and websites to supplement his learning at school. This isn't simply about accessing information, for Connor it's also about finding a way of learning that suits him which in turn builds his sense of self-efficacy:

> It's like ever since high school I always had people telling me, you know, I was thick. I was dumb. I was stupid. I didn't understand things, this, that and the other…and that started getting me to just think like, 'Yes, these things are true.' I'm not doing well in school, my grades are always low. I'm always in the lower sets. And then whilst on YouTube one day I just stumbled across a channel called Game Theory.
> Yes, basically, it just…it sort of helps me to get past all these… all the stuff that people were saying, because it's just one guy who you never actually see in person, it's all made out of different animations on the screen. And he basically takes a video game and

applies like maths and science to it and stuff like that. He makes up little theories about things and it sort of helps. He teaches people stuff in a way that some people actually understand, by taking something that people understand and then adding real life stuff to it…

Ruth described how finding content online to help her with her studies was a useful means of reducing her stress and helping her to keep focused:

> I'm doing my A-levels at the moment and if I'm looking for something and I can't find it in the textbook or I can't find it on a worksheet, you can end up getting a lot more stressed than you need to do, but I think it's good, that there's so much…where they just simplify it and then you can kind of, if you know you're in that mode where you're just stuck and you don't know where to start? Just watch one of those simple things and then you're just back into it again. Instead of just sat there stressing out and not knowing what to do.

Through our conversations with young people, we found that many use the internet in a multiplicity of ways beyond simply chatting with friends, in order to learn new skills, develop their confidence and self-efficacy, and to supplement their learning at school. We were struck, as were were throughout writing this book, by the many, varied and sometimes ingenious ways young people were exploiting the internet to increase their sense of self-efficacy and improve their wellbeing.

Vlogging – the relatable and the aspirational

The practices of blogging (online journals) and vlogging (video diaries) afford young people with mental health problems an opportunity to chronicle their experiences, to educate others and to share support with peers. They can enable a teen's voice to be heard and their experiences shared in the public domain in a way that was not so readily available to them in an analogue world (Blum-Ross and Livingstone, 2017). We were surprised by the extent to which YouTubers played a significant and positive role in the lives of almost all the young people we spent time with. YouTube routinely came up as the most important social network to our participants, alongside Instagram and Snapchat.

Children aged 5–15 say they spend more time online than they do watching television on a TV set. Twelve- to 15-year-olds are more likely to use a mobile phone to watch television programmes or films. Eighty-seven per cent of 12- to 15-year-olds consume YouTube content such as music videos, funny videos/pranks and content posted by vloggers, either on the website or via the app. When asked, children say they prefer watching YouTube to the TV (Ofcom 2016b, p.6). In their qualitative longitudinal study Ofcom found that young people experience YouTube as 'entertaining, comforting, aspirational' (Ofcom 2016a, p.27) and that they often used vlogs as a means of exploring issues that they themselves are dealing with as adolescents. Lifestyle and beauty YouTubers with massive numbers of followers sometimes use their reach to talk about mental health and reduce stigma. Mind has teamed up with YouTube star Zoe Sugg AKA Zoella as a digital ambassador. She has used her vlog to share accounts of her own experiences of anxiety and panic attacks, and launched an initiative called #DontPanicButton (NHS England, 2015, p.36). Zoe describes how she can across Zoella by accident, and how she has had a positive impact on her own mental health and in developing strategies to manage it:

I think I've come across without realising, especially because in my day and age my parents don't really get it but I watch a lot of YouTube. One of my favourite YouTubers, Zoella, suffers with anxiety and panic attacks. I discovered her and at the time I was feeling quite alone and isolated and it definitely helped me find out that I'm not the only one. Even though I didn't realise that at the time, looking back on it now I understand. I definitely found that just generally searching through the internet and people opening up really helped me find ways of coping. I think I got into photography when I started really watching Zoella and she was talking about how it helps her, and writing, I did start a journal of writing down emotions.

 Ruth describes what she gets from following vloggers who she feels can relate to and empathise with, and who at the same time feel like a peer:

Having access to people that aren't necessarily an authoritative figure or from a specific organisation and making it feel like, you know, it's not someone official telling you what to do. It gives you the access to…hear other people's stories that are real people. Whether it's someone that has been suicidal and they talk about how they coped and how they got through it and you get to see it from a personal point of view or whether it's someone who has an eating disorder or something…a hang-up about their body and there are people out there to help and advocate the fact that there are things out there that can help, and that's with discussion and meeting people who have suffered like you have.

Aliya told us enthusiastically about her favourite YouTuber, Nikki Blackketter, who is a fitness vlogger and model. In describing the YouTuber, Aliya alluded to similar qualities that Ruth had admired – someone who is both aspirational and relatable and also someone who is not an authority figure:

[She] vlogged during her breakup and did happiness challenges, promoting a lot of self love and acceptance. She is a lot of fun to watch, has a massive fan base who see her as a friend. She is very true to herself and doesn't care about looking pretty or acting a certain way. She is a brilliant role model to a lot of people due to not only her active lifestyle, but her outlook and values…without trying hard to preach.

Aliya explains why she followed the celebrity and activist Russell Brand's YouTube channel, and how his background of mental health issues appeals to her:

> He uploads frequently about current issues and often relates them back to his own addiction and mental health struggles, but always providing deep insight, discussion and a realistic optimism that I find both insightful and hopeful.

Ruth signals that the value of YouTubers is that they are both relatable but at the same time distanced: 'And what I've found is that they don't know you and you don't know them. So it's kind of anonymous.' This suggests that some young people enjoy the warmth of feeling they get from feeling they *know* a YouTuber whilst simultaneously not having to engage with them in person. Teens we interviewed tended to have a preference for following YouTubers who vlog about a whole range of topics and only happen to occasionally talk about mental health:

> Just like a general YouTuber who is going through a rough time in their life and they're open about it. And you might see them, someone who you are inspired by so much anyway, or you look up to so much, you see them going through a tough time and how they handle it…just how they were open about it, was quite motivating just to see how they were handling it…[that's] really good – because when it's unexpected as well.

Young people described how these sorts of vloggers remind them that it is possible to focus on other things than mental health, and that it is possible to have mental health difficulties and be successful. YouTubers weave ongoing first person narratives which chronicle the ups and downs of their lives.

Only one of our interviewees told us about actively creating content and he was doing so to raise awareness of mental health. Amen produces online material and described how he uses his Facebook and Instagram to talk about his experiences of mental distress and to campaign for greater awareness:

> Campaigning has massively helped my own mental health. Being so open is helping me accept what I should have accepted over almost a decade ago. People support mental health when someone famous dies due to a mental health condition or suicide, whereas this is my daily life. I'm not famous, I don't want to be famous, all I want to do is help people understand what so many people go through. Having social media as a platform allows me to connect with many people miles away, I am still at the very beginning of this campaign and I am already noticing how expressing myself online is helping my physical self and mind.

He is a young activist who has made YouTube films about his experiences to inspire others and set up Imagine Bradford which campaigns to improve mental health support and services for young people. He is actively using the internet to share his story in order to help other people.

Our interviewees gave us a strong message about the importance of relatable peer-created video content that they can understand and connect with. Whilst some do look for authoritative information online through institutional websites, they also want to hear from people like them and they want to develop a relationship, albeit at a distance, in order to feel connected to another person's life. They are looking for people they can aspire to, but also relate to.

The power of distraction

Despite the fact we found little evidence of this in the literature, one of the most common themes that young people shared with us was the affordance of the internet to facilitate distraction from troubling emotions. Time and again they told us how they use the ubiquitous functions of social media, games and websites to provide a distraction from distressing emotions. Many of the teens we had conversations with described how distraction provides a means of escapism and the ability to remove oneself from overwhelming feelings. Ava uses distraction as an active means of managing her anxiety:

> On Snapchat you can also read different articles on stories made by companies like BuzzFeed. Sometimes, sitting down and reading one of those, like a funny one or an interesting one, can help. Sometimes my thoughts will go back to [the thing that] I'm worried about or anxious about. Because [I love being] distracted, now I'm a bit calmer and I'll be able to think about it more reasonably.

Developing the habit of distracting oneself from troubling emotions is a feature of cognitive behavioural therapy (CBT) and dialectical behaviour therapy (DBT). CBT is described by the charity Mind (2017), as:

> a type of talking treatment that focuses on how your thoughts, beliefs and attitudes affect your feelings and behaviour, and teaches you coping skills for dealing with different problems. It combines cognitive therapy (examining the things you think) and behaviour therapy (examining the things you do).

DBT is described as a type of talking treatment. It's based on cognitive behavioural therapy (CBT), but has been adapted to help people who experience emotions very intensely. This extract from a blog by journalist Polly Allen for Mind describes how she uses distraction to tackle negative thoughts:

> We all know there are loads of well-publicised ways of trying to combat negative thoughts. I'm sure you've read about meditation, mindfulness, and the importance of exercise, but these activities can seem like impossible challenges when you're having a

tough time. I've tried them all, and found them difficult to approach during depressive episodes. Learning to concentrate, let alone banish all negativity and worry, seems like an impossible challenge… However, small-scale distraction techniques – the really manageable ones – can really help when you're surrounded by ruminating thoughts and waiting for talking therapy. (Allen 2015)

While the examples that Polly offers are analogue in nature, the teens with whom we had conversations had any number of digital means of distraction which they told us they found useful. This example from Aliya, is just a digital version of reading a book, but perhaps is one that she finds more accessible in the format of an app on her smartphone:

[When I'm] struggling to sleep at night, and it's just a distraction, I really like listening to audiobooks…I love watching cartoons to help me sleep or just distract myself in a way, that's completely unrelated to my life, which is good as well.

Aliya describes how she users Tumblr, a blogging and curation platform, to escape from her reality when she is finding it overwhelming. She uses the simile of going on a walk on which you get lost without even having to go anywhere, which conjures up an impression of a pleasurable but safe experience:

I use Tumblr as a bit of an escape as in I like to…it's easy to get lost in Tumblr, so whenever you really need to get lost or whenever you need an escape, it's just a place that you go to. It's kind of like going on a walk without actually leaving your house.

Whilst Conrad enjoys watching mental health vloggers on YouTube, he tells us that there are times when he needs a break from mental health-related content, preferring instead to watch on demand TV or cooking channels on YouTube:

Because sometimes you don't want to do more mental health stuff and even though it is for my mental health, it is unrelated, if that makes sense, so that really quick, simple access is, you know, for me, really, really helpful. And it's something quite small and I know you could probably get that from the TV, but it's just…I don't know why, it's a weird thing, just knowing I can go and watch either *The Simpsons* On Demand or like I have loads of subscriptions on YouTube to food cooking channels.

However, whilst distraction can be helpful, it is also has its limits and Martha describes how she avoids it tipping over into what she regards as time wasting:

I think if I'm wasting time because of the way that I get when I'm feeling down, often there's not a lot I can do about that. I actually have a lot of Chrome plugins on my laptop. I have one that you can set your websites that aren't that good and then you set a time limit. So it can be like half an hour and then after you've spent half an hour on one of your blocked websites, it stops you from going on them anymore.

Zoe accesses music on her smartphone to lift her mood and remind her of her passion as a dancer. She uses the music to spark her imagination and visualise dance moves:

Music has often pulled me through a lot. I think also because I'm a dancer, so anything to… I visualise choreography in my head and stuff. So I think music has always lifted me up because when you hear jazzy songs and whatnot, pop songs…I don't know, I have a different music taste to all my family so they often think my music is a load of tripe but it lifts me up, so I'll just keep listening.

We were struck by how often young people cited multimedia online content as an easy and accessible way to find a distraction from troubling feelings. It left us thinking that this insight may be useful for practitioners who can perhaps help young people curate content so that they can access it when they are feeling down. Multimedia content on a smartphone is accessible, private and clearly can be a powerful tool to manage distressing feelings and create a distraction when it is needed. As with any distraction, it should be proportionate and balanced with other positive activities to cope with distress. In Chapter 7 we focus in more depth on how practitioners can undertake a holistic assessment of young people's use of social media, digital tools and the internet.

Mental health digital tools and services

With an increase in the prevalence of mental health problems and associated pressure on services, digital technologies are seen by many as a way of providing scalable tools to widen access and meet demand for care and support (Hollis *et al.*, 2017). Digital mental health interventions can be defined as:

> Interventions that provide information, support and therapy (emotional, decisional, behavioural and neurocognitive) for physical and/or mental health problems via a technological or digital platform (e.g. website, computer, mobile phone application (app), SMS, email, videoconferencing, wearable device). (Hollis *et al.*, 2017, p.2)

Digital tools offer the option for asynchronous and synchronous delivery of therapy, as well as active self-monitoring (such as diary keeping) and passive monitoring of activity, sleep and mood. Educational content can be delivered through video as well as quizzes and games, and can be accessed on multiple devices. Digital tools offer the possibility of reducing barriers to face-to-face help-seeking, such as stigma or embarrassment about discussing one's own mental health (Grist, Porter and Stallard, 2017). Research indicates that some young people value the fact that digital tools can be discreet and easy to conceal, the ability to personalise an app is also important, alongside being easy and pleasing to use (Grist *et al.*, 2017).

Common sense suggests that digital technologies will be welcomed by young people who are already mediating many aspects of their lives through their smartphones. However, as we discuss in Chapter 5, access to and use of digital technologies is not evenly distributed and investment in digital technologies runs the risk of exacerbating existing inequalities as much as it may also solve them.

Future in Mind, NHS England's strategy for children and young people's mental health, sets out an aspiration to empower young people to self-care through increased availability of 'quality assured apps and digital tools' (2015, p.12). In the strategy it is argued that the use of apps and other digital tools can empower self-care, giving children and young people more control over their health and wellbeing and empower their parents and carers. Harnessing the potential of the web to promote resilience and wellbeing aligns with the principles set out in the Government's framework for digital in the NHS Personalised Health and Care 2020 and the priority it has given to young people's mental health (HM Government 2014, p.36).

What about the role of practitioners in recommending digital tools or using them in their practice? Mental health practitioners are enthusiastic about the role of digital tools in their work. However, they are concerned about issues such as security, privacy and risk, as well as worried that they are not equipped to guide the people they support in identifying good quality apps. They are also concerned about having to provide technical assistance and about digital technologies adding to their workload (Schueller *et al.*, 2016). When digital tools are recommended and blended into therapeutic work then they are much more likely to be used by people they support (East and Havard, 2015, p.3). Practitioners therefore have a pivotal role in the diffusion of digital technologies amongst people accessing services. However, there remain many barriers to use of digital tools amongst practitioners, not least through variable access to smart devices, lack of WiFi and non-permissive social media policies.

Despite the increased emphasis on digital tools to support young people's mental health, we were struck by how few teens that we spoke with were making use of them. In our participatory work with young people we have found that digital tools for mental health are competing for phone storage space with the likes of Instagram and Snapchat. Many teens have limited storage and data that are easily swallowed up through their use of social media. Young people are often reluctant to download applications that they do not see as central to their lives, and can be worried about having apps on their phone which could signal to others that they have a mental health problem. Practical issues of access along with concerns about privacy create basic barriers to use of dedicated tools for mental health. It is for this reason that we believe it is more promising for practitioners to focus their efforts on leveraging the tools that teens do already use, rather than solely focusing on digital mental health tools and services.

Along with the barriers set out above, another reason for slow uptake of digital tools by practitioners is the limited evidence that underpins them. A review of digital health interventions for the most prevalent conditions identified by the World Health Organisation found more than 1536 apps for depression, but only 32 published articles. There is a legitimate concern that many digital mental health tools are not supported by evidence-based research and may not follow evidence-based treatment guidelines (Grist *et al.*, 2017). The gold standard of randomised control trial research is not easy to deploy in a rapidly shifting environment whereby digital tools are regularly changed and where technology can quickly become outdated.

Two recent systematic reviews have found that, to date, there is limited evidence for digital technologies in improving young people's mental health; there is a notable lack of evidence concerning the cost effectiveness of digital technologies in mental health (Grist *et al.*, 2017; Hollis *et al.*, 2017). The Hollis and colleagues review shows some positive benefits for cCBT (computerised CBT) with a key insight that guided therapy is more effective and encourages greater adherence than non-guided interventions

(Hollis *et al.*, 2017). Blended or guided therapy enables an individual to work on their mental health in between face-to-face or telephone sessions and may encourage them to trust in their own abilities to self-manage and adapt (Wentzel *et al.*, 2016). Our experience as practitioners aligns with the evidence – when practitioners use digital tools to enhance or extend care then they are more likely to be accepted and used by young people. When they are used by young people independently or without being embedded as a tool by practitioners, they are more likely to be forgotten about and discarded.

There is a need for more research into the benefits and cost effectiveness of digital technologies to assist young people in managing mental distress. The heterogeneity of existing research means that it is hard to draw firm conclusions about the benefits. Furthermore, the lack of an agreed classification system, or taxonomy, for digital mental health means it is difficult to group interventions and identify active components. However, feedback from young people suggests that the ability of digital technologies to offer personalised interventions and to provide guided therapy through an avatar are both highly appealing (Hollis *et al.*, 2017). It is clear that research is, in this field in its infancy and there is still much to be understood about the efficacy of digital technologies as part of mental health care for young people.

Online peer and professional support platforms

Earlier in the chapter, we described a number of social media platforms which enable young people to produce content and engage in peer-to-peer interaction. Some of these platforms are being used by young people to discuss mental health and to offer and receive support. There are also a number of dedicated mental health-orientated peer-to-peer support platforms in existence in the UK which we consider in this section.

The internet has a number of facets which can make it easier for some young people to seek help from peers than in person – it allows young people to connect with others they would not be able to offline; the reduced social cues enable differences in gender and ethnicity to be reduced; anonymity can facilitate increased self-disclosure; the ability to control how much is shared and to take time to respond to others (Prescott, Hanley and Ujhelyi, 2017). Olivia, a 17-year-old with a diagnosis of autism, describes her preference for the distance and privacy afforded by online services:

> I definitely think it would be more helpful to publicise online stuff to adults and the kids, especially through mental health services like CAMHS and other things, because sometimes it might not be the child's best way to speak face to face to someone that they have to see every week. For me, I always had that fear that they'd speak to my mum about things or if I didn't want it bringing up again, they'd bring it up next week. I think it's good for someone to speak to someone that doesn't necessarily know the person but they still feel comfortable in speaking to them.

Online peer support platforms enable young people to access support from wherever they are and often provide 24/7 availability. Olivia told us that the knowledge that support is available whenever she might need it provides reassurance:

> Yes. It's just like that comfort, no matter what time it is or the problems, there is going to be someone there to speak to.

Participation in online peer support can normalise distressing experiences and help young people feel less alone. Ruth shared how she chooses online communities over face-to-face services because she finds the quality of support better than her local crisis service:

> I use more kind of like online communities and online support, support services. So, basically, in [name of city] the ones who do provide online support it's just basically the best option instead

of going through the… How can I say this? The crisis team, who I'm not a big fan of at all. [Through online support I get] a better quality of support and understanding as well.

A systematic review found that there is some evidence for the positive benefits of online peer support for young people, but there is a lack of good-quality evidence and further research is required. It is not as yet clear for whom online support is effective and under which conditions (Ali *et al.*, 2015). However, the teens we spoke to were largely positive about online peer support. Ella told us:

Basically, those online communities, they really helped me feel less lonely, because I think that's something that mental health affects quite a lot. That's a really big part, I think, what it plays for me, like if I am cut off from everybody then that's my communication. Do you know what I mean? And I also think, I don't know, it's… they always say it's sometimes easier to talk to strangers.

Children and young people are increasingly accessing both information and support online and some organisations are adapting accordingly. For example, two-thirds of Childline counselling sessions are now delivered online and their website incorporates messageboards where young people can offer support to each other. The charity is building its presence on Facebook, YouTube and Instagram in order to increase access to their services (Childline, 2016). Childline report that young people tell them they find accessing online support more acceptable than via a phone call (Childline, 2016).

Kooth is a well-established UK-based online counselling service for young people aged 11–25 who are experiencing emotional and mental health problems. It offers drop-in and one-to-one chats with trained counsellors, a themed moderated messageboard, a secure web-based email and an online magazine. Young people register on the site using an anonymous username. An evaluation of Kooth, using data over a two-year period, found that users post a blend of non-directive and directive informational and emotional support. Non-directive approaches comprised young people sharing their own experiences and what has worked for them in response to a particular emotion or situation. The directive approach comprised more practical advice in response to young people asking for advice. The researchers hypothesise that both posting and responding can have therapeutic benefits for users, although this requires further investigation. Importantly, they found that directive support could be construed as inaccurate or unhelpful and as a consequence they note the important role of moderators who can step in where appropriate (Prescott *et al.*, 2017). Ruth shares her thoughts about the value of online support communities in managing her mental health:

> Yes, you get involved in online communities that can really make an impact on your life, making friends and having experiences that you wouldn't meet in the everyday life.

Practitioners should consider gender differences in how teens seek help from adults. One study found that whilst as teens grow older they are more likely to seek support from peers than parents when experiencing something troubling online, teenage girls are still more likely to talk to their mothers and teenage boys continue to seek support from parents over friends (Mascheroni and Ólafsson, 2014). There has been comparatively little research into gender differences in accessing online mental health services. An Australian survey of 1038 young men aged 16–24 found that respondents were drawn to websites with video and music content and were more likely than women to play computer games. The researchers suggest that insights from the survey indicate that online mental health services aimed at men should be action-orientated (as opposed to simply information or talk-based) as well as being informed by the everyday technology practices of young men (Ellis *et al.*, 2012).

A comparative study of a web-based versus face-to-face counselling intervention for 12- to 25-year-olds found a much higher prevalence of females (almost 80%) accessing web-based services over males. The authors relate this difference to a common reluctance on the part of males to contact mental health services, along with reliance on family and friends to make initial contact. This apparent need for encouragement, according to the authors, makes it more likely that males will engage with in-person services. In contrast, web-based services are more dependent on self-motivation and so may better suit female preferences (Rickwood *et al.*, 2016). The young people accessing the web-based counselling service had greater levels of mental distress than the in-person service but they had also sought help earlier. The high levels of reported distress can be explained by the likelihood that the service use is closer to the time at which the symptoms are distressing, whereby in-person services have to wait for an appointment. All this evidence suggests that web-based services may enable easier and earlier access for some groups of young people.

A qualitative research study into the use of digital channels for communication between young people with long-term conditions and practitioners found that both patient experience and outcomes were improved:

> Young people and clinicians reported that timely digital communication enhanced engagement, reduced patient anxiety, and improved trust between the young people and their clinicians. Young people felt they received personalized care and valued the continuity of care they received by being able to contact the clinicians who knew them when they needed to. The timely access prompted activation and better self-management by the young people. (Griffiths *et al.*, 2017, p.6)

Including four mental health teams, the research results showed that the benefits of digital communications are dependent on the context. For example, text messaging is useful for raising less urgent concerns and reminders, and email is useful for sending complex information and summaries of discussions. This ability to communicate in a timely fashion can help build trust and motivate a young person to engage more in their care. It should be noted that the research found that digital communications are a useful adjunct to face-to-face contact and that the former create more space and time for the latter.

Whilst research is in its infancy, the emerging evidence, alongside insights from the young people we had conversations with, suggests that online peer and professional support has a salient role in helping some young people manage mental health problems. It therefore makes sense for practitioners to familiarise themselves with online resources that exist and to help young people they support determine if they might be useful to them.

Emerging technologies

As we go about our everyday lives, we are both actively and passively generating data through sensors. Increasingly ubiquitous in our environments, we generate data traces through sensors in our phones, in our debit card purchases, in our website searches and in our status updates. Our location is tracked when we log on to public WiFi, the accelerometer in our phone can track our activity, wearable devices can map our physiological functions, and apps can access the microphone in our smart devices to gather paralinguistic information such as volume, intonation or speed (Mohr, Zhang and Schueller, 2017).

Can these byproducts of our day-to-day lives play a useful role in our mental health? Emergent technologies are attempting to draw on these data to generate salient information about our mental health as well as our physical status. For example, sleep quality is commonly associated with a range of mental health difficulties; smartphone apps can detect common events which interfere with sleep such as movement, coughing and ambient noise and these data can be correlated with reported experiences of, for example, increased stress. Some apps aim to detect stress through paralinguistic features of speech such as pitch and speaking rate. Increasingly, work is underway to develop tools which can indicate relapse in relation to diagnoses of bipolar disorder and schizophrenia (Mohr *et al.*, 2017).

This field is in its infancy, but research and development in this area is increasing. Along with it come a whole range of ethical issues related to consent, control, privacy and security, along with acceptability and accuracy. Whilst passive monitoring may be appealing insofar as it requires minimal effort from the user, we must consider what this continual surveillance might mean to individuals who use it. The ethical implications of such emergent technologies must be carefully addressed to ensure governance keeps pace with the speed of technological capabilities.

The next generation of digital health interventions, informed by augmented and virtual reality, artificial intelligence and machine learning, are seeing a move towards 'chatbots' or digital coaches that interact with a young person via automation (Hollis *et al.*, 2017, p.21). Chatbots are automated conversational agents that act as personal assistants, helping the user navigate to the information they require. For example, Transport for London has created TravelBot for use in Facebook Messenger through which you can text questions to navigate to relevant transport information. TravelBot responds through text and by showing relevant images such as Tube maps. More controversially, the NHS in North London is trialling a chatbot alternative to the non-emergency 111 number whereby patients type their symptoms into a smartphone app and receive a response based on a database of illnesses (Plummer, 2017).

A number of chatbots that aim to act like a therapist are beginning to emerge on the app stores. It is claimed that they use evidence-based therapies such as cognitive behavioural therapy in a similar way to mobile phone apps, but are more engaging because of their interaction with the end user, which mimics a text-based conversation with another person. The interactional quality that is lost in online CBT programs may be retained to some extent through a chatbot. One such chatbot is called Woebot, which has been subject to a randomised controlled trial in use with young people who have a diagnosis of depression or anxiety. The study compared outcomes from two weeks of CBT delivered via Woebot with an online information control group in a non-clinical college population. The results showed a significant reduction in depression as measured by the validated tool PHQ-9 and had a high level of engagement over the two-week period. Qualitative feedback from users indicated that Woebot was viewed more favourably than the information-only control. The study is limited in its scope and it should be noted that the second author has a financial interest in Woebot Labs Inc. (Fitzpatrick, Darcy and Vierhile, 2017).

In an opinion piece about chatbots, Miner and colleagues argue that these conversational agents, who often interact through text message, have the potential to reach people who are less likely to be willing to speak to a person about their mental health, even anonymously (Miner, Milstein and Hancock, 2017). However, there is a risk of chatbots interacting in ways which are inappropriate or might increase distress, could cause harm and decrease the willingness to seek further help. Algorithms used to power chatbots and other technologies that process natural language have been accused of bias because they often draw on data sets which exclude certain groups, such as ethnic minorities. Issues of artificial intelligence, bias, fairness and transparency must all be considered in this developing field. This is therefore an area of digital development in its infancy and which requires much more research and development.

Conclusion

In this chapter we have considered the creative and inventive potential of social media, digital tools and the internet. Through our conversations with young people we have identified ways in which they are using ubiquitous platforms such as YouTube to manage their mental health; we have also seen how digital mental health therapies are increasingly becoming available to young people and their families. Lastly we have summarised emerging technologies and their role in the future of mental health support.

In conclusion, we set out key takeaways from the chapter which we believe are salient for practitioners supporting teens who have mental health problems.

Increasing self-efficacy

The internet affords the opportunity for teens to engage in creative production and civic activities. These can enable young people to develop their self-worth and self-efficacy. Practitioners may wish to consider how they can help young people balance passive consumption of social media with more active creation of content, blending online knowledge with offline activities.

Relatable vloggers

YouTubers are significant in the lives of many teens and provide peer-orientated and relatable information about mental health and other topics. Practitioners should be aware that YouTube may be the primary source of mental health information for teens and they may wish to leverage this knowledge to help young people both access and critique this information. Some young people are generating their own content about mental health and can find campaigning a positive aspect of living with a mental health problem.

The role of mental health digital interventions

Digital technologies for mental health, such as online therapy, appear to offer a scalable means of reaching out to and helping young people. They may be more acceptable to young people who are reluctant to seek help in person. However, evidence is limited and many practitioners are concerned about issues of information governance and security. Young people may be less likely to download digital mental health apps and so it is important that practitioners also pay attention to general use of the internet and not just specific mental health interventions.

The affordances of online peer support

Emerging evidence suggests that peer and professionally led online peer support forums can be efficacious for some young people. They can often be accessed at any time and from anywhere. Practitioners can employ this knowledge as part of their everyday toolkit.

Understanding emerging technologies

Artificial intelligence, virtual reality and conversational agents are all emerging in the field of mental health. Whilst evidence is limited, it is worthwhile for practitioners to be aware of these trends for future practice.

Useful resources

BBC Make it Digital contains creative content and activities from the BBC – www.bbc.co.uk/makeitdigital

Code First Girls aims to help girls to learn to code – www.codefirstgirls.org.uk

Coder Dojo is global network of free coding clubs for children – https://coderdojo.com

Fab Labs is a global network of makers – www.fabfoundation.org

Raspberry Pi Foundation is a UK-based charity that aims to put the power of digital making into the hands of people all over the world – www.raspberrypi.org

Chapter 4

Developmental frameworks and perspectives

Introduction

The internet provides an important and almost constant context for teens to play out and experience the transition from childhood to adulthood. This is a very different context to that which practitioners will be familiar with, both in terms of our own childhoods and in terms of our own learning about child development through whichever route we became practitioners.

The particular facets of the internet in respect of spreadability and searchability, along with the persistence of content, means that impulsive decisions can remain visible and are not easily reversed or left behind. It follows that engagement in online social networks may harm as well as benefit teens' cognitive and emotional growth; adults therefore have a vital role in helping young people navigate their interactions in respect of their healthy development.

Empirical research examining the interplay between social media and child development is in its infancy and has yet to be consistently embedded in the curricula for practitioners who work with children. However, whatever our personal views and experiences, it is clear that the internet is a factor in adolescent development which cannot be overlooked or ignored. As Barth argues: 'For clinicians, the question is not whether or not to address these issues, but when and how to do so' (Barth, 2015, p.201).

Bio-psycho-social perspectives of adolescent development

We know that the brain goes through significant changes during adolescence. The social and behavioural aspects of teens' lives that are presented to us as practitioners are underpinned by an imperceptible structural and functional reorganisation of the brain. An understanding of the brain changes at this age of child development is an important component of a bio-psycho-social approach to discerning how young people might be affected by their engagement with social media, digital technologies and the internet. In this section we summarise what the evidence tells us about the bio-psycho-social development of teens.

Developmental psychology holds that teens' cognitive self-control systems are not sufficiently mature to balance their emotional reward pathways, which increases the potential to make poor decisions influenced by a desire for immediate social rewards (Gabriel, 2014). The prefrontal cortex is the part of the brain that contains those self-control systems. It is also referred to as the seat of executive function because it helps us evaluate situations, judge risks, plan options based on potential outcomes, and make decisions, whilst inhibiting impulses from our brain's emotion and reward centres. During adolescence, the prefrontal cortex undergoes significant change, resulting in it containing a smaller number of neurons that have greater and more selective connectivity with each other. This increases its power at controlling the impulses from our social reward and emotion centres, such that as young people reach late adolescence, they are able to make more considered decisions.

The emotion and reward centres are contained within parts of the brain collectively referred to as the limbic system (see Figure 4.1 for a simple diagram of the limbic system and the prefrontal cortex). During adolescence this system becomes more sensitive such that it responds to a greater degree to sensed emotionally charged events. There is research that suggests brain changes of adolescence may occur at different times in males and females, in keeping with the broader difference in onset of puberty. Exploring these differences in detail is beyond our scope.

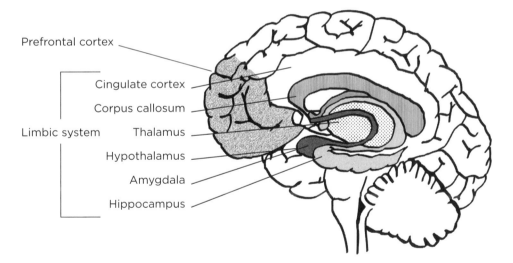

Figure 4.1 The prefrontal cortex and limbic system: Important areas of the brain that go through significant changes in adolescence

The prefrontal cortex

Referred to as the seat of executive function in that it helps us evaluate situations, judge risks, plan options based on potential outcomes, and make decisions, whilst inhibiting impulses from our brain's emotion and reward centres.

The limbic system – Key parts

Cingulate cortex

Through connections with other parts of the brain, it helps us make the link between our behaviour, its outcome, and subsequent motivation to carry out behaviours in the future.

Corpus callosum

Links the two halves of the brain, or cerebral hemispheres, together.

Thalamus

Acts as a relay for sensory and motor signals from receptors to other parts of the brain, and is important in sleep and consciousness.

Hypothalamus

Important to hormonal control, and regulation of body temperature, hunger, sleep and circadian (daily) rhythms of the body.

Amygdala

Key to emotional processing, behavioural responses to emotions, processing of memory and motivation.

Hippocampus

Critical for turning short-term memories into long-term ones.

Taking a closer look at how the brain works, research has highlighted two important functional networks of the brain; these are linked parts of the brain that fire together in a coordinated way when we are in certain situations or undertaking certain tasks. The Default Mode Network (DMN) is the functional network frequently activated during tasks that involve *mentalising* (Buckner, Andrews-Hanna and Schacter, 2008), such as thinking about others possible mental states and reflecting on our own experience. The DMN is sometimes considered the seat of *self-talk* in the brain and its activity has been shown to be affected by regular meditative practices (Brewer *et al.*, 2011; Taylor *et al.*, 2013) – showing more coordinated activity between the brain regions that make up the network in response.

The Central Executive Network (CEN) is the network that becomes activated when we are actively doing a purposeful task, such as completing a piece of coursework. Increasing activity within this task-focused network has been seen to occur with a decrease in activity in the Default Mode Network. The CEN may even directly inhibit the activity of the DMN. We can be involved in day dreaming, reflective self-talk or single-mindedly focused on a task.

Adolescence is a critical period of maturation in these two networks. They become more connected within their own networked parts and they become more distinct from each other. These distinct changes appear important in development; for example, there is evidence that good connectivity within the CEN is associated with a higher IQ (Sherman *et al.*, 2014).

Early trauma has been shown to have an effect on the structural and functional development of the brain. For example, the regulation of the limbic system can be significantly affected. Research has shown that experiencing repeated trauma in early childhood over time leads to a blunting of the hormonal response to everyday stress through life, but greater responses to significant, specific trauma.

Teens who have experienced early childhood trauma are more at risk of developing poorer mental health (Grant and Lappin, 2017). It seems likely that the combination of existing structural and functional change developed through early adverse childhood experiences and the later changes to the brain that take place during adolescence act to increase the sensitivity of individuals to social stressors and reduce their ability to cope with it in terms of resilient executive function.

It is important to acknowledge the research, albeit limited, into how social media and technology use may affect brain function. This is an area that is likely to grow and continue to be reported widely in mainstream media. Lauren Sherman at Temple University and colleagues in the United States have published several studies on the interaction between teens' responses to social media *likes* and changes in brain activity (Sherman *et al.*, 2016; Sherman *et al.*, 2018). Whilst they were undergoing an MRI scan, the researchers asked teens to review images on an image sharing social media platform and measured their brain activity in response. The teens were presented with different types of images, including images they had submitted themselves. The number of *likes* associated with each image was determined by the researcher, and teens could add a *like* or move on to the next image. One of the strongest findings was that when viewing images they submitted with high numbers of likes, teens were much more likely to like them too, and showed significantly increased activity in a part of the brain called the Nucleus Accumbens. This part of the brain is considered to be central to the reward system and important in implicit learning of culturally specific cues. The suggested implication by Sherman and colleagues is that this reflects the primacy of teen concerns about their sense of self over their view of others. When reviewing risky images, for example of alcohol or drug paraphernalia, teen participants showed reduced activity in areas of the brain linked to cognitive control, with the implication that there was less of an inhibitory response in engaging with the behaviours pictured. In the second of their two studies, comparing high school teens with older young adults, they found that older students showed greater changes in Nucleus Accumbens activity in response to highly liked photos but increased activity in cognitive control centres when viewing risky photos. This highlights that peer endorsement of our view of ourselves continues to be important, but control over risky impulses gets stronger with age.

Likes, or *quantifiable social endorsement* as Sherman refers to them, are only one aspect of social media, but one that is common across platforms. Whilst there is no current research into the effects of social media on brain activity in teens with mental health problems, we can begin to imagine that this might be a complex mix of the persistent effects of any adverse early childhood events, the changing sensitivities of adolescence, and any specific changes that may be related to a mental health problem.

In considering the full bio-psycho-social context for teens experiencing mental health problems and their use of social media, recognising the brain changes, particularly in executive function and emotional regulation, that occur during adolescence offers some part of the puzzle in understanding how or why young people might report the experiences they do in the quotes throughout the book; for example, the use of purposeful distraction through online activities activating the CEN, thus reducing the activity in the DMN and the self-critical reflective thoughts from it. Whilst not necessarily currently offering a mechanism for intervention, helping young people understand the changes that are happening to their brains may be helpful in motivating young people to try different behaviours, which if kept up will ultimately change the patterns of connections between neurons, i.e. the function of their brain.

Holding in mind the underlying brain changes that are occurring at this time, in more psychological terms, development from a child into an adult is characterised by a tension between the need for protection and autonomy; the desire to push boundaries and to take risks; and the need to make mistakes and learn from them – these are all necessary aspects of developing towards adult maturity (Gabriel, 2014). As young people shift their emotional locus away from family and towards their peer group – so separation, development of identity and a drive towards independence become key aspects of development (Best *et al.*, 2014; Wood *et al.*, 2015). Teen development is a time of conflict, transgression and change, and the internet provides an important context for these normal experiences to be played out.

However, in addition to providing a context, the internet also shapes the behaviour of teens and is shaped by them. For example, the need to respond immediately and to continually hold people in your awareness who are not physically present with you is a particular facet of online social networks (Gabriel, 2014). Social media are designed to be persuasive, that is to keep users' attention for as long as possible, which can mean other important aspects of life are neglected. Whilst teens are working through a developmental period of transition, so does the internet provide a context in which boundaries such as private and public are similarly collapsed. By keeping theories of child development in mind, we can deepen our understanding of the motivations of young people to go online and appreciate how they experience the internet. It is also worth reminding ourselves that teens do not hold a dichotomous relationship between on- and offline experiences, and indeed evidence shows that many of the issues and problems that arise through online communication mirror those found in teen's face-to-face experiences (Valkenburg and Peter, 2011).

Matt, who feels socially awkward around others and who would like to have more friends, talks about the upsides and downsides of attention on Facebook Messenger:

> I know I've done this a few times now, where I've just mass sent the same message to about five people, hoping to get a response. And when you get it back, it's like, particularly for me, who's wanting to socialise more, if you can show a jolt of excitement, you're like, 'Ooh'. It's all going back to the whole paying attention thing, like, I'm not going to lie, I do love getting attention, basically. But if you don't get it, you feel really worse about yourself: it's like you see other people, and they're getting all that, and you get kind of envious, because you just feel like, 'Well, why aren't them lot looking at me?' really. I know it's not a negative, not really, if you're talking about boosting, but when it's you, it's like your, it's like your heart always skips a beat.

Mirroring the research by Sherman and colleagues described earlier (2016, 2018), Martha reported that she similarly relies on 'likes' as a social currency that has an impact on her sense of self-worth:

> Sometimes if I post something I don't get upset if I don't get likes, I'm not like-oriented, but if something does get a lot of likes, sometimes it can make you feel like, 'Oh, people are interested in what I'm doing.' Just that what I've posted was worthwhile.

What do we know about young people's shifting use of the internet as they develop through their teenage years? Ofcom's qualitative longitudinal study of the same 18 children aged 8–15 (first undertaken in 2014) has found evidence of evolving media habits that occur with age. Through in-depth interviews they found that changes in media use are influenced by cognitive development, taste and social awareness. Younger children are more likely to use the internet for entertainment purposes; as children develop an increasing cognisance of the world around them, so they increase their engagement in the online world, managing many and varied social relationships. The study has found that social media play an important role in identity formation in which 'children learned how to grow into themselves, both on and offline' (Ofcom, 2016a). As teens become young adults, there is a shift again in internet use. Work responsibilities and cohabiting relationships are associated with a reduction in messaging as well as a reduction in engaging in fan-type activities (Jenkins *et al.*, 2017).

Drawing on the UKCCIS publication (2016) on child safety online, Table 4.1 describes key facets of child development at different ages, the related activities they engage in, and what this means in terms of their attitude towards taking risks. Setting out the biological, psychological and social change makes clear how dynamically related they are. As children all develop at different rates, it is worth considering these as much as stages of development that may occur sooner or later for any individual.

Table 4.1 **Bio-psycho-social perspectives of child development**

Age	Social development	Psychological development	Brain development	Key online activities	Attitudes towards risk and moral development
3–5-year-olds	Highly influenced by effectiveness of parenting and development environment Beginning to learn that there are social rules to follow Starting to build up friendships but peer pressure remains low	They can put themselves in others' shoes, but they are still quite fooled by appearances Growth in language ability and vocabulary towards adult fluency Very questioning about things Cooperative play and sharing	Continued development of visual, auditory and motor abilities Continued development of left hemisphere (in right-handed individuals) greater than right hemisphere Continued rapid Glial cell and myelin sheath development started in post natal period – this increases the power of brain	Entertainment, particularly games and TV Access potential limited by lack of reading ability – can be overcome via use of voice recognition technology	They may be unaware of risks
6–9-year-olds	Becoming socially more sophisticated; the need to fit in and be accepted by the peer group becomes more important Learning about the complexities of relationships; if they can't manage these it can lead to alienation, bullying and loneliness They are now frequent users of the internet but with limited information on staying safe online, which may make them vulnerable	Play is mainly pretend/role-play, moving towards greater rule-based reality play At around 7, they undergo a significant shift in thinking to more order and logic, and can understand concepts of time, space and dimension. Referred to as Concrete operational stage Learning how to manage their thinking and their emotions and recognise that they are different from others	Ability to learn increasingly complex coordinated tasks – playing musical instrument, playing sports – underpinned by greater connection between hemispheres of the brain via corpus callosum Important exposure to varied environmental experiences to help develop skills	Entertainment and fun – games, films, TV, video. Communications largely with family only	Children largely compliant with messages from school/home – although if risks aren't explained clearly, they imagine their own explanations – towards more their own judgement about what is right and wrong

10–13-year-olds	Very aware of social pressure and expectations; will change aspects of themselves in order to fit in and be accepted by peers Friends are becoming more important. More aware of what's 'cool' or not, including brands Early teens show a decrease in self-esteem as they compare themselves to others around them	Moving towards more adult ways of thinking but still not making decisions the way adults would Hypothetical and logical reasoning developing – can develop ideas regarding potential consequences of thought and action and then test them out. Can reject ideas based on logic	Increasingly selective activation of brain regions during tasks – diminishing ability to readily pick up new skills	Communications with friends; games (for boys), gossip, TV/films, shopping. Open communication across a range of sites Visual communication becomes key. Development and honing of self-image	Developmentally, the strong desire for immediate rewards triggers risk-taking behaviour
14–18-year-olds	Still have difficulties realising that others can have a different perspective, so may find it hard to work out interpersonal problems Highly dependent on peers for a sense of wellbeing They need to feel as if they are part of a group – yet also want to be viewed as unique Can appear to shun adult influence but still require clear boundaries and support from parents and teachers	Developing ability to think in more abstract ways as well as more complex hypothetical and logical thought processes Developing ability to think about thinking – self-reflection, as well as insight into others perspectives Mental health difficulties such as anxiety and depression can intensify A time characterised by idealism, with a tendency towards all-or-nothing thinking	Increasing density and reduce volume of the prefrontal cortex – reciprocal relation with risk taking and learning from outcomes Sensitivity of limbic system to social stressors Developments in the prefrontal cortex may contribute to the increase in risk-taking behaviour seen during adolescence	Communications with friends; games (for boys), gossip, TV/films, shopping. Open communication across a range of sites Visual communication now vital and the 'currency' of likes and ratings is very important	More settled within peer groups. Beginning to get better at the risk/reward equation Most adolescents will reach adult appreciation of the rule of law and social conformity to it. Some may develop beyond this to a greater insight

In the rest of this chapter, using a psycho-social approach and drawing on evidence, case studies and interviews, we further explore aspects of child development and consider what this means for understanding teens' use of the internet.

Developing independence

The drive to develop independence whilst retaining connectedness to family is a key feature of development in teens. Digital technologies play an important role in this drive towards independence by simultaneously enabling teens to stay in regular contact with parents whilst experimenting with separation. As Tom takes the first steps towards autonomy by catching the bus into the town centre with his friends, he feels more confident knowing that he can message his dad if he needs him. His dad feels similarly reassured that he can easily check how Tom is doing via a quick message, and be on hand if needed.

However, this constant connectedness between teens and parents has mixed impacts. Rosie's mum travels away regularly for her work but keeps in touch via WhatsApp and FaceTime throughout the day. Rosie checks in with her mother during the school day with updates and occasional requests for help. Whilst this constant contact is reassuring to both mother and daughter, it also sometimes means that Rosie relies on adult guidance in preference to making choices and decisions for herself. This example exemplifies how the internet offers both the possibility of premature separation and of extended dependence, both of which can have negative as well as positive consequences for the developmental tasks of adolescence (Barth, 2015).

In helping teens with mental health difficulties it can be helpful to pay attention to the micro day-to-day interactions between family and friends, how they are experienced, and what positive and negative effects they may have from a child development perspective. Helping families shine a light on these interactions and leverage those which have a positive effect is a powerful way in which practitioners can help teens and their families exploit the internet.

The internet offers teens access to characteristics associated with the adult world such as autonomy and privacy (Jenkins *et al.*, 2017) and indeed enables teens to experiment with an adult identity. A healthy sense of identity emerges from successfully balancing connectedness with separation and in the ability to regulate emotion. Both of these tasks benefit from adult involvement, despite the fact that teens are inclined to push for autonomy and independence. Cultural pressures to provide more space and less hands-on involvement are problematic, alongside a tendency towards secrecy which is amplified by the private and hidden nature of online social networks (Barth, 2015). Respecting the rights of teens for privacy and autonomy whilst setting age-appropriate boundaries and helping them learn skills in managing impulsivity and peer influence are important tasks for parents and practitioners. These judgements are not straightforward, there are often no rights and wrongs, and boundary decisions can have unintended consequences.

It should be taken into account that adolescent orientation towards risk taking, novelty seeking and heightened emotional responses are all natural developmental aspects of teens moving away from the family towards new social worlds with peers. During this time of transition the ability to detect threat (especially within social relationships) is critical and this is assisted by heightened emotional reactivity (Hansen and Holmes, 2014). Our interviewees gave us many examples of the central importance of social media as a context where the highs and lows of their emotional lives are played out. Matt describes the pain of feeling left out by his peer group:

> Like, I'll go for days without getting a single text off someone, and it just makes you think, because then you hear, like… Like I hear at college, when they're all talking about conversations they've been having on Messenger or Snapchat, and it just makes you feel a little bit left out.

Zoe similarly talks about how she avoids looking at her Instagram timeline because she feels her life compares badly to her peers:

> [I avoid] looking at people's social feed because that kind of gets me down a bit, I'm not going to lie. Everybody having amazing lives and whatnot and I'm just there like, 'I'm at home.'

Mariam describes how, other than talking to close friends which she regards as positive, she finds social media amplifies her mood when she is feeling down:

> Yes, if you look at social media when I'm upset, I think it does make me feel, generally, it makes me feel worse. My mood will go, like, not, yes… I think, things, on social media, it's really easy to trigger your emotions.

She gives an almost visceral account of the distress she experiences when she witnesses missing out by seeing it on social media:

> I guess, one thing would be, hearing about what friends have done, and then the feeling of missing out. And then going on social media and seeing, physically seeing it, is worse than hearing about it. Which has upset me in the past.

And then how she manages what appears to be an overwhelming surge of desolation:

> But in those situations, I've had to learn to log off social media, wait for that tidal wave to pass, and then just go back

Worries about friendships, loneliness, jealousies and peer comparisons are nothing new, but social media are providing a pervasive context for them to be performed and experienced. The young people we had conversations with were aware this was the case, and routinely commented on the artifice of it, however they were unable to extricate themselves because the social norm of using social media was all pervasive.

Self-presentation and identity

The internet affords a degree of control and self-presentation for teens at a stage in their lives where they can be especially self-conscious. For teens experiencing mental distress these affordances can be particularly important and often beneficial. One study found that lonely teens are more likely than non-lonely teens to experiment with their identity as means of finding connectedness with others. The researchers found that lonely teens positively benefit from the anonymity of the internet to practice social skills, which they are then able to apply to their relationships in an offline context (Valkenburg and Peter, 2008). Studies have found that one in three teens prefers online communication over face-to-face communication to talk about intimate or embarrassing topics. Matt describes how his social awkwardness makes it painfully hard to even post on a friend's timeline:

> And it's, like, I struggled to send a comment on someone's post the other day, because she's going to an audition for a drama school, and I was going to wish her good luck, but I didn't want to come off as creepy. It's just, like, I struggled to send it, and I had to, like, I actually covered my eyes and pressed enter.

The ability to control presentation online can create a sense of security and the ability to overcome hindrances in everyday face-to-face situations (Valkenburg and Peter, 2011). The internet also enables teens to access information and engage in conversations about topics which are associated with stigma and shame, such as mental health difficulties (Best *et al.*, 2014).

Whilst adults often associate online anonymity with danger, the internet affords different types of anonymity which young people can find helpful in information seeking and interaction with others. First, young people can search for information online and engage in chat rooms or online support networks without having to share their identity. Second, whilst they may choose to share their identity, they can nevertheless remove or reduce certain cues (such as visual or auditory) which gives them greater control over self-presentation (Valkenburg and Peters, 2011) along with the ability to plan communications due to their asynchronous nature (Wood *et al.*, 2015). Mariam finds web-based communication easier than using the phone when discussing mental health:

> I feel like it's easier to talk over a website, rather than on the phone, about when you're struggling in a situation. I think personally, for me, it's more about being able to slowly tell [someone] how you're feeling. And having the time to think about what you're going to write. I think, on the phone you feel more pressured, into telling people… Like telling the person how you're feeling in that situation. And I think sometimes you forget to say things. So if someone asked me what was wrong, I'd probably forget the actual point that I was upset about. And then when, say, the phone call finished, I'd probably remember it again, and it would come back even worse though.

Control of self-presentation can have a disinhibiting effect in both helpful and unhelpful ways. Less positive affects may be impulsivity in sharing information that an individual later regrets or engaging in bullying behaviour. Sometimes it can be about engaging in behaviour that you know is not beneficial but can be hard to resist when the barriers are low. As Mariam describes:

> If I think there is one thing that makes you feel better about yourself, it sounds really bad, but judging what they're [peers]

doing, and then making yourself feel better. But then, if you think about it, it's making you feel worse.

A positive benefit is being able to take productive risks in sharing aspects of identity which may cause shame or embarrassment. This control over one's environment and the ability to optimise approval and acceptance from others can have a favourable effect on young people's self-esteem (Valkenburg and Peter, 2011). However, over-reliance on likes and follows from friends may have a negative effect on self-esteem, although this can be countered by having a strong sense of purpose independent of an online context (Burrow and Rainone, 2017). For young people with low self-esteem, this can be a big issue, as Rod describes:

> I tend to overthink what I'm saying and I can't really socialise on the internet, as they [friends] tend to do. You've probably heard of Snapchat? It's like, I don't tend to get a lot of Snapchats: I've got it, but I don't tend to get a lot. And I want to be able to talk to people on it, but it's, it's a kind of, just afraid what they'll think of me.

Rod goes on to describe the positive effect of getting likes when he updates his status:

> I don't particularly do this often, but I know that a lot of people do it, which is post a status on Facebook and you get likes, it comes back, and you feel nice, because you feel like people are paying attention to you, and they're complimenting you and stuff like that. I know I've done this a few times now, where I've just mass sent the same message to about five people, hoping to get a response.

Martha finds the compulsion to fit in and conform to normative behaviours online problematic:

> If you're within the crowd and all your friends are posting pictures of them in their underwear and stuff, you feel like you have to conform to that because you're part of that. That can be really negative.

The pressure to conform can be overwhelming insofar as it can have real-world consequences of being cast out from friendship groups:

> People find it hard to post what makes them happy and be individual with what they post or even the things they say to other people, through fear of being disliked or cast out or something like that.

One survey of 1500 young people aged 12–17 found that they can find it hard to separate fact from fiction in content they come across online; around a third of children said they found it easy to check if images and videos are truthful (UK Safer Internet Centre, 2017). However, even when they are aware of the editing process, it does not necessarily mean they are not negatively affected. As Sophie describes:

> I know quite a lot of it is fake or they've spent 50 billion hours on that make-up or something but I don't know, it just kind of gets me down. I'm kind of like, 'I'll never be able to do that.' This idea of a perfect woman or what everybody aspires to be, that definitely stresses me out.

A practitioner's helping role is twofold in this regard – helping young people think critically about their use of the internet whilst at the same time helping them boost their self-esteem and sense of identity so that their reliance on external approval is lessened. The internet is only one part of the problem and can at the same time be part of the solution. Rod reinforces the fact that adults do have a valuable and important role in assisting young people; he points to a situation that he was unable to resolve without help from his counsellor:

I think there are certain things that people can handle on their own, but there are, but they may need advice on it, like I said with making group chats, I wouldn't have known to do that. I probably would have figured it out sometimes, but it would have been very much later on when it might have been a lot more of an anxious time for me, or something like that. But I feel like there are certain things that, you don't really need to directly intervene with unless it's proper, proper serious.

Valkenburg and Peter (2011) argue that online communication allows for the controllability of self-presentation and disclosure that results in a sense of security, which is not necessarily possible with face-to-face interactions. Moreover, they go on to state that the internet provides: (1) anonymity of one's identity (for example, in chat rooms) and audiovisual anonymity (such as reduced visual or auditory cues that may be overwhelming); (2) asynchronicity (for example, one can change what one was going to write); and (3) accessibility (for example, large opportunities to share information). All of these factors are particularly important for preadolescents and adolescents, who may be especially self-conscious at this stage in their lives.

Young people's development of identity is a learning process which is inevitably be filled with challenges along the way. We need to find a balance in understanding that young people will make mistakes online and that learning comes with some degree of risk. A healthy adult identity is formed through a learning process in which one takes measured risks and manages the consequence of one's decisions (Jenkins *et al.*, 2017). We must step back enough to enable this to happen or we may be exacerbating problems of the present or creating problems of the future.

The importance of friendships

Friendships with peers take on increased importance during adolescence and the associated dramas of conflict and resolution can be all-consuming. Friendships are of great importance to the psycho-social development of young people, and in adolescence are characterised by the primary importance of social status and social acceptance. Positive adjustment during this period in a young person's development is influenced by the extent to which they have broad social skills that help them navigate this difficult terrain. Teens are living out all of the normal developmental aspects of conflict, anxieties and distress through their interactions online as well as in person (Barth, 2015). Social comparisons and jealousies can be amplified online, where carefully curated Instagram accounts give the impression of a perfect life. Even though Zoe appreciates this is constructed, she still feels the weight of comparison with her peers:

> The same with girls in school, they have all these social lives that they post everywhere and show off all their different friends and how many they have. Stuff like that definitely gets me down quite a lot.

As teens primarily use the internet to communicate with friends, it therefore provides an important context in which developmental aspects of teen identity are experienced and played out. Indeed, the most popular teen social networks, such as Snapchat and Instagram, are primarily concerned with peer-to-peer communication amongst peers. A longitudinal study of young people's use of Facebook found that it is used primarily as a tool for staying connected with friends (Alloway *et al.*, 2013). Multiple studies have found that engagement in online social networks can have positive effects in enhancing and strengthening friendships amongst young people (Wood *et al.*, 2015). Danah Boyd's ten-year ethnographic research on the social life of networked teens in America led her to conclude that:

> Most teens are not compelled by gadgetry as such – they are compelled by friendship. (Boyd, 2014, p.18)

She argues that as parents increasingly control and constrain teenager's freedoms in the physical world, so they look to find new spaces to come together with their peers. Livingstone's year-long ethnography of a class of 13-year-olds in a London school reached a similar conclusion:

> The more we know about teenagers' lives the clearer it becomes that young people are no more interested in being constantly plugged in than are the adults around them. What they want is to have the choice of when and where to disconnect from the often rule bound and conflicted world of grown-ups they find themselves in. (Livingstone, 2016)

Close friendships are characterised by sharing of secrets and disclosing parts of oneself that one would not share in the public domain. In a study of Dutch teens, Valkenburg and Peter (2008) found that the internet is a significant facilitator of self-disclosure and therefore can play a positive role in developing and maintaining close friendships. Teens who use the internet to communicate with their existing friends tend to feel closer to them. The researchers also found that lonely and socially anxious teens are more likely to communicate about intimate topics via the internet as means of compensating for perceived difficulty in doing so face to face.

One of our interviewees, whilst declaring it usual teen behaviour, was prepared to share how she indulges in mean behaviour online:

> And then you might use social media to have a bit of a bitch to other people about this person, and you might be like, 'Oh, look at her.' I don't know, it gives you something which makes you feel better about yourself, to show that you might be better than this person about something, or the other. And I think it just happens to everyone, I think.

Sexual development and gender identity

Adolescent development is the time during which young people become used to feelings of sexual desire, define and accept their sexual orientation, and learn how to engage in mutual and safe sexual contacts and relationships (Valkenberg and Peters, 2011).

The anonymity afforded by the internet enables young people to seek information and obtain advice as well as discuss sensitive issues safely. This can be particularly advantageous to teens exploring issues of sexual orientation and gender identity who can explore their feelings and practise public acceptance in a safe way. Childline report that young people who are exploring issues of sexual orientation and gender identity are increasingly turning to online networks in search of support. In addition to their own content on this topic being well used, they describe how frequently young people build close friendships with peers going through similar experiences online. This has positive effects in reducing isolation alongside feelings of being different or abnormal and increases a sense of belonging and self-acceptance (Childline, 2016).

An Australian study of lesbian, gay, bisexual, transgender, queer and intersex (LGBTQI) teens found that the internet was an important means of accessing information about sexual orientation and gender identity. Participants valued making connections with peers online whilst retaining a preference for face-to-face contact with other LGBTQI young people in safe spaces. Online technologies were not sufficient to overcome isolation experienced by this group of young people (Robinson *et al.*, 2014). In another study young LGBTQI people reported that they found offline spaces more risky because of victimisation, violence and isolation as a result of their sexual and/or gender identities; online spaces enabled supportive connections and relationships to be developed which were not so readily available in their face-to-face social groups (Craig *et al.*, 2015). This research suggests that public discourse about dangers online often fails to address the very real in-person risks to safety experienced by teens from minority groups.

There is strong evidence that whilst teens are less likely to post information about sexual health, they value the ability to search anonymously for sexual health information. This is particularly the case for vulnerable teens and numerous studies show that young people who are from lower socioeconomic backgrounds are more likely to use the internet to search for sexual health information (Livingstone and Mason, 2015). There is comparatively sparse research about what teens want to know about sex, sexual development and sexual health and it has been argued that this should be a priority for developing online information and services that meet young people's needs and preferences (Livingstone and Mason, 2015). However, the research that does exist indicates that young people want a comprehensive rights-based approach to sex that incorporates education about relationships, sexuality, gender equality and pleasure (Ketting and Winkelmann, 2013).

Whilst adults are most often concerned about solicitation, plenty of young people meet future partners through social networks. Online dating apps such as Tinder are popular and there are a number of platforms dedicated to teenage dating, such as Yellow. Practitioners supporting vulnerable teens in respect of their romantic relationships need to be aware of new contexts in which they are taking place and provide help which is relatable to teens' experience. A focus group-based study with Flemish teenagers found that social media are an intrinsic part of initiating, maintaining and ending relationships. First, information gleaned from social media profiles is used to assess potential partners before relationships are initiated; second, romantic interest is signalled through liking posts and updates; third, private messages and use of emojis are a means of developing conversation. Romantic relationships are signalled through shared selfies, status updates and mutual check-ins using GPS location apps. Surveillance, jealousy and control are all aspects of being able to track activity of a romantic partner through the traces they leave online which can have negative effects. Passwords can be shared between romantic partners as a symbol or trust but can then also be used to control behaviour by having access to private channels of communication such as direct messages. Unfollowing and blocking were common behaviours on dissolution of a relationship, along with attempts to make an ex-partner jealous through status updates.

Young Scot[1] has useful advice for teens using such apps or generally chatting with people online whereby they are thinking of dating. In their dos and don'ts of online dating they recommend that teens take precautions such as being careful what personal information they make available, be honest about who they are, take steps to check the identity of the person they are chatting to, and be safe when meeting in person.

Conclusion

In this chapter we have considered the developmental bio-psycho-social changes that teens go through across different domains. Appreciating the interaction between the biological, psychological and social changes that happen in adolescence helps us to understand the difficulties and potential benefits of social media during this period. We have not covered the interaction between common forms of atypical development, such as autism and social media. Whilst there are some overarching themes to how practitioners can approach any young person, not least keeping it centred in the reality of the specific young person you are supporting, specific approaches to tasks may need to be different as a result of different capabilities.

In conclusion, we set out key takeaways from the chapter which we believe are salient for practitioners supporting teens who have mental health problems. They are as follows:

---

1   Young Scot is the national youth information and citizenship charity. They provide young people, aged 11–26, with a mixture of information, ideas and incentives to help them become confident, informed and active citizens. See https://young.scot

Bio-psycho-social development

Understand the bio-psycho-social changes of adolescence and consider them as stages that individuals may progress through in broad bands of ages, not narrow points in time. Rather than getting caught up in the details of the problematic use of a particular social media platform, practitioners should focus on getting a sense of an individual's context and abilities at their developmental stage that will shape their use of social media. Hold this framework in mind as you are reading through the next few chapters on literacy, rights and adverse experiences.

Peers not parents

Understand the pivot toward peers becoming the significant source of influence, but that it is the sense of self in the context of peers which is the most important. This is reflected in what teens find most rewarding on social media.

Purposeful versus ruminative activity

Different networks in the brain light up depending on whether we are engaged in purposeful activity or in non-purposeful, self-reflection at rest. It is worth holding this in mind when thinking with young people about what state they are in when approaching online activity. Purposeful or self-reflective? How does this change their emotional response to content?

Rewards of risk

Taking risks is important for teens; accurately judging risks is harder and having the cognitive abilities to fully test out possible outcomes in abstract ways comes with later adolescence. Helping teens to think through risks using developmentally appropriate frameworks and to reflect on risks they have taken will help them develop psychological resilience as well as the underlying brain mechanisms that support it. There is a shorthand saying in neuroscience: brain cells that fire together, wire together. In helping create the right connections, we build patterns of thought and behaviour that are more adaptable for life.

Anonymity, asynchronicity and accessibility

The common capabilities given by social media of anonymity, asynchronicity and accessibility allow teens to both explore and control their developing identity, whether through the perfected visual image or repeatedly rewritten message, or access to information that helps portray or develop a certain understanding they may not have had otherwise. As practitioners, we have all been asked questions we weren't certain of the answer to, and where able, many of us have probably searched the internet for the answer rather than immediately confess our ignorance. We have managed our identity and sense of self using the affordances of the internet. In honestly reflecting on our own use of technology in such situations, we might gain further insight into the anxieties that teens experience.

Me, myself and SoMe

The affordances of the internet and social media (sometimes abbreviated to SoMe) allow the exploration and control of identity; whilst beneficial in terms of self-expression it can also pose risks, particularly around intimate relationships.

#FOMO

Quite simply, ask young people what they are doing online. Honestly, you don't know what you are missing out on #FOMO – yes you can google it, we won't tell!

Chapter 5

From digital natives to digital differences

Introduction

Digital literacy entails being able to manage information, communicate, transact, solve problems and create content online – this can include everything from using a search engine to find information through to verifying sources of information and creating something new from existing online content. With digital media as a pervasive means of communication, in everything from making an appointment through to banking, digital skills are fundamental to participating in a connected society (OECD, 2015; Wilson and Grant, 2017). Developing digital skills and confidence is key aspect of participation in contemporary life and is an important way in which practitioners can help vulnerable teens:

> The importance of digital skills or literacy, sometimes widened into the concept of digital citizenship, cannot be overstated. Skills enable children to use the internet more widely and deeply,

enhancing a wide range of opportunities to learn, participate, create and have fun. Skills can also help children to behave well and wisely online, both in maximising their own opportunities and in evading or dealing with online risk. (Livingstone *et al.,* 2012, p.8)

It is easy to assume that because young people are enthusiastic adopters of social media, they must by default have intrinsic digital skills. However, in the UK, it is estimated that there are over 300,000 young people aged 15–24 who are not as digitally literate as we might expect (Nominet Trust, 2017). It therefore important, when considering use of social media, digital technologies and the internet, that practitioners consider issues of equity – who is included and who might be disadvantaged or left behind.

In this chapter, we explore the issue of equity from two vantage points: first we explore issues of *access* to smart devices, broadband and digital technologies; second we explore issues of *digital* and *health* literacy which are sometimes referred to as eHealth literacy: 'the ability of people to use emerging information and communications technologies to improve or enable health and health care' (Neter and Brainin, 2012). We frame both of these issues in the context of health inequalities which relate to the conditions in which people are born, grow, live, work and age; and to social determinants of health which relate to the social and economic circumstances in which people live and which influence the quality of people's health.

The Nominet Trust has identified three factors that create a barrier to young people developing digital skills and confidence:

- **Personal skills** – factors such as poor literacy and numeracy can prevent young people from using digital technology for formal communications such as job applications.

- **Circumstantial barriers** – household poverty and poor credit ratings can deny access to home broadband; long-term family health conditions can mean peer and formal support to use technology are not readily accessible.

- **Systemic barriers** – young people living in households with intergenerational unemployment can lack motivation to develop digital skills through formal training programmes.

These barriers are further compounded by disruptions such as experience of the care and criminal justice systems, family breakups and addiction or violence in the household (Nominet Trust, 2017). The most important indicators of non-use and limited use of the internet include age, disability, social class, income and the age at which people leave education (Yates, 2017). In the UK, one in six children lives in a home where no parent is employed and 10 per cent are deemed to live in poverty (Livingstone and Sefton-Green, 2016).

We know that there are similarly strong links between mental health problems in children and young people and social disadvantage; with children and young people in the poorest households three times more likely to have a mental health problem than those growing up in better-off households (Murphy and Fonagy, 2012). The absence of internet at home limits young people's access to information that is important for their cognitive development and which can support access to knowledge and learning as well as entertainment and connections with family and friends (OECD, 2017). Children who do not have access to the internet are disadvantaged in their reduced access to educational resources such as online encyclopedias for school work (OECD, 2015).

It is therefore important that we do not further exclude teens who are already disadvantaged. In this chapter we consider issues of digital exclusion and associated implications for young people experiencing mental health problems. We show how practitioners in helping roles with vulnerable teens have a legitimate role in supporting their digital inclusion and participation.

Are teens digital natives or digitally naive?

The notion that children and young people are *digital natives* and that adults born before 1980 are *digital immigrants* was first introduced by American educationalist Marc Prensky. He made the case that, as a result of their ubiquitous engagement with digital technologies, young people:

> think and process information fundamentally differently from their predecessors. These differences go far further and deeper than most educators suspect or realize…it is very likely that our students' brains have physically changed – and are different from ours – as a result of how they grew up… Our students today are all 'native speakers' of the digital language of computers, video games and the Internet. (Prensky, 2001, p.3)

This notion has become deeply embedded in popular discourse and we hear it routinely articulated in discussions about young people and the internet. But is it a helpful characterisation or does it mask profound differences and divides in internet access and use? And does it abandon older people to an essential digital disconnect that can never be overcome, along with an inherent inability to bridge a generational gap?

A dichotomous separation between natives and immigrants belies empirical evidence which points to a continuum of engagement which is predicated on a variety of factors including not just age, but also gender, education and socioeconomic status (Helsper and Eynon, 2010). In this chapter we explore issues of digital differences in detail and challenge the normative assumption that young people are inherently digital natives. We promote a more nuanced understanding of teens' connected lives which accounts for the wider social contexts in which they live.

Equity and access

Evidence indicates that age is not the most significant indicator of breadth and depth of internet use. Socioeconomic status is an important predictor of how people are incorporating the internet into their everyday lives, with those from more privileged backgrounds using it in more informed ways for a greater number of activities (Hargittai, 2010). Many of the young people we spoke with described how they are expected to use the internet for homework by their school. When asked to tell us her top three uses of the internet, after social media and online shopping, Mariam told us how she uses the internet for homework:

> School use textbooks, as well, on the internet. So that's for research things, at school.

Children aged 5–15 in lower-income households are less likely to have internet access at home, either through a fixed broadband connection or a mobile network signal (Ofcom, 2016b). They are also more likely to have a phone that does not connect to the internet and therefore less likely to use the internet when they are out and about (Mascheroni and Ólafsson, 2014).

One study found that 94.8 per cent of 15-year-olds in the UK use social media before or after school, with children with a lower socioeconomic status more likely to use social networks before the school day begins (Frith, 2017). Compared to the average, children aged 5–15 in more wealthy households are more likely to have ever made their own music, while those in lower income households are less likely to have made an animation, moving picture or image (Ofcom, 2016b). Socioeconomically advantaged young people are more likely than their disadvantaged peers to think that the internet is a great resource for obtaining information (OECD, 2017) which indicates differences in benefit gleaned from the internet.

There are also differences in parental supervision of children's use of the internet. Less-educated and less digitally skilled parents are more likely to rely on more restrictive approaches to use of the internet and prefer more technical restrictions (Livingstone *et al.*, 2017). These figures show that digital divides are not simply about access to the internet but also relate to how people engage with and make use of the internet.

Access can be more nuanced than simply having broadband and a smart device. For example, although the vast majority of young people own a mobile phone, they will not necessarily have credit for accessing voicemail and making phone calls, and may not have sufficient memory or data to download a particular app. Although it is tempting to assume that all young people own their own smartphone, we interviewed one 15-year-old who had a basic phone for text messaging and calls, and then shared his mother's smartphone to go online. In a participatory project to codesign a mental health app with young people, we found that the amount of data storage required by the app was a critical factor in whether they would download it and keep it on their phone – if it was a choice between Instagram and a clinically provided and endorsed mobile app, then there was simply no competition in their minds. In another project with teens accessing Child and Adolescent Mental Health Services (CAMHS) we discovered that young people were unlikely to pick up a call from the service because it displayed 'number withheld' on their phone, and then they would think twice before picking up an answerphone message and responding to it as it would incur a charge from their network provider.

Digital differentiation

How do young people access and make sense of mental health information online? Young people often find it hard to ask for and to access help when experiencing mental distress. A systematic review found that the most common reason for teens not seeking help is anticipation of stigma and associated shame. Other reasons for not seeking help are a desire to be self-reliant, a lack of awareness that help is needed, a belief that no one could help and a dislike of sharing personal information with a stranger (Gulliver, Griffiths and Christensen, 2010; Clement *et al.*, 2015). One of our focus groups participants described going online as an alternative to face-to-face services when she is unable to get an appointment:

> Say if you can't get an appointment to the doctors or something, so what I usually do is I just go on NHS Choices or Boots has one as well, I think it's called WebMD…so you just go on that and look through stuff.

Martha describes how she follows up a visit to her GP by looking for information online to supplement the appointment:

> Occasionally, after I've been to doctor's appointments and stuff, I'll look at the NHS, the mental health part of the NHS.

It is not surprising then that young people often prefer the internet over face-to-face contact to find out about health conditions. The perception that online information is more up-to-date than books, the ability to explore a topic from a variety of different perspectives, the convenience of accessing information when and where you want to, along with avoiding the embarrassment which can be associated with talking to a health professional, are all salient factors. Also important is being able to find out about mental health issues online to mitigate anticipated experience of stigma (Gray *et al.*, 2005).

In one American qualitative study with 50 college students, participants identified that they searched for health information in order to inform a decision about whether to make an appointment with a doctor, which in turn they used to inform their discussion with the doctor, and then to cross-reference what they were told by the doctor (Briones, 2015). It is clear that the internet has many facets that are appealing to young people wanting to find out more about mental health – but have they got the combination of digital and health literacy skills to do so?

Mascheroni and Ólafsson argue that being digitally literate means 'having the ability to develop a critical relationship with media, and to engage in communication in an autonomous, competent and safe manner' (2014, p.47). Digital skills can be conceptualised as an interplay between having technical knowledge, an appreciation of how the media works and an understanding of social norms:

- **Technical literacy** – being able to successfully navigate technologies with technical skills.

- **Media literacy** – understanding the opportunities new technologies can open up; working knowledge of available platforms; capacity to make judgments about the quality and reliability of online sources.

- **Social literacy** – an understanding of the social norms that apply in online settings (Cooper 2012, quoted in Third *et al.*, 2014, p.35).

Mariam, who often feels depressed, shares how she was recently told about the Childline app by her school nurse. Her description suggests that whilst she had the technical skills to download the app, it appears to be lack of motivation and confidence that inhibits her from fully exploring it as a potentially helpful tool:

> I didn't actually have a look at it, but I knew that it was there, so I knew that there was an app there. Like, on the App Store, when I looked at it. I didn't actually download it, but I looked at it, and it didn't have very good reviews. I didn't actually read the reviews, but I was just like, I don't really feel like it. But, yes. But they're the only things that I've actually ever heard about, digitally.

What exactly do we mean when we talk about digital skills? A taxonomy of digital skills has been developed by the charity, Go ON UK (which has now merged with the charity, Dot Everyone) that sets out five basic digital skills and a set of associated competencies as follows:

- **Managing information** – which is characterised by the ability to find, manage and store digital information and content; assessing accurate sources of information and using security tools when browsing the web.

- **Communicating** – which is characterised by the ability to communicate, interact, collaborate, share and connect with others; understanding how to manage your identities, protecting yourself from scams; using the right security settings (including parental controls); protecting your data.

- **Transacting** – which is characterised by the ability to purchase and sell goods and services; organise your finances; register for and use digital government services; using secure websites for financial transactions; protecting your personal data; respecting the privacy of others.

- **Problem solving** – which is characterised by the ability to increase independence and confidence by solving problems and finding solutions using digital tools; using accurate sources of support; avoiding malicious websites, scams and pop-up windows.

- **Creating** – which is characterised by the ability to create basic digital content in order to engage with digital communities and organisations; being aware of copyright law; protecting your personal data; respecting the privacy of others (Tech Partnership, 2015).

In addition to these five digital skills, we would also add that the know-how to engage critically and reflectively with the internet is also salient. This includes an appreciation of the internet's production and consumption processes. We explore this aspect of digital literacy in more detail in Chapter 7 where we consider young people's digital rights and online resilience.

Hargittai identifies three different interdependent factors that influence digital skills, namely demographic, socioeconomic, and contextual. Through a survey of American college students, the researcher found that white and Asian students report knowing more about the internet than their African American and Hispanic counterparts. The number of access locations, number of use years, and weekly web-use hours are all positively related to online skills; however they do not account fully for the relationship of gender, education, and race/ethnicity to skills. All of this reinforces the fact that online know-how is more than just about having technical skills (Hargittai, 2010). Practitioners should be alert to the demographic and social factors that may influence access and utilisation of digital media.

Another, and perhaps more helpful, approach to conceptualising digital access is the notion of 'digital differentiation' which focuses on differential use patterns of the internet that result from unequal socioeconomic, cognitive and cultural resources. One study found that differences in formal education had a direct impact on how teens use the internet. Teens with lower educational attainment tend to focus more on entertainment than seeking information, as is the case with traditional media (Peter and Valkenburg, 2006a). Practitioners have a valuable role to play in helping young people figure out how they can make use of the internet to promote positive mental health and social inclusion, for example through engaging in peer communities and creative activities.

eHealth literacy

Health literacy is defined by the World Health Organisation as: 'the cognitive and social skills which determine the motivation and ability of individuals to gain access to, understand and use information in ways which promote and maintain good health'. In this definition, health literacy addresses the environmental, political and social factors that determine health. Combined with digital literacy, health literacy enables people to make use of digital technologies to improve or enable health (Neter and Brainin, 2012). The sheer volume of information available on the internet, encompassing everything from self-published blogs on specific health conditions through to institutionally mediated information, can be overwhelming and the ability to navigate it requires a degree of skill and confidence.

Despite the fact that the internet increasingly contains multimedia content such as video and animation, it remains a largely text-based medium and therefore requires basic reading literacy in order to make sense of it. One observational study of low literacy adults found that they encountered a whole range of barriers including difficulty in generating precise search terms to answer health questions, difficulty in interpreting and retaining health information, reticence to click on links, a preference for sponsored sites and limited critical comprehension or evaluation of material (Birru *et al.*, 2004).

A similar study of college educated teens found that this more capable group avoided sponsored links and advertisements, but still used overly general search terms and did not always find it easy to find the information they were seeking. The observed teens tended to scan quickly, jump from site to site, and often missed the salient information they were looking for. Spelling errors were another reason for failing to find relevant health information. When Zoe first found information about mental health, she stumbled across it through following vloggers on YouTube. She describes how by watching young people vlog about their mental health, she came to understand more about what it was as well as help her feel less alone:

Even though it didn't stop my anxiety and panic attacks being so severe, it definitely helps me to know that I'm not alone. Even though it was still really severe, I still couldn't get out of this frame of mind, it just helped to understand really, and get really a big concept. Because obviously having it from such a young age, I didn't really understand…and me not understanding led to me having a food disorder, an eating disorder, but obviously I was very young so I didn't understand that it was an eating disorder.

Something as simple as knowing how to search for information via an internet search engine is an important basic skill and we shouldn't underestimate how opaque and inaccessible mental health services can be to a young person. Sam, an 18-year-old, remembers when he was first referred to CAMHS in his early teens. In his first attempt to find out more information online he was unable to find anything about the service because he hadn't seen the acronym written down and so misspelt it into the search engine. It was only on his first visit to the service that he realised he had been searching for the wrong term and understood what had happened. Mariam, who is aged 14, wishes she'd been pointed to trustworthy online information a lot earlier:

Even the school nurse didn't really know much about [the Mindmate website] and she deals with a lot of mental health issues at school. I'd been struggling for a long time. I was struggling since I was about 11 or 12, and then to find out that there was this website, five years later, it was a bit like… I don't know.

Several of our interviewees seemed to be unaware that they could find mental health information online. For example, Martha told us: 'resources aren't really readily available for mental health type stuff. You go on the internet and it's all just social media and stuff like this.'

Similarly, in our interview with Olivia, a 17-year-old with autism, it was apparent that she had never thought to search for mental health information online: 'No, I've never really looked. You see a lot of things being advertised on Facebook but it's not really relevant things that could help young people.' Olivia told us that practitioners hadn't suggested online information to her and that she would be reluctant to search for it herself without a recommendation to a trustworthy site. A eating disorders practitioner told us how young people she supports are often naive about how promoted posts and advertisements work on sites such as Instagram, not realising that because they follow diet and fitness accounts, they inevitably receive a barrage of related advertising. We were struck by the fact that the motivation and know-how to search for and find out information about mental health online was highly variable amongst the young people we had conversations with.

In their systematic review of the literature, Diviani *et al.* (2015) identify four characteristics of eHealth literacy, which are:

- **evaluation** – being able to evaluate online health information

- **perception** – the extent to which an individual can evaluate quality of online health information

- **trust** – the extent to which an individual trusts the internet as a source of online health information

- **evaluation criteria** – the extent to which an individual uses criteria to evaluate online health information.

The review found people with low health literacy are less likely to have or deploy the above attributes. For example, one study found that people with low health literacy were most likely to associate the position of a website in health results or the quality of images as evaluation criteria for the trustworthiness of the information. This contrasts with the evidence which shows that institutional sources are likely to be more accurate, whilst position in search results and image quality are not good criteria. The studies in the review tended to conclude that people with lower education levels have worse actual and self-rated skills to evaluate online information and lower trust in online information than those who are more educated.

A Canadian survey of young adults aged 18–35 who had experienced a first episode of psychosis aimed to understand how technology could assist in their recovery. Respondents, asked to rank barriers to accessing mental health information and support online, identified the following: lack of knowledge on how to perform an internet search (31%); the way in which information is presented online (27%); no interest or need (22%); lack of time (19%); and cost of internet access (19%). Just under a third of respondents reported no barriers to accessing information and support online (Lal *et al.*, 2015). This mix of access, motivation and absence of basic digital skills aligns to other evidence about skills gaps in young people. Assumptions can be made that those with diagnoses such as schizophrenia and psychosis may be less able to engage with digital technologies due to the impacts of paranoia, disorganisation and/or cognitive impairment. However, this is not borne out by the evidence and there are many apps available on the apps stores specifically targeted towards people with those diagnoses (Firth and Torous, 2015).

Does eHealth literacy reduce people's utilisation of health services? The global evidence is mixed and inconclusive, with some studies suggesting that people with greater health literacy engage in more preventative behaviours and are more likely to seek help early. Other studies have shown little or no significant difference between those with high and low health literacy (Schulz *et al.*, 2017). Some evidence suggests that poor eHealth literacy can contribute to adverse health outcomes, such as lower take up of screening programmes or low adherence to treatment; this points to the fact that eHealth literacy should be a concern of practitioners helping young people (Diviani *et al.*, 2015; Schulz *et al.*, 2017). We set out how practitioners can support young people in Chapter 8 and how services and organisations can approach this in Chapter 9.

Conclusion

In this chapter we have reviewed the evidence about the digital literacy of teens. We have found that, despite popular discourse which situates young people as digital natives, there are many who are more likely to be digitally naive.

In conclusion, we set out key takeaways from the chapter which we believe are salient for practitioners supporting teens who have mental health problems. They are as follows:

Digital exclusion

Digital exclusion is not only about access to digital technologies and broadband, but is also about having the skills, motivation and confidence to use the internet in order to participate in society.

Uneven distribution

Over 300,000 young people aged 15–24 are affected by digital exclusion. Digital skills and confidence are unevenly distributed and are influenced by demographic and social factors. The same social and economic disadvantages that increase the risk of mental health difficulties also carry implications for digital exclusion.

Digital inclusion

Promoting digital inclusion is associated with helping young people develop the confidence to undertake everyday social, civic and participatory activities, such as connecting with friends and family, finding information for homework, and verifying information in respect of their health and wellbeing. These are all important aspects of positive mental health and wellbeing.

Critical digital literacy

Digital literacy not just about being able to transact and participate online, it is also about being able to engage with the internet critically – understanding its benefits and also its downsides.

Digital differentiation

Evidence suggests that teens have differential use patterns of the internet that result from unequal socioeconomic, cognitive and cultural resources.

eHealth literacy

eHealth literacy enables people to make use of digital technologies to improve or enable health. Even teens who are confident in participating in social networks may be less assured when it comes to seeking information about their mental health. Teens have variable basic knowledge about how to search for health information online. Sometimes young people do not find the information they need because they spell terms incorrectly or they are not sufficiently motivated to spend time searching for, and appraising, different sources of information. eHealth literacy can be hit-or-miss for many young people and practitioners may wish to consider how they can help young people develop the requisite skills.

Benefits of eHealth literacy for teens with mental health problems

Variability in eHealth literacy is more problematic than it might first appear, as it is evident that online information may have particular benefits for teens affected by mental health difficulties. The ability to search for information anonymously, access online services and discover experiences from peers all have the potential to mitigate shame and stigma which is commonly associated with mental distress. Helping young people develop digital confidence is a relevant and legitimate practice for practitioners to engage in and may contribute to improved health and social outcomes.

Useful resources

Digital Exclusion Heatmap is an online map showing likelihood of digital exclusion throughout the UK – http://heatmap.thetechpartnership.com

Doc Ready is a digital tool that helps young people to prepare and make the most out of mental health related GP visits. It helps young people to know what to expect during a GP consultation, plan what to say and record the outcomes of their appointments. Doc Ready has been designed and developed with young people – www.docready.org.

Good Things Foundation is a charity dedicated to supporting digital skills – www.goodthingsfoundation.org

Ada is a national college of digital skills – www.adacollege.org.uk

Barclays Digital Eagles provides digital inclusion resources and learning tools – www.barclays.co.uk/digital-confidence/eagles

Media Smarts is a not-for-profit company that creates free educational materials for schools and youth organisations, for teachers, parents and guardians, to help young people think critically about the advertising they come across in their daily lives – www.mediasmart.uk.com

Digizen provides information for educators, parents, carers, and young people to strengthen their awareness and understanding of what digital citizenship is and encourage all users of technology to be and become responsible DIGItal citiZENS – www.digizen.org

Digital Inclusion Guide for Health and Social Care is a guide for commissioners and developers of digital health technologies. The guide aims to help them ensure digital products and services and products are accessible to everyone – https://digital.nhs.uk/widening-digital-participation/digital-inclusion-guide

Chapter 6

Understanding adverse experiences online

Introduction

With the internet permeating almost every aspect of teens' lives, it is unsurprising that adverse as well as positive impacts are coming to the fore. In this chapter we consider a range of adverse experiences that teens may encounter online. This includes exposure to pornography, bullying, unwanted contact from strangers, troubling content and sharing of sexually explicit images. It also includes either witnessing or engaging in self-harming behaviours and sharing suicidal thoughts online. We briefly touch on the impact of marketing and advertising on young people's wellbeing, although this is explored in more detail in Chapter 7. Our focus is on online behaviours between young people and so we do not address online child exploitation by adults (for a summary of research on this topic, please see Livingstone *et al.*, 2017).

Evidence shows that generally children have a low level of concern about about online risk and regard the channels they engage with as simply another media through which everyday dramas are played out, initiated or continued (Young Minds, 2016). The UK is neither especially high nor low in relation to other European countries with regard to children's online risks or negative experiences as reported by their parents (Livingstone *et al.*, 2017). In this chapter we focus on the more problematic aspects of adverse effects rather than everyday ups and downs that teens experience both online and offline. Through our conversations with young people, it became apparent that many are well attuned to adverse effects and want help to avoid them and to manage them when they do occur. As Aliya explains:

> Because [the internet] is becoming such an integral part of our lives…there does need to be that aspect of kind of safety and not necessarily monitoring and controlling everything, but like the example of cars – you're driving a car and when cars first came in, they were obviously dangerous. They were great, but they were dangerous and people had to learn how to use them. With the internet, you just to adapt to it and we all do too, but I think it can't be brushed under the rug and ignored like no one is going to suffer any negative health effects from it.

The experience of organisations such as Childline suggests that adverse effects may be on the increase. In their 2015–2016 annual report, Childline describe a hike in requests for support by young people about issues they are encountering online, which include online grooming, sexting and viewing sexually explicit images (Childline, 2016). In contrast, the young people we spoke to had few examples of practitioners or organisations taking active steps to help them manage adverse effects. As Mariam describes:

> It has come up at school. With things like cyberbullying, with other students, and teachers giving everyone *the* talk about it. Or like how people use social media against other people. But it's never come up, like, personally.

Mariam's comment suggests a certain frustration with adult reductive messages that fail to resonate with teens' realities. She goes on to suggest that the way schools broach the topic of social media and adverse effects may be worse than not broaching them at all:

> I wouldn't say so, no. I think they do, I think sometimes, in certain situations, they can make it worse. The way they approach it, and the way that they use it with young people. Because obviously, essentially, they have different outlooks on social media than young people do. Because usually young people use it more often than, essentially, the older generation might.

Much of the literature categorises experiences, such as contact with strangers online, as inherently as *risky* or *harmful* to individuals. However, adverse experiences are both subjective and vary in their impact from person to person. It is for this reason that it has been argued that we should avoid simple reductive terms which obscure this diversity of experience (Przybylski and Nash, 2017). As an example, it is often assumed that online contact between strangers is essentially both risky and harmful; however, two teens who connect on the basis of shared interests is qualitatively different to contact with a stranger who wishes to cause distress. It is therefore important that adults seek to understand the nuances of teen practices before categorising and judging their online experiences.

We argue that a wholly risk-focused approach to teens' online lives runs the risk of reducing their ability to take advantage of the many positive affordances of the internet. A UNICEF global child-focused research study entitled Children's Rights in a Digital Age found that the sorts of adverse effects identified by young people are not always the same ones that dominate adult's imagination:

> Children's direct references to cyberbullying nevertheless remained few and far between, which suggests that cyberbullying does not preoccupy children to the same extent that it often features in public and policy debates. (Third *et al.*, 2014, p.41)

The researchers propose the development of child-centred definitions of the opportunities and risks associated with young people's digital lives. Our adolescent interviewees similarly gave us a clear and consistent message – *listen to us, understand and don't jump to conclusions.*

Throughout the rest of this chapter, we interweave what young people told us with what the research tells us in respect of the most common adverse experiences encountered by teens online:

- bullying

- self harm and suicide

- gender identity and sexual exploitation

- sexting

- pornography

- body image and disordered eating

- excessive use of the internet

- other adverse effects including radicalisation.

Current guidance and advice for parents and other adults often focuses on the negative aspects and adverse impacts of the internet (Third *et al.*, 2014). We believe this needs a counterbalance if parents, carers and practitioners are to help their children use digital technologies to enhance their lives – for learning, building relationships and having fun (Farrugia, 2017). We therefore approach the theme of adverse effects from the perspective of our our original proposition set out at the beginning of this book, in which we ask how we would approach these issues if we considered the internet as an asset to be leveraged rather than simply a problem to be solved. We include stories from young people and practitioners to illustrate both negative experiences and how some teens are resisting adverse effects. We help you think about what you can do in your everyday practice to help teens in their connected lives.

What risks are there online and how concerned should practitioners be?

Practitioners supporting teens with mental health problems are rightly concerned about the impacts of witnessing or engaging with troubling content online. The EU Kids Online project (2014), which surveyed more than 25,000 children and their parents in 25 European countries, generated significant insights into the impact of negative experiences online. They found that children who encounter more risks online are not necessarily those who experience more harmful consequences. Although rather counterintuitive, they found that teens who encounter more risks are often more skilled and as a consequence develop more resilience. When asked what insight about her connected life that she would like to share with an adult, Ava alludes to this surprising effect:

> Probably [I would tell an adult] that sometimes you see things that upset you or you shouldn't really see, but it can make you more mature in what to do about things like that. It gives you a sense of the wider world outside.

Children who are less exposed to both opportunities and risks tend to be more negatively affected when they do have adverse experiences online (Third *et al.*, 2014). It is also the case that children and young people who are vulnerable offline as a result of psychological problems or social characteristics are more negatively affected by online risks. It shouldn't be any surprise that online and offline vulnerability are closely associated (Mascheroni and Ólafsson, 2014). A typology of adolescent vulnerability to adverse online effects sets out the following four characteristics:

1. **Adapted adolescents** – this group is the largest and has the least number of risk behaviours online or offline, are the least vulnerable and least likely to receive sexual solicitations from an adult online.

2. **Inquisitive non-sexual adolescents** – this group has lower risk taking offline but higher online risk taking. They are at low likelihood of receiving sexual solicitations or sending sexts.

3. **Inquisitive sexual adolescents** – this group demonstrates the highest rate of receiving requests for sexual information. They have a high likelihood of receiving sexual solicitations from adults. This group also has the highest likelihood of meeting up in person to engage in sexual activity.

4. **Risk-taking aggressive adolescents** – this group is the smallest and exhibits the highest risk taking on- and offline, and are most likely to both harass and be harassed. They demonstrate real-world antisocial behaviour such as problems with authority (parents and teachers), truancy, school exclusion, drug and alcohol misuse. They have the highest levels of online/offline aggression towards others, including peers. They also have a heightened level of experiencing online/offline victimisation at the hands of others (Livingstone *et al.*, 2017).

Reproduced with permission from Professor Sonia Livingstone

This typology can be useful for practitioners wishing to assess the degree of vulnerability a young person may have towards adverse online effects. Practitioners working with teens who are already vulnerable as a result of mental health problems should seek to understand their online lives and try to help them navigate both the positive and detrimental aspects. The internet has many benefits but it takes skill and literacy to gain from the positives and minimise the negatives. Young people want adult guidance but they also require that adults suspend their judgement and walk alongside them. This requires practitioners to manage your own worries about and risk and governance in order to have helpful and non-judgemental conversations.

The types of risks encountered by young people fall into three broad categories (Young Minds, 2016):

- **Content risks** – these are risks associated with encountering either mass-produced or user-generated content which are likely to cause distress.

- **Contact risks** – these are risks where a young person participates in activities that have been initiated by an adult (either voluntary or non-voluntary).

- **Conduct risks** – these are risks whereby where a young person is either a victim or perpetrator of peer-led online activities which are likely to cause distress.

So for example, in the case of online pornography, a *content risk* may be sexual images, a *contact risk* may be exploitative, and a *conduct risk* may be sexting. The relationship between exposure to risk and actual harm is not a straightforward one. However, evidence appears to suggest that young people with mental health problems may be more likely to turn to the internet and social media for interaction and that excessive internet use may exacerbate their problems. Young people experiencing mental health problems tend to encounter a higher level of online risk and be more upset by it when it occurs (Young Minds, 2016). It is also the case that young people have a high threshold for seeking help about upsetting online experiences and that boys are less likely to ask for help than girls.

Protective factors for vulnerable young people include peers and friendship networks, engaged and supportive parents, parents who are themselves online, accessible sources of age-appropriate information and access to relevant authorities where children have been provided with appropriate information (Livingstone and Palmer, 2012). Practitioners can actively help young people leverage these protective factors whilst helping them work through the risks. We discuss how practitioners can support vulnerable young people in more detail in Chapter 8.

Bullying and online hate

It is well accepted that face-to-face bullying is a risk factor for the social and emotional adjustment of teens who are on the receiving end as well as for perpetrators (Cowie, 2013; Görzig, 2016). Children who are bullied are more likely to report an increase in depression and anxiety over time, and bullying in childhood is linked to depression in adulthood (NHS England, 2015; ONS, 2015). Bullying is therefore an important consideration for any practitioner working in a supportive capacity with teens affected by mental health issues.

Cyberbullying occurs when internet-based applications are used to systematically intimidate or insult a person in order to cause them humiliation, embarrassment or hurt; it entails intended repetitive actions designed to cause distress (Valkenburg and Peter, 2011). There is emerging evidence that children and young people are seeing hate speech online and/or being targeted in relation to their identity characteristics such as gender and gender identity, sexuality, race, religion and disability (Livingstone *et al.*, 2017). In one study, 64 per cent of children and young people aged 13–17 reported having seen people posting images or videos that are offensive to a particular targeted group (UK Safer Internet Centre, 2017). When asked to describe which particular groups they had seen targeted by hate speech online, the largest group was related to religion (55%) followed by Black, Asian and minority ethnic groups and lesbian, gay or bisexual people (42%). Just over a fifth of online hate was directed at disabled people (UK Safer Internet Centre, 2016).

In our focus groups, young people were attuned to concerns about online bullying and took steps to avoid it. Atiya told us about her worries:

I think I'm a bit paranoid, especially with Instagram as well. There's this sort of thing where things go viral and I think I'm paranoid about, I think people can manipulate things, people can screenshot things. I've seen instances where things have gone viral and people have tried to humiliate someone, and I think I'm just super paranoid about stuff like that because you get these awful pages, I think they're called 'banter pages' or something on Instagram and they repost things of young people who might have been, I don't know, whatever they were doing, and it goes viral across Instagram and everyone knows and people's lives get turned upside down and I don't like that aspect of it.

Whilst bullying is nothing new, the internet enables 'banter' or 'beef' as, our interviewee Rose describes it, to be searched for, shared and amplified. It is this persistence that is qualitatively different to the time and spatial boundedness of bullying that takes place in person. Throughout conversations with young people, we found that certain social media platforms have facets that enable specific forms of bullying. Zoe describes how the fact that images disappear from Snapchat meant that people who bullied her could avoid leaving a digital trace of their mean behaviour:

I've had them on Snapchat before because they can delete. Because once you've read it, unless you save it or screenshot it, they can see that you screenshot it. So as soon as you've opened it and you go off, it's completely wiped and you can't recover it. I find that if I do screenshot it, then they know [Snapchat alerts the poster when someone has taken a screenshot].

Face-to-face bullying can no longer so easily be left in the school playground and online bullying can permeate every aspect of a young person's life. Mariam describes how social media exposes her to the lives of people who she would rather not have contact with and which have a negative impact on her sense of wellbeing:

I guess other things would be, people that you avoid, on a day-to-day basis. But then go on social media and seeing those people, it kind of just, fuels something, I don't know...this person, and seeing what they post. I kind of don't want to, but then you do want.

Ava, who experiences anxiety, describes how witnessing bullying behaviours can negatively impact her mood:

[I feel less good] when people are arguing online or if you see someone being cyberbullied or things like that.

A survey of 2515 young people by anti-bullying charity, Ditch the Label, found that 57 per cent of respondents had experienced bullying whilst playing online games. One respondent said:

I get bullied constantly for my skill level while playing games. I get told to kill myself and that I'm lesser of a person because I can't play games as well as others. (Ditch the Label, 2017, p.9)

The survey also found that 20 per cent of respondents said that they had perpetrated online bullying whilst playing online games. One respondent said:

Back in the days, I used to bully people in games to make myself feel better from all the hate and negative vibe in real life. To make me feel better about myself, I bully others and make them feel sad and insecure. (Ditch the Label, 2017, p.11)

The 2016 Ofcom annual survey of parents' and children's attitudes to, and use of, media found that the number of teens who say they have had negative online experiences remains relatively low. The survey found that 12- to 15-year-olds are as likely to be bullied via social media or group chat or text message as they are to be bullied face to face. Only 13 per cent of teens reported they had been bullied in the past 12 months and levels of bullying are the same across social media, chat or text messages at 6 per cent. Only a tiny amount (2%) of 12- to 15-year-olds also reported that they have been bullied via online games. Overall, research suggests that between 6 and 25 per cent of children and young people in the UK experience cyberbullying (Livingstone, 2017).

Despite popular public concerns, surveys of teens routinely indicate that the advent of the internet has not significantly affected the extent of bullying (Jenkins *et al.*, 2017). However, cyberbullying is often the top concern cited for parents, above topics such as spending too much time online (Farrugia *et al.*, 2017). It seems that adult fears may be disproportionate to the actual lived experience of teenagers. However, this is not to suggest that cyberbullying is not harmful when it takes place. Young people report that they are unsure about what action is taken when they make a report about cyberbullying to social media platforms, and some feel that their concerns are not taken seriously (Livingstone *et al.*, 2017).

The ways in which bullying behaviours are mediated can be qualitatively different online than they are in person. In particular, the use of group chat platforms such as WhatsApp is leading to new forms of bullying. According to Schenk and Fremouw (2012), cyberbullying is characterised by the following behaviours:

- **Flaming** – angry or rude messages.

- **Harassment** – sending insulting or threatening messages.

- **Cyberstalking** – threats to harm or intimidate another person.

- **Denigration** – spreading rumours and putting people down.

- **Masquerading** – pretending to be someone else and sharing information intended to damage a person's reputation.

- **Outing** – sharing private information about another person which has been shared in confidence.

- **Exclusion** – deliberately leaving a person out of a group online with the intention of causing distress.

- **Ganging up** – on another person.

Children interviewed for Ofcom's qualitative research on attitudes towards media were increasingly aware that online behaviours can leave a trace which shows evidence of bullying behaviour. As a result, a number of children in the research described how some of their peers were finding new ways of being mean without leaving evidence, such as excluding someone from a chat. Often the functionality of group chats indirectly facilitates exclusion, as children exploit the ability to add or delete people from these groups in order to exclude or hurt them (Ofcom, 2016b). Danah Boyd refers to such practices as 'hiding in plain sight' to describe how teens can use encoded techniques to avoid leaving a trace of mean behaviour.

Ruth explains that 'exposing' is a behaviour whereby she might put a private photograph in the public domain that had been shared in confidence. According to Ruth this is a common practice that takes place when friendships have broken down and to 'get back' at someone who has hurt your feelings. Whilst Matt is not the subject of bullying, he does find that the *banter* that is common in group chats can be confusing and worrying:

Like there's a whole craze of group chats at the moment, and being in them is really great and all, but when people have banter – I get some for it – banter, and it gets a bit too harsh and stuff, and people are rude to you, and you're just, I've had to go on and just say, 'I don't understand what I said is wrong. I only said, like, a few jokes.' I think it's because then people can be very sensitive, and they'll take it the wrong way, and then they start fighting back, or they try to overpower you, especially in a group chat, because always the ones would be the alpha of the pack.

As practitioners, we cannot hope to be up to speed with ever-changing teen practices, which are virtually impossible to police, even if this were desirable or possible. A pragmatic way to make sense of this landscape is to have conversations with teens through shared inquiry in order to help them work out how they best navigate the terrain. This approach transcends the rapidly shifting online environment and means that practitioners can be helpful to young people whatever online context they are experiencing.

Whilst we propose that active support is the most helpful response, it is the case that controls and sanctions are available to some practitioners. In the UK strategy for children's mental health, it is noted that schools can help to contain cyberbullying during the school day by banning or limiting the use of personal mobile phones and other electronic devices. Schools also have the power to search for, and if necessary delete, inappropriate images (or files) on electronic devices, including mobile phones (NHS England, 2015). However, these sanctions and surveillance methods are severely limited in their scope or impact, particularly given young people's ability to encode meaning which is not immediately understandable to adults and for them to subvert and obfuscate. Studies show that some teens avoid discussing experiences of cyberbullying with adults because they fear they will have internet access revoked or controlled or because they believe their parents lack understanding of online practices (Cowie, 2013). Practitioners helping young people manage bullying have to consider young people's fears about sanctions and find ways to have conversations that help young people be open and search for ways forward together.

The internet is not simply a place where bullying can be perpetrated, it can also be a useful resource for young people who are experiencing bullying. A search using the phrase *bullying story* on YouTube shows multiple YouTuber vlogs sharing personal stories about experiences of bullying. In Chapter 2 we explore the valuable role of YouTubers in providing relatable and aspirational stories that young people can both identify with and which help them feel more hopeful.

Self-harm and suicide

Self-harm and suicide are of significant concern to parents and practitioners helping young people with mental health problems. It is not surprising then that the internet is an associated source of concern, providing easy access to pro-suicide information, forums and chat rooms focused on this topic (Bell, 2014). Stories of livestreamed suicides on social media sites such as Facebook and apps such as Periscope are not uncommon and are well publicised in mainstream media. Evidence from practice suggests that lack of understanding on the part of nursing staff regarding information given to them by young people about their online activities may mean that risks go undetected (Livingstone and Palmer, 2012).

According to recent psychological, behavioural, and self-reported data, young adults may engage in self-harm to regulate negative emotions or to punish themselves (Klonsky *et al.*, 2015). Self-harm serves as a coping mechanism to deal with affective, cognitive, and social stress (Nock, 2010). Stigma and lack of understanding of self-harm can result in teens being unwilling to seek help for their behaviours (Seko *et al.*, 2015). The internet therefore affords the opportunity for young people to find out information and to access help in ways which can overcome barriers in face-to-face contact.

It is not uncommon for teens who self-harm to post images of self-harm on the internet. This performative aspect of self-harm suggests that the internet provides both an outlet and an audience to bear witness (Gabriel, 2014). In qualitative interviews with 17 young people who self-harm, Seko and colleagues identified two major themes in the motivations for young people posting images of self-harm online. The first theme focuses on individual benefits such as expressing the self, reflecting on the self-harm experience and soothing the urge to self-harm. The second theme is more socially orientated towards offering emotional help, seeking support from peers and raising social awareness. The internet can be perceived by self-harming teens as a safe place where they can *vent* and seek support. Feeling accepted online can contrast with fear of not being understood by family and practitioners (Seko *et al.*, 2015).

The phenomenon of 'digital self-harm' has been coined by Danah Boyd in a blog post exploring an increase in young people writing nasty messages anonymously to themselves and then answering them online through a social media site called Formspring (Boyd, 2010). One study found that both male and female respondents were mostly likely to say they engaged in self-harassment to gain the attention of a peer. Girls were more likely than boys to say that their motivation was 'proving I could take it', encouraging others 'to worry about me', or to 'get adult attention'. Boys were more likely to say that they did this because they were angry or as a way to start a fight (Englander, 2012, p.3). Hannah Smith was a teenager from Leicestershire who took her own life after suspected cyberbullying. However, an investigation found that most of the bullying messages had been sent from her own IP address on the Ask.FM social media site (Davies, 2014).

So how can parents and practitioners help young people navigate the internet when it comes to making positive choices in relation to self-harm. A systematic review found that young people who self-harm have a preference for informal support over help via health care professionals. It has also been found that health care professionals tend to have a negative view of people who self-harm (Dyson *et al.*, 2016). In contrast, there is a rise in self-harm and suicide prevention activity online and a mounting body of evidence to show they can be helpful to young people. Such resources enable young people to engage in peer support without geographical and temporal barriers and to tell their story. This can help normalise feelings of distress and reduce social isolation (Bell, 2014). A small qualitative study which created an online discussion forum called SharpTalk found that young people participating in the site found it easier to talk to strangers than family and friends, valued the anonymity the forum provided, felt more able to disclose and less likely to be judged by others (Jones *et al.*, 2011).

How are online social network platforms addressing the issue of self-harm and suicide amongst their users? Many of the major social media platforms, such as Facebook, Tumblr and Instagram, have developed policies whereby posts can be reported and self-help resources triggered, or where certain content is unsearchable or banned (Dyson *et al.*, 2016). However, young people quickly find ways to circumvent such restrictions and some platforms do not have any policies at all. This context makes it all the more important for practitioners to take a permissive stance in respect of social media use as opposed to a censorious one.

Bell asserts that research that takes users' views into account tends to emphasise the helpful elements of self-harm and suicide-related online exchange. Research from a professional perspective tends to emphasise the concern that some professionals have about triggering and other harmful information (Bell, 2014). In our conversations with practitioners, we found significant concern that discussion about online behaviours related to self-harm might increase risk for the young person. Practitioners were also concerned about their exposure to managing risk which they are not sure how to respond to.

Just as teenagers go online to create communities of friendships and interests, so distressed young people can find people in similar circumstances and reach out to not feel so alone. Practitioners should gather online resources that they can point young people towards and help them make positive choices about how they use digital media in respect of self-harm. Practitioners should seek to understand how young people are already using the internet in respect of their self-harming and suicidal feelings in order to help guide them in making helpful choices. These approaches are timeless and can be deployed whatever the context and in spite of changing practices and the emergence of new social media platforms.

Calm Harm is an app that helps young people reduce the urge to self-harm. Developed by a clinical psychologist Nihara Krause who runs the charity Stem4, Calm Harm provides Dialectical Behaviour Therapy-related tasks that help the user resist or manage the urge to self-harm. It is private and password protected.

The apps helps the user learn to identify and manage their 'emotional' mind with positive impact. The app enables the user to track their progress and is an aid in treatment but does not replace it. The four categories of tasks target the main reasons for why people self-harm:

- **Distract** – helps to combat the urge by learning self-control.

- **Comfort** – helps to care rather than harm.

- **Express** – helps get feelings out in a different way.

- **Release** – provides safe alternatives to self-injury.

The app has been approved for inclusion on the NHS Apps Library.[1]

Gender stereotypes and sexual harassment

As teens begin to explore their sexuality and gender identity, the internet affords opportunities to access information and engage in a process of discovery online. The internet expands possibilities whilst simultaneously creating new pressures and tensions for young people to manoeuvre their way through. Sexual harassment exists on a continuum from use of gendered and sexual insults, unauthorised sharing of images, through to threats and coercion and sexual violence (Livingstone *et al.*, 2017). Research about offline sexual harassment suggests that it is commonplace for girls and young women and that it

---

1   https://apps.beta.nhs.uk

is accepted by many as a normal part of everyday life and is therefore under-recognised and under-reported (Livingstone *et al.*, 2017).

Whilst there is limited research about online sexual harassment, the results of European qualitative research show a similar pattern, with 'slut-shaming' and homophobic comments viewed as normalised. Whilst these behaviours are more often experienced by teen girls, boys also report the normalisation of online homophobic bullying (Livingstone *et al.*, 2017).

Sexual experimentation is a normal facet of child development, and in a connected world it is accompanied by the potential for sexual solicitation and harassment online. Adolescents are more at risk of online sexual abuse than younger children insofar as they have more unsupervised use of the internet, along with an increased propensity for risk taking, impulsivity, sensation-seeking and sexual interest common to this developmental stage (Hansen and Holmes, 2014).

A review of evidence related to teen sexual development found that gender stereotypes of masculinity and femininity are routinely reproduced online with associated pressures to conform for teens of both sexes (Livingstone and Mason, 2015). The authors found gender differences encountering sexual experiences online, with girls more likely to be targeted online, receive direct requests about sexual activities, report being upset by these interactions or receiving images, and more likely to be victimised than boys. The researchers argue that more research is required to understand the extent to which conforming to a masculine identity impacts on boys' sexual development; a number of studies suggest that boys may have more reservations about sexually explicit content online than might be expected, and that they face stigma in reporting abuse (Livingstone and Mason, 2015).

Not surprisingly, online vulnerability is often connected to offline vulnerability. Lesbian, gay, bisexual and transgender (LGBT) teens are more likely to be targeted by online solicitations and sexual requests (Livingstone and Mason, 2015). Research suggests that teens most at risk are boys who are gay, adolescents who have been sexually or physically abused, teens who engage in risky offline behaviour, and those who talk to strangers about sex online in, for example, chat rooms (Valkenburg and Peters, 2011). Communicating with strangers online can have adverse effects whereby young people are vulnerable to being coerced into doing things to prevent intimate details about their sexuality being exposed (Childline, 2016).

A systematic review of evidence related to teens accessing sexual content via social media found a positive correlation with risky sexual behaviours but was not able to establish if one is caused by the other (Smith *et al.*, 2016). It is not clear if teens who are more likely to engage in sexually risky behaviour then choose to seek out content online; or if seeking out such content leads to more risky behaviour. Rather than assume causality, the evidence indicates that practitioners should seek to understand context, meanings and the interplay between online and offline behaviours in order to gain grounded insights into young people's experiences of sexual experimentation online.

The potential for online sexual harassment and solicitation is particularly problematic given that the internet can equally be an important means of accessing information and support for teens – paradoxically, spaces that can be liberating can simultaneously expose vulnerable teens to abuse. Those promoting children's rights argue that many internet filters aimed at protecting children get the balance wrong in placing protection over teens' rights to access information. Such filters can block educational, political and advocacy information and may prevent teens from engaging with these topics, forming their own opinions and developing resilience to problematic content (Livingstone and Mason, 2015). Practitioners should seek to balance an awareness of the risks associated with digital media against the positive benefits of accessing useful information and resources. Open and ongoing conversations with young people about these issues is an important way of helping young people both navigate immediate pressures as well as develop resilience for the future.

Sexting

Sexting is the term that describes sending nude or partially nude images via digital media. It is illegal for children to create such pictures, transmit them to others, and for others to possess, download, store or view them. A young person is breaking the law if they (1) take an explicit photo or video of themselves or a friend; (2) share an explicit image or video of a child, even if it's shared between children of the same age; or (3) possess, download or store an explicit image or video of a child, even if the child gave their permission for it to be created. However, current policy guidance and Crown Prosecution Service policy are not to prosecute consensual transmission or possession between older children. The focus is rather on safeguarding, health and online safety promotion (Martellozzo *et al.*, 2017).

In a survey for the NSPCC it was found that most young people interpreted sexting as writing and sharing sexually explicit words with people they knew, normally a boyfriend or girlfriend (Martellozzo *et al.*, 2017). Evidence suggests that sexting is not widespread, with only a small minority of teens sharing nude images online. In the NSPCC survey 14 per cent of participants had taken nude or semi-nude pictures of themselves and only half of those (7%) went on to share those images with others. However, a much greater number of young people (49%) had been asked to share their picture online and this is more the case for girls than boys (Martellozzo *et al.*, 2017). A literature review (Cooper *et al.*, 2016) of sexting behaviours found the following motivations behind young people sending sexually explicit images:

- a means of flirting

- consensual activity within a relationship

- part of an experimental adolescent phase

- as a result of pressure from partner and/or friends.

It should be noted that, despite media and public discourse focusing on the adverse psychological and social harms from sexting behaviours, research with young people suggests that many teens perceive a range of positive aspects such as exploring sexual identity and as an expression of intimacy in a romantic relationship.

Non-consensual sharing of sexual images online can have a range of negative impacts from shame and humiliation through to bullying and blackmail (Cooper *et al.*, 2016). The risk of an image being shared without consent, or mistakenly forwarded to others, can result in shame and humiliation both for the person sending the image and the subject of the image. Young people may not always think through the consequences of their actions before it is too late and it can be almost impossible to remove photos once they are online (Ahern and Mechling, 2013).

Research suggests that certain groups of young people are more likely to become subject to unwanted sexual solicitation and exploitation. A history of offline physical or sexual abuse, depression, isolation or lack of support within the family may all lead to increased vulnerability (Cooper *et al.*, 2016). Gender and ethnic differences also appear to play a role in sexting behaviours, with girls more likely experience more sexual solicitation than boys, and Black girls more likely to receive requests for sexual pictures of themselves (Tynes and Mitchel, 2013, quoted in Cooper *et al.*, 2016). Sexting behaviours are taking place in a cultural context whereby gender inequality exists and boys are more likely to be held in high regard for showing off pictures of girls whereas girls are more likely to be criticised or seen as putting themselves at risk.

None of the participants in an NSPCC study knew how to take action to remove nude images on digital media and where to go should they become worried about their own images. They all felt that not enough information is available to children and young people on this issue (Martellozzo *et al.*, 2017). Ruth accepts that sharing of nude images is an ordinary part of everyday teenage online life that has to be navigated. Her approach is to limit the damage of a shared sext rather than tell an adult – if a photo gets posted then just pretend you don't care and it will get less traction:

> If you admit it then no-one can use it against you. People can only throw shade on you if you get upset or don't admit your flaws.

Ruth worries that a consequence of telling an adult might result in excessively prying parents or, worse, having a phone confiscated. She also believes that sexting between teens in a relationship is a comfortable way of exploring sexuality if they are less confident in person. Her attitude towards sexting is likely to be very different than that of her parents.

The NSPCC recommends that organisations working with children and young people should have a policy to deal with sexting and provides a series of useful resources. They argue that organisational approaches to managing sexting should be part of their wider approach to safeguarding. The NSPCC also provide advice on how to go about removing sexually explicit images from the internet. Recognising that teens may choose to sext, the charity Young Scot, has useful guidance on *safe sexting* that helps young people make good choices and avoid harm. They advocate a harm minimisation approach as follows.

If you do send explicit images to your partner, you can agree on how to stay safe together:

- Have a secure app on your phone to avoid anyone else looking through it.

- Keep your face out of any photos.

- Keep other distinguishing features hidden too, such as a tattoo.

- Make sure your bedroom and any indication of where you live is out of view.

- Agree to delete the images after you've viewed them.

- Before you hit send remember, even if you trust your partner not to share the photos, there's always the risk they could lose their phone or be hacked.[2]

Whilst we may be tempted as practitioners to shut down or avoid this difficult topic, the above guidance offers a commonsense way to have practical conversations which are non-judgemental and help teens make sensible choices. As we have previously seen, banning and blaming can be counterproductive, and a pragmatic approach which opens up conversation and encourages young people to be honest about issues such as sexting will go a long way to helping them develop online resilience.

Pornography

Many practitioners are concerned about young people's easy access to pornographic content via digital media. Evidence suggests that there does seem to be a relationship between viewing pornography and poorer mental health. In one study among 10- to 17-year-olds, those who sought internet pornography were twice as likely to report the clinical features of depression and less positive relationships with caregivers compared to those who used offline pornography and non seekers (Ybarra and Mitchell, 2005). Online pornography can be defined as:

> Images and films of people having sex or behaving sexually online. This includes semi-naked and naked images and films of people that you may have viewed or downloaded from the internet, or that someone else shared with you directly, or showed to you on their phone or computer. (Martellozzo *et al.*, 2017, p.16)

---

2   This is reproduced with permission from the Young Scot website, see https://young. scot/young-scot-extra/articles/safe-sexting

In a mixed methods study for the NSPCC, researchers found that young people tend to encounter pornography through a mix of actively searching for it online and through encountering it as it 'popped up' whilst they are online. Around a fifth of young people report seeing pornography when it is shown to them by someone else without asking for it or expecting it (Martellozzo *et al.*, 2017). Research findings suggest more children are more likely to report unintentional rather than intentional viewing of pornography. This may happen through a number of different ways such as pop-ups, misleadingly named websites or advertising on illegal streaming sites (Livingstone *et al.*, 2017).

By the age of 15–16 more young people report having seen pornography than not having seen it. More boys (59%) than girls (25%) actively search for pornography online. Older teens are significantly more likely to agree that pornography is unrealistic or exploitative and boys are more likely to agree that pornography is fun or amusing, arousing and exciting; girls are more likely to agree that it is shocking, scary or upsetting (Martellozzo *et al.*, 2017). Exposure to online pornography shapes both male and female teens' conceptions about what *real-life* sex is supposed to be like, with girls often being concerned about body image and boys concerned about sexual performance (Livingstone and Mason, 2015).

The focus group element of the NSPCC study, which considered how institutions should respond to online pornography, led to a consensus about the importance of education and the need to revisit the school curriculum in response to increased access to pornography online. Participants emphasised the need for information and education on this topic to be relevant and engaging (Martellozzo *et al.*, 2017). In their review of the literature, Livingstone and Mason conclude:

> Researchers concur that young people and especially adolescents deserve age-appropriate, informative materials on sex and sexuality, and critical tools for interpreting pornography.

SEIM [sexually explicit internet material] in itself appears to be an inept and harmful source of information about sex. At the moment young people do not receive the appropriate tools to help them critically assess pornographic images, nor do they receive relationship-based sex education that discusses the positive potential of sex in a consenting, affectionate relationship. (2015, p.38)

When Ruth was 12 years old a male friend showed her a pornographic video trailer containing explicit images. The film has become infamous amongst comedy YouTubers whereby people film themselves watching the video to share their reactions online. Ruth laughs as she tells this story and says she finds it both funny and disgusting in equal measure. Her attitude is that the friend shared it with her as a joke and she took it in that spirit. Ruth assured us that her experience is not uncommon.

So how can practitioners help young people who seek help and guidance in respect of online pornography? Below are some useful pointers for parents and practitioners:

- Keep yourself informed about online pornography.

- When discussing pornography with a young person, use language appropriate to their age.

- Acknowledge and show appreciation that a young person is discussing pornography with you in order to keep an open dialogue.

- Avoid approaching the topic in a way which may blame, punish or invoke shame in a young person.

- Help young people prepare themselves for the fact that they are likely to encounter pornography when they go online.

- Keep communication channels open so young people can can turn to you for help should they need it.

The above pointers promote open dialogue and a proactive approach whereby we should assume young people will encounter pornography, and we should aim to prepare them for when this happens. Avoiding blaming and shaming and helping to minimise harm is a useful way for practitioners to approach this difficult topic.

Body image and disordered eating

Eating disorders are a group of diagnoses in which individuals experience issues with body weight, shape, everyday diet and attitude towards food. A survey by the UK's leading eating disorders charity, Beat, found that eating disorders are most commonly first seen in teens under the age of 16. Eating disorders tend to continue for around six years and can cause significant disruption to a young person's education along with longer-term impacts on health, employability and lifetime opportunities (PwC, 2015). Websites and chat rooms promoting anorexia and other eating disorders have caught the public imagination as a worrying aspect of the internet for vulnerable teens. How right are we to be concerned and what do parents, carers and practitioners need to know?

According to sociocultural theory, idealised images of beauty and body image are pervasive in mainstream media and have a powerful effect on teens. A substantial body of research demonstrates a link between fashion magazines, television consumption and body dissatisfaction associated with disordered eating (Tiggemann and Slater, 2013). An Australian study which focused on girls in the first two years of high school, found that internet exposure was associated with internalisation of the thin ideal, body surveillance, and a drive for thinness. The researchers found that social networking sites, which are characterised by developing a personal profile and multiple comparisons via peer-to-peer engagement, had the most substantial negative effects on body image (Tiggeman and Slater, 2013). A systematic review of of evidence regarding Facebook use and disordered eating in girls and women concluded that there is a positive association between the two (Holland and Tiggemann, 2016). Zoe, a 14-year-old with an eating disorder, describes how she follows celebrities on Instagram that feed negatively into her sense of self:

> I've always suffered with body image and I've always found it very hard. When I see these things on Instagram, it's like, 'how to get a smaller waist' or 'do this and you'll get this' and 'this is bad' and it's like a normal body type. It's like completely photoshopped. Or you see the Kardashians with perfect make-up and hair every day and everything is goals and they show you all these amazing, glorious moments. Even though I shouldn't, I do compare myself a lot to these things and even though all these celebrities have been edited, they've had really good lighting, they've had makeup and stuff, you don't see that when you look at the image. You just see you and then you compare your body or your makeup and everything. You always want what you can't have, in a way. You're always looking and like, 'I want my hair to be blonder', or, 'I want a figure like that', or, 'Their clothes.'

Even though Zoe is aware that the celebrities that she follows have carefully curated appearances, and that they edit images to manufacture an idealised body image, she nevertheless finds that looking at them makes her feel bad:

> You feel almost put down because that's what the media always portrays as goals and what women should have and people like. Obviously, no one is ever going to like you in life but I'm always super paranoid about making a good impression.

As we can see through Zoe's description, social media platforms such as Instagram and Snapchat are highly visual media through which idealised images of appearance can be promoted. Furthermore, the interactive nature of online social networks provides ever-present opportunities for young people to compare their appearance with others (McClean *et al.*, 2017). Posting photos of oneself, otherwise known as a 'selfie' is common practice, with 91 per cent of teens who use online social networks posting images of themselves. Sharing of selfies has been linked to greater internalised body dissatisfaction that other forms of activity on social media (McLean *et al.*, 2015). Zoe describes her sister, who also has an eating disorder, who has a complicated relationship with photo sharing:

> She's so scared of being judged or photographed – obviously she suffers with body dysmorphia, but being taken a photo of or something, she can't go out unless she's perfect. She'll have a breakdown if her hair's not curled enough. But I'm not just saying breakdown, I mean full on screaming, shouting. It's distressing.

However, such studies do not always illuminate the more nuanced activities of some teens that can be more easily elicited through qualitative means in order to understand how they may play with and subvert the platforms they engage with. One example of this subversion is the rise of *Finstagram*. Otherwise known as *Finsta* this is a fake Instagram account which takes the form of an alter ego profile to a young person's real Instagram or *Rinstagram*. Through their Finstagram account, teens subvert the social norms of a carefully curated and presented profile, to share images and updates which are more mundane, less attractive and with secret jokes. Whilst Maddy declares her public Snapchat is for 'bragging' she uses the platform's private chat and video function to goof around with her friends, often chatting to them whilst she is dressed in her pyjamas and without the carefully made-up face she shows to the outside world.

Whilst we traditionally associate the private sphere with the home and the public sphere with spaces external to the home, Snapchat affords both personal and public spaces in one platform. Rosie can simultaneously brag and show off through her carefully curated *story* on Snapchat whilst messing about through the same platform with her close friends – a nuanced blend of public and private, curated and carefree, pressured and personal.

It is perhaps overly simplistic to assume that young people are passive consumers of consumer culture. A group of Black and Asian young women in Bradford have established a campaign with the hashtag #iamperfectasme which is focused on taking control and promoting body confidence amongst their peers. The group uses the hashtag to share positive messages on Twitter and blend online activities with performances and workshops in a city-centre social temporary meeting space called Speakers Corner. It seems in a whole variety of ways, young people are finding their own ways to subvert social media platforms to present multiple and various facets of themselves and to challenge reductive representations of their bodies. The adult refrain that social media has made young people narcissistic and vain does not necessarily hold up under close interrogation.

Practitioners should help young people become aware of the possibilities of creative civic engagement that challenges stereotypes connected to young people's bodies. However, we must recognise that celebrity and mainstream media accounts have the resources and the reach to be all pervasive and that practices which intend to subvert them will reach much smaller audiences. The key is equipping teens to engage with media critically and to develop their sense of self-worth to the extent that they are less buffeted by the normative portrayals that they are likely to consume.

For those with disordered eating, social networking platforms can be a means to share, discuss and consume idealised body images. A review of Twitter's timeline using the popular pro-ana (short for pro anorexia) hashtag #thinspo reveals numerous tweets promoting anorexia along with photos of exceptionally thin girls and women.

The tone of the tweets is often aspirational and some accounts have tens of thousands of followers. Zoe describes how her sister engages with commercial online content that promotes an ideal body image:

> Obviously, my sister, she's bought corsets and all these fit pills and stuff that all the celebrities promote. They're like, 'I get this amazing waist with my waist trainer.' Obviously, they're sponsored, they're being paid to say this, but this is all over social media.

A study of Twitter accounts in English, French and Spanish found 341 pro-ana Twitter accounts. The most popular hashtag used by the accounts was *#thinspo* (an abbreviation of *thin inspiration*) followed by *#thinspiration*, *#Thin15*, *#EDprobs* (eating disorders problems) and *#proana*. Other hashtags were *#bonespo*, *#annatips*, *#anamia*, *#abcdiet*, *#thigh gap* and *#LovemyED*. The study found that most account biographies indicated that they belonged to teens (Bert *et al.*, 2016). The study points to a sub-culture of teens using social media to promote disordered eating and to create peer support and encouragement to sustain associated practices.

Whilst a desire for thinness is a predominant feature of disordered eating, dissatisfaction with body image can come in many shapes and sizes. Rachel is a white British 15-year-old whose best friend, Tika, is a first generation African Muslim. Having met in primary school and now living in separate cities, they maintain contact through daily FaceTime chats as they get ready for school each morning, carrying their smart device from bedroom to bathroom and kitchen as they get ready for school with an air of amiable companionship. Both teens share a love of R&B music and scour YouTube and Snapchat for celebrity updates and music videos. They compare their slight frames with to the more curvy bodies of celebrities such as Beyoncé and Kim Kardashian. They endlessly look at articles, like *How to Get a Bigger Butt, According to Kim Kardashian's Trainer Gunnar Peterson* and have found 'fitness' syrups for sale online, along with countless blogs in which women claim to have transformed their bodies. Tika's mum has ordered the syrup online for her daughter whereas Rachel's parents have been more cautious. An online search found that it contains antihistamines and has a whole range of unpleasant side effects. This story of two teens longing for curvy bodies and lunging after apparent solutions exemplifies how media can amplify body dissatisfaction and online articles and blogs can offer off-the-shelf fixes. A potentially toxic mix for teenagers in search of a simple answer and without the skills or motivation to critically appraise the information they are presented with.

How do practitioners navigate this online terrain? Our interviews uncovered a high degree of ambivalence and significant concerns about risk. Practitioners sometimes worry that by talking about the internet with teens they may inadvertently lead them towards the very websites they would like them to avoid. One practitioner told us:

> There are a lot of staff feeling out of touch and worried about issues such as information governance. We need to be less risk averse with this and we direct teens to good information. There is a risk in not doing it, that they'll go on to sites that aren't appropriate and find their own way through to it. We need to embrace it.

So how can practitioners help teens negotiate aspects of online social networking which appear to encourage negative body image and increased body surveillance? One experimental study with adolescent girls deployed an intervention combining media literacy and peer components in order to prevent disordered eating. The media literacy component aimed to encourage critical thinking about the media in order to deconstruct and reduce its pervasive influence; the peer component focused on peer interactions as a risk factor for body dissatisfaction and aimed to reduce pressure to adhere to norms and ideas related to appearance. The intervention, Boost Body Confidence and Social Media Savvy (Boost), consisted of three class-based 50 minute lessons, with before and after measures taken using a number of validated instruments. A control group was used as a comparison. The study showed improvements in body esteem and reduced pressure to alter appearance. Whilst a small experimental study, the results suggest that practitioners can play a helpful role in assisting teens in their navigation of the internet along with helping them develop critical thinking about how social media and media more generally can promote idealised images.

In an article for *Eating Disorders: The Journal of Treatment and Prevention*, Tierney (2007) argues that practitioners should take time to get to understand pro-ana websites and forums on the basis that they can be the one place where teens feel understood and respected. She goes on to make the case that people experiencing an eating disorder are more likely to be open about their beliefs and behaviours on fora than they are to professionals. We would suggest that practitioners working with teens who are affected by eating issues should familiarise themselves with the types of content available online. For example an internet search for *pro-ana tips and tricks* reveals dedicated websites that present anorexia as a lifestyle choice along with strategies to reduce weight. However, there are also many peer websites which actively challenge pro-ana content and provide alternative viewpoints. The national charity, Beat, has moderated messageboards for adolescents and for adults along with online support groups. Both messageboards and support groups have ground rules for participants and are professionally moderated, providing an addition or alternative to peer-to-peer fora.

Practitioners should recognise the reality that pro-ana forums may have positive as well as negative effects on participants (Teufel *et al.*, 2013). The affordance of online fora for anonymity, to find like-minded people and develop a sense of belonging and acceptance may all be experienced positively by participants (Tierney, 2008). As Siobhan explained, seeing a middle-aged male psychiatrist once a week feels insubstantial when you know you have a peer group available to you 24/7 who understand and support you. Enabling teens such as Siobhan to engage critically and reflectively with her peers online is a key task of practitioners helping teens affected by eating disorders. Endeavouring to understand teens' engagement with those sites by seeing the world through their eyes means suspending the reflex to judge and condemn.

During the course of our focus groups and interviews, teens told us time and time again that their smartphones and the internet can be an invaluable distraction from feeling down or distressed. They were often frustrated that adults too readily criticised them for going on their phones without understanding this important facet of how they use them. Edward, an eating disorders service practitioner, told us how teens that he works with regularly use their phone as a helpful distraction during mealtimes – either chatting to friends for support and encouragement or playing games or scanning Instagram to view updates from their friends. Whilst this can be a means of getting through a mealtime for a young person, it is often criticised or forbidden by parents and carers. Edward understands parents' concerns, but believes that they should make every effort to reduce the barriers to eating and support means of helping young people begin to increase their intake of food. He is therefore an advocate of the smartphone as a helpful distraction for some young people in the early days of recovery where weight restoration is the immediate priority.

It is clear that the internet has both positive and problematic qualities for teens who are vulnerable to or have disordered eating. The internet can be a source of valuable information and peer support. In contrast, it can be a place where teens can access information and support to continue and even deepen harmful behaviours. The challenge for parents and practitioners is to help young people make decisions which promote good mental health whilst recognising that they may gain positive benefits from sites which, on the surface, appear highly destructive.

Excessive use of the internet

Concern that the internet is inherently antisocial and that young people are engaging with their phones in preference to in-person relationships is familiar trope within popular discourse. However, this dominant view is inconsistent with evidence from research, which finds that young people primarily use digital technologies to extend their interactions with friends from school and other face-to-face social settings, or to engage with traditional media such as music and film (Common Sense, 2016).

A UNICEF research project noted that child participants often expressed nostalgic views about a time when face-to-face relationships were the norm, even though this could not reflect their own lived experience which does not precede the existence of the internet. The authors argue that this nostalgia for a time that young people cannot have personally experienced suggests that it has been imposed by the adult world rather than necessarily being grounded in young people's lives (Third *et al.*, 2014).

The notion of internet addiction has taken a firm grip on public consciousness and the effects of problematic internet use are regularly scrutinised in the media. Take for example, an article in *The Atlantic* entitled: 'Have smartphones destroyed a generation?' (Twenge, 2017) which posits that smartphone use is precipitating a mental health crisis in teens. However, there is ambiguity about what constitutes internet addiction, given that smart devices can be used for many different activities from watching videos through to playing games and chatting with friends. Focusing simply on time spent online is problematic when so many activities can take place via the internet (Common Sense, 2016). The fifth edition of the American Diagnostic and Statistical Manual of Mental Disorders (DSM-5) does *not* include a diagnostic category of internet addiction, but does include a new category of Internet Gaming Disorder (IGD). In the 11th revision of the International Classification of Diseases (ICD-11), the World Health Organisation has classified digital and video gaming as a mental health disorder (WHO, 2018). However there remains controversy both about the diagnostic category itself and the associated symptoms (Common Sense, 2016). The term Problematic Interactive Media Use among Children and Adolescents (PIMU) has entered the lexicon in this field and there is an increasing number of academic studies exploring this topic area.

An international OECD study found that most teens are balanced in their use of the internet and generally report beneficial effects from being online (OECD, 2017). Zahid's reflections exemplify a sensible approach to achieving on/offline balance:

> Yes, I would say that the internet is good for so many purposes for different people, it depends on everyone and what the internet brings to their lives, you know, but it's just maybe over using it for maybe some people, who maybe use it for unnecessary stuff and that is not really, really important. That doesn't help other people as well. So I think if you use the internet for a better purpose, it will bring a positive thing to you. But if you use it for a negative purpose, then, obviously, it doesn't help.

An OECD study identified a small number of 'extreme' internet users who go online for more than six hours a day. They found that excessive internet use has a negative relationship with life satisfaction, with teens reporting feeling more lonely at school, and being bullied alongside a greater risk of disengagement from school (OECD, 2017). Research to date about excessive media use is largely correlational rather than causational, making in hard to establish whether problematic use of the internet is causing negative outcomes or whether mental distress results in teens spending more time online (Common Sense, 2016). Martha describes how she uses the internet more when she is feeling down:

> When you feel low or just not in a good place, it's easy just to go on the internet. So usually I would spend more time on the internet if I was feeling not very good than if I was having a great

time... I can just consume, scroll through and not have to think about anything else.

It should be noted that digital media companies incorporate persuasive design features that encourage users to stay on their sites for as long as possible. With advertising as their primary source of revenue, it is in their interests to keep us actively engaged on their platforms and producing data which can then be monetised (Nodder, 2013). A critical awareness of the internet entails an awareness of the ways in which we may be persuaded to stay online at the expense of other activities. This is important to be aware of in helping young people who are not happy with their levels of internet use or for whom it is causing problems.

To help explore with a young person whether their use may be problematic, it would helpful to consider the components of addictive behaviour (Griffiths, 2009) that have been identified as:

- **Salience** – where the addictive behaviour, or thinking about the addiction, becomes the most important activity and is prioritised over others with a negative impact on the person's function.

- **Mood modification** – the addictive behaviour alters the subjective experience of mood and not doing it leads to a significant negative change in mood state.

- **Tolerance** – increasing frequency or intensity of a behaviour is required to achieve the same positive effects (a reward or 'hit').

- **Conflict** – the behaviour and its consequences are a source of conflict between the person and those around them, or within the person's own mind, potentially leading to a loss of social relationships and status.

- **Withdrawal** – the person experiences physical symptoms or mental distress when the behaviour is stopped.

- **Relapse** – following a period of abstinence, a person quickly returns to the previous levels of excessive use when they re-start the behaviour such that moderated use is difficult to sustain.

Reflecting these universal components to addictive behaviours, Mascheroni and Ólafsson (2014) identify five characteristics of excessive internet use in children and young people which may have adverse effects:

- sacrificed eating or sleeping because of the internet

- felt unhappy or bothered when not able to go on the internet

- surfed the internet even when not really interested

- spent time on the internet in preference to doing school work or spending time with friends or family

- tried and not succeeded in spending less time on the internet.

As indicated by the above traits, internet use can become problematic when young people feel compelled to go online and feel out of control in how they engage with it. Young people can become preoccupied with the internet and experience withdrawal symptoms when they are not online. They may use the internet to escape from negative feelings and internet use results in conflict both with others but also with oneself (Van den Eijnden *et al.*, 2008). Though they may not have physical symptoms of withdrawal, psychological difficulties, such as high levels of anxiety, may be experienced.

Getting sufficient sleep is both important for a child's physical and emotional development and for them to be able to learn well at school. Despite a concern from some parents that children are engaged in social media until late at night, the Children's Digital Day report found that the peak evening time for young people between 11–15 to be on social media is at 8.15pm and by 9pm, 15 per cent are still doing so. At 10pm, the percentage of 11- to 15-year-olds communicating via social media has decreased to 9 per cent and by midnight it is 2 per cent (Ofcom, 2016b). Setting clear boundaries around sleeping times has well established benefits for both children and teens and this should be a consideration for practitioners helping young people who don't feel in control of their internet use.

One in five children report at least two behaviours or feelings associated with excessive internet use as set out above and young people in the UK report the highest levels (29%) compared to other countries (Mascheroni and Ólafsson, 2014). Ella describes how it can be easy for internet use to become unhelpful but it isn't always easy to exercise self-control and step away:

> It can be so brutal sometimes and I think sometimes, as well, for me, anyway, when I'm in a certain mind frame, I can relate anything to what is going on. And, particularly, when you're in that mind frame, when you're comparing yourself as well, it's so easy to just let it spiral by going online and looking at stuff and kind of torturing yourself a bit. And sometimes I will be good and have some self-control and not do that, because I know – I can catch myself and be like, 'What you doing? You're making yourself feel worse.' And sometimes I won't even realise that I'm doing it, you know?

She goes on to describe how reducing her use of the internet had a positive impact on her mental health:

> I just stayed away and that was really, really helpful. And I've noticed as I've started integrating back in it has brought back my anxieties and just things like, you know, waking up and checking

your phone for things and stuff like that, which are habits that I don't feel are healthy for me. And that I do want to change, but it's kind of hard to, because of the main things for me, that I find difficult, especially when I'm struggling is being contactable all the time.

Whilst a medical interpretation of excessive internet use is seen as a pathology similar to gambling, other approaches favour a compensatory model of internet use, whereby some people may use the internet as a means to escape from problems and to compensate for psychological difficulties (Mascheroni and Ólafsson, 2014). Mary has distressing experiences associated with her diagnosis of Borderline Personality Disorder and routinely uses online games as a distraction from suicidal feelings. When she is unable to sleep at night, she uses Twitter to connect with people on the other side of the world where it is daytime and with whom she can chat.

Rather than taking a punitive approach to teens who are excessively using the internet, we would argue that a more helpful approach would be to redirect their efforts towards using technologies for purposeful activities (OECD, 2017). Leveraging the internet for educational, creative and civic participation may help young people to re-orientate themselves from adverse to positive associations with the internet. Connecting online activities with offline activities can also be a useful strategy for achieving more balance in internet use. Parents and practitioners also have an important role in helping self-regulate their activities online. Aliya told us how she has a strategy in place with her mum to take some time away from the internet:

If I'm feeling particularly stressed or something, me and my mum and have got something called 'going to ground', which is basically like your phone is on airplane mode, your laptop is off. We'll turn the router off if necessary, where it's literally just stay in the house, with the cats and just watch TV and read a book. So you don't have anything from outside making you feel worse.

Ella had a whole range of strategies for managing her time online to help her feel in control of her internet use:

> I like to do something where you can't do anything else, if that makes sense? So I end up going to the gym and just putting headphones in, turning the phone off. And going to the cinema is one of my favourites and because you can't see your phone, if you can everyone else gets annoyed…it's just dark and then I'm in that but then for the rest of the evening I'm thinking of what the next [book] will be or thinking of what – because I like to write a lot, so I always get ideas to write and then that just extends out for the rest of the evening. I like that kind of thing. Like going for a drive. I go for a drive with my dad and we'll just put on a random album like really loud and then we'll just sit there or I'll just have a really random discussion about something.

Practitioners have a valuable role in helping young people recognise when they are spending excessive amounts of time online. Supporting teens to develop strategies for a more balanced engagement with digital media is an important feature of a holistic approach to developing good mental health and wellbeing.

Extremist content and other adverse effects

A range of additional adverse effects can be experienced by teens, which we mention briefly here. These include, but are not limited to, online fraud, viruses and malicious software, hacking of personal information (for example, the term *Frape* blends the words Facebook and rape, when a personal account is violated) fake profiles, people pretending to be someone else (otherwise known as *catfishing*; Mascheroni and Ólafsson, 2014). The potential to be influenced by radicalisation is another online adverse effect; this is a process whereby an individual:

Comes to embrace values and opinions about a certain topic… that gradually become more extreme and hence start to deviate more from the normative opinions, while at the same time finding it more difficult to accept opposite opinions. (Geeraerts, 2012, quoted in Livingstone *et al.*, 2017, p.54)

The internet appears to play a considerable role in facilitating an increase in radicalisation amongst young people on topics from politics through to religion. It can be facilitated online and at scale without in-person contact. At its most extreme, it can lead to ideological violence such as terrorism (Livingstone *et al.*, 2017). The research is sparse in regard to online radicalisation of young people in the UK and characteristics that may make young people vulnerable are not clear. A review of the evidence by the Youth Justice Board (2012) sets out existing evidence in detail.

It is possible that teens, who are still honing their critical thinking, may find it hard to separate what is true from that which is fiction. This may increase vulnerability to propaganda, fake news and extremist content. One survey of 1,500 12- to17-year-olds found that only a third report that they find it easy to critically appraise information online (UK Internet Safety Centre, 2017). An example of fake news that was quickly propagated, by mainstream media such as the BBC as well as via social media, is a news item about a fictional Blue Whale Game. The game, which in the event turned out to be fake, was supposedly one in which players were encouraged to take their own life. It was reported that several suicides had taken place as a result. However, on investigation by the UK Safety Internet Centre and others, it transpired that there was no substance to the story. This incident underlines the need for young people, parents and practitioners to develop good digital literacy skills. We discuss digital inclusion and literacy in more detail in Chapter 5.

Cybercrime is a relatively new phenomenon and there are limited UK crime statistics on prevalence rates. However, the National Cyber Crime Unit has stated that the average age of suspects arrested in cybercrime investigations is 17 (Livingstone *et al.*, 2017). Cybercrime appears to be mostly perpetrated by boys, and many do it for fun without appreciating the consequences of their actions or the criminal justice implications. Online gaming can be a pathway to cybercrime, whereby gamers join forums to source game modifications through which criminals can groom them to participate in illegal online activities (Livingstone *et al.*, 2017). There is an opportunity to recognise and harness the skills and talents of young people to take up careers in the ever-growing tech sector. This requires adults who are interested in their online behaviours, willing to engage in conversation about them, and can route them towards legitimate educative and career pathways to make the most of their skills and interests.

As with all adverse implications of the internet, practitioners who take a creative and optimistic approach to helping young people navigate the risks, will, simultaneously, help teens realise the many benefits.

Conclusion

In this chapter we have seen that teens' adverse experiences of the internet can have varied impacts which are not always obvious. It is desirable for teens to be exposed to some risk and to learn how to manage it in order to develop both digital skills and resilience. Practitioners can take a number of approaches to help teens anticipate, minimise and manage adverse experiences online. First and foremost we advocate that practitioners adopt an inquiring orientation and an open dialogue with teens.

In conclusion, we set out key takeaways from the chapter which we believe are salient for practitioners supporting teens who have mental health problems.

Everyday ups and downs

In general young people have a low level of concern about about online risk and regard the channels they engage with as simply another media through which everyday dramas are played out, initiated or continued. It is important that practitioners keep this in mind when weighing up concerns about adverse effects, and seek to understand the nuances of teen practices before categorising and judging their online experiences.

Balancing positives and negatives

Social media platforms have multiple features that enable a range of activities that are both private and public. For example, whilst we may associate Instagram with sharing images with followers, it also enables private messaging between individuals; Snapchat enables private video calls between friends as well as public image posting. This means that the same platform may afford both positive opportunities and negative effects simultaneously.

Resilience through experience

Children who encounter more risks online are not necessarily those who experience more harmful consequences. Teens who encounter more risks are often more skilled and as a consequence develop more resilience and are more able to manage difficult or unpleasant situations when they encounter them.

Vulnerability

Teens who are vulnerable in their everyday lives are more likely to be vulnerable online. Practitioners should be alert to how vulnerabilities expressed in the offline lives of young people they support may manifest themselves online.

Limitations of surveillance

Filters, surveillance and sanctions have a role in minimising the risk of adverse effects. However, given that young people's encoded practices are not always obvious to adults, these approaches can be limited in their scope or impact. Filters can block educational, political and advocacy information and may prevent teens from engaging with these topics, forming their own opinions and developing resilience to problematic content. Teens may avoid discussing adverse experiences with adults if they fear the will have internet access revoked or controlled or if they believe adults lack understanding of online practices.

The internet as a resource to counter adverse effects

As well as being a sphere in which adverse effects can be experienced, the internet is replete with resources to help young people inform themselves, understand, and work out how to counter negative experiences. Practitioners should help guide teens to access these resources so that they can equip themselves to negotiate the downsides of their connected lives.

Informing and educating

An educative approach that anticipates adverse effects and helps young people become informed and educated is a means of countering adverse impacts and helping young people think critically about encountering material such as pornography online. Information should be age-appropriate and engaging for young people. It should help young people develop their critical faculties so they are able to appraise and interpret materials that they access or are exposed to.

Minimising harm

Certain risky practices with potential negative impacts, such as sexting, are not uncommon amongst teens. Practitioners may therefore wish to consider a harm minimisation approach to supporting vulnerable teens in which they help them reduce the risk of negative effects. First and foremost this entails helping young people understand and appreciate the risks of engaging in a risky behaviour. Second, this may entail giving advice about how to minimise potential harm, for example, advising a young person to avoid showing their face or features which may distinguish them if they do choose to sext.

How much is too much?

For some young people, time spent online becomes problematic when it is out of balance with other activities. Practitioners may wish to help teens critically appraise the persuasive features of many social media platforms that aim to keep them engaged even when it may not be satisfying to do so. Rather than taking a shaming or blaming approach, helping young people balance activities which blend on- and offline (for example, engaging in activities which blend on- and offline) is one approach to achieving balance. Another is to take an holistic view about what young people may be compensating for by excessive internet use and to help them understand and articulate how they feel about it, as a precursor to taking steps to rebalance.

Keeping communication channels open

Encouraging dialogue and welcoming disclosures about accessing problematic content online is important so that teens feel safe to discuss adverse experiences. This requires practitioners to manage their own anxieties about risk and information governance in order to keep communication channels open. Practitioners should avoid invoking shame, blame or punishment when young people open up to them.

Useful resources

Webwise provides information, advice and free resources on a range of internet safety issues and concerns – www.webwise.ie

CEOP Think u know provides information and resources about online safety along with information about how to report concerns – www.thinkuknow.co.uk

Internet Matters provides information and advice to help parents keep their children safe online – www.internetmatters.org/

UK Safer Internet Centre provides advice and support along with a helpline and a hotline for reporting concerns – www. saferinternet.org.uk/safer-internet-day/2017

Childline cyberbulling resources is a dedicated website page on the topic of cyberbullying – www.childline.org.uk/info-advice/ bullying-abuse-safety/types-bullying/online-bullying

Beat (beat eating disorders) is a national charity that supports young people and parents and practitioners. The website has information, advice and access to a phone line, messageboard and online support groups – www.b-eat.co.uk

Ditch the Label is an international anti-bullying charity – www.ditchthelabel.org

Centre on Media and Child Health has a toolkit for parents and practitioners about how to promote healthy use of social media and the internet – www.cmch.tv/clinicians

Full Fact is an independent fact checking charity – www.fullfact.org

#chatsafe is a young person's guide for communicating safely online about suicide – https://www.orygen.org.au/Education-Training/ Resources-Training/Resources/Free/Guidelines/chatsafe-A-young-person-s-guide-for-communicatin/Guidelines_Orygen_ Final_WebLG.aspx?ext

Chapter 7

Digital resilience and digital rights

Introduction

In this chapter we explore how practitioners can help teens develop resilience in respect of their internet use. We believe that a rights-based approach to thinking about young people's online practices is a helpful one – this orientation recognises that adults, and their perspectives, often dominate public debates about digital rights and responsibilities which affect young people. A rights-based approach not only includes the right for young people to express their views about digital technologies and the internet, but also the right to form those views in ways which are not dominated by adult points of view:

> Children's right to form their own opinions must guide our approaches to developing online safety initiatives that can balance harm minimisation with the promotion of children's right to participation. (Third *et al.*, 2014, p.42)

This chapter considers digital resilience, digital rights and a quest for proportionality in terms of curtailing young people's freedom to engage in the online public sphere. We explore how practitioners can harness a rights-based approach to the internet which promotes positive mental health in teens and which fosters resilience for young people affected by mental health difficulties.

We make the case that if we aspire to a culture in which young people and adults alike make an active contribution to public life, then we must help them foster the skills to do so in their formative years (Jenkins *et al.*, 2017). In order for young people to learn the skills to engage in the online public sphere, practitioners need to step back enough to let young people experiment and learn through their mistakes. We also need to ensure the right safeguards are in place to protect teens in their online lives as we would expect to be the case in other aspects of their lives.

A global participatory research project with children and young people, led by UNICEF, found that adult points of view about risk and protection dominate young people's thinking about the internet. This predominantly negative frame for conceptualising the internet has the potential to undermine young people's capacity to conceptualise or imagine the benefits digital media offers them in realising their rights (Third *et al.*, 2014). It is important that practitioners helping young people with mental health difficulties similarly step back, check our own position, and endeavour to understand teens' use of the internet from a rights-based perspective, rather than simply through the lens our own experiences and assumptions. It is in this way that we can help young people make the most of the advantages of the internet and contribute to civil society.

Just as in other aspects of life, inequalities are pervasive within the sphere of digital technologies. Digital media can replicate and perpetuate imbalances in power between different groups. The values encoded into digital platforms reflect the values of the people who develop them and it should be noted that the tech sector does not equally reflect all societal interests (Wilson and Grant, 2017).

For example, mainstream media have reported claims of sexism made by women who work in influential tech companies such as Google. We should therefore think critically about how dominant social values and structural inequalities influence the design of digital technologies and encourage young people to do the same. This rights-based approach extends the case for digital literacy as set out in Chapter 5, to one which comprises a critical awareness of rights and unequal power distribution.

The ability to actively contribute to the online public sphere is just one aspect of contemporary civic participation. As well as being active agents, young people are increasingly becoming the objects of a wide range of monitoring devices that collect data about them in a multitude of different ways, often without them having an understanding of the implications. We consider how data is being collected about children and young people and describe a number of related issues for practitioners to consider. We conclude the chapter by introducing the *Digital 5 A Day* framework for promoting digital resilience in young people.

The opaque world of Terms and Conditions

How often do you fully read the terms and conditions before ticking the consent box that enables you to download an app? In her report on growing up digital, the UK's Children's Commissioner asked a group of teens to review the Terms and Conditions for Instagram, which at the time of assessment ran to a whopping 17 pages and 5,000 words. Unsurprisingly, the young people found the content boring, overly long and impenetrable; this meant that they were unlikely to read it despite the fact that those Terms and Conditions require the user to agree to a variety of terms in respect of privacy, buying and selling of data and tracking (The Children's Commissioner, 2017).

The task force behind the report worked with a law firm to develop a simplified version which they were able to distill to a single page using clear and plain language. The simplified version includes statements such as: 'we can force you to give up your username for any reason' and 'when you delete your account, we will keep this information about you, and your photos, for as long as is reasonable for our business purposes'. The results showed how unnecessarily opaque such terms and conditions can be and how it is clearly not viable for young people to understand and exercise their rights when they are so difficult to make sense of.

Both the data that young people actively generate and the data that are generated about them have implications for their rights. The UN Convention on the Rights of the Child (CRC), which was ratified by the UK in 1991, agrees that public bodies should consider the best interests of children when doing anything that affects children. Whilst the CRC protects the rights of children in all areas of their lives, it is not yet the case that it has adequately taken account of the implications of digital technology related practices to protect children (Lupton and Williamson, 2017). When the General Data Protection Regulation (GDPR) came into force in Europe in 2018, it required that:

> When services are offered to a child, you must ensure that your privacy notice is written in a clear, plain way that a child will understand (The Children's Commissioner, 2017, p.12)

Many social media platforms require children to be aged 13 before they can set up an account. The reason for restricting user access below this age is because this is how companies such as Facebook have chosen to respond to a law known as the Children's Online Privacy Protection Act (COPPA). This law regulates how commercial websites can collect and use information about children under the age of 13. Many companies avoid these obligations by restricting use of children under the age of 13 through their Terms of Service. However, many parents are complicit in supporting their children to lie about their age when they sign up to such sites. They do this unaware of the reasons underpinning the restriction and because they believe it is to do with with relative maturity of a young person (Hargittai, Schulz and Palfrey, 2011). In a survey of 1000 US parents, it was found that the majority of parents who knew their children had set up social media accounts under the age of 13 either helped or allowed them to do so so; furthermore, parents believe it acceptable to violate those restrictions if they believe that the social media platform enhances their children's education, family communication and/or social interactions with peers (Hargatti *et al.*, 2011).

In our discussions with young people we did not find anyone who routinely opened and read through Terms and Conditions when setting up an account with a social media or gaming platform. Young people did not even think to consider what they might be consenting to in agreeing to Terms and Conditions and they defaulted to a group norming process whereby they assume they are reasonable because their friends use the application.

The lengthy and complicated Terms and Conditions found in many mobile applications result in a relationship between the provider and user of the service that are less than clear and transparent. Personalised or targeted advertisements generated by tech companies selling data to marketing companies is common practice and the default business model for companies such as Google and Facebook. Despite most teens being aware of personalised online advertising, research shows that they are not always able to identify this in practice, especially on social media when it looks similar to other content (Ofcom, 2017). In one study, a dislike of seeing too many adverts was the top concern of 12- to 15-year-olds (Livingstone *et al.*, 2017). An exploration of Terms and Conditions leads us towards a consideration of issues of ownership, along with production and consumption models underpinning social media platforms. A critical awareness of these underpinning models is increasingly an important feature of being able to navigate our connected lives.

How much do young people actually care about online privacy?

Battles over privacy between parents and children are nothing new – both of our childhoods featured arguments over parental access to our bedrooms and fears that our secret diaries might be secretly read behind our backs. Rose goes to great lengths to ensure her parents are blocked from all her social media accounts and, to be on the safe side, she makes sure her friends block them too. When her mother walks into the kitchen, Rose puts her FaceTime call on pause and when she's sitting at the dining room table her phone is placed face down so no updates can be inadvertently observed. Rose is meticulous about keeping her online social life private from the adults around her. Rose's experiences are not uncommon; participatory research with young people around the world has uncovered universal concerns about *nosy*, *overprotective* and *spying* parents who teens feel compromise what is most important to them in respect of their privacy (Third *et al.*, 2014).

Popular platforms, such as Facebook and Snapchat, require contact requests to be made and accepted before profile information can be seen by each party. Despite a common parental concern that young people do not value privacy, the evidence does not actually back this up. One study showed that two out of three young people only add new contacts when they know them (49%) or know them very well (18%), one in four accepts requests from people with whom they share friends in common, and just 9 per cent accept all requests (Mascheroni and Ólafsson, 2014). Many of our interviewees described the lengths they went to in order to maintain their privacy and manage boundaries online. Nadia, who is 16, told us:

> I'd say I'm extremely private on my social media, to be fair. Even if I don't know anyone, I just won't add them. I'm actually like acting on social media, you'll get like three Facebook statuses from me and that'll be it, and that's if you're lucky. You'll get about two Snapchat stories in about four weeks.

Atiya describes how the functionality of Snapchat, which enables a user's story to automatically disappear after 24 hours, is one of the most appealing aspects of the platform:

> Bringing it back to Snapchat, I really like the fact that it disappears after 24 hours. The main reason I deleted my Instagram and my Facebook was that I could see embarrassing things popping up all the time. I was like, 'Oh, yes, I remember I did this,' and then I had to delete it. In regards to Snapchat, it deletes itself so I don't really have to do the effort.

Many of the young people we spoke with were highly concerned about their social media presence and went to some lengths to control and contain their public visibility. Aliya has stringent practices for managing the people she connects to on Snapchat:

> Recently I've deleted my Instagram because I thought that it was too revealing and people could find out anything about me. Now I only have Snapchat and I only add people who I know, and if someone adds me and I don't know them, then I just block them.

Aliya's experience is not uncommon and, in addition to peers, young people also desire privacy from adults, particularly those in positions of authority (Livingstone and Sefton-Green, 2016). As Martha asserts:

> I wouldn't want an adult to sit there and listen to my conversations with my friends in real life, not because I have anything to hide but just because that's weird. If I had my friends round and [an adult] sat in the same room as me, just literally sat there listening, that would be weird, in the same way it would be weird if you just read our conversations or something.

Despite this exacting concern for privacy, it is not uncommon to hear adults bemoan young people's lack of care about their private lives online. Parents see how their children appear to capture and share their every move on Instagram and continually curate and broadcast their day via Snapchat. It is the case that teens are mediating many aspects of their lives in public and online. Parents worry about their children's safety and are concerned that they are unwittingly giving away personal information about themselves. So how accurate is this concern and how worried do adults have to be?

A recent Ofcom survey of UK teens paints a different picture to the one that many parents assume is the case for their children. They found that many teens are cautious about the sites they use and the data they give away, with most 12- to 15-year-olds (77%) who go online saying that if they did visit a new site they would make checks first if they were unsure whether they could trust it. They are also cautious about the data they provide about themselves. Just 17 per cent of 12- to 15-year-olds agree that 'I will give details about myself to a website or app to be able to get something that I want' and just 13 per cent of those with a social media profile agree that 'getting more followers is more important to me than keeping my information private' (Ofcom, 2016b). During one of our focus group sessions, Aliya volunteered a story about troubling consequences of online tracking and personalised adverts:

> I had a friend that suffered with a miscarriage … before that, obviously, she was twelve weeks pregnant at the time and was searching lots and lots of really wonderful things about, you know, she's going to be a future mum. And with the internet history it records and remembers things…and sends data off to places and then you get flooded with things and after her miscarriage she really suffered and constantly, whenever she'd go on her phone scrolling through Facebook, it was adverts for Mothercare, and Mamas and Papas and Clearblue and for her it was a constant reminder of how – what she had and what she lost. So she decided to avoid that for quite a while.

One study showed that 52 per cent of teens keep their profiles private so only their friends can see their information, 29 per cent keep them partially private, and just 19 per cent keep them public (Mascheroni and Ólafsson, 2014). When Rose takes photos of her birthday cards to share on Instagram, she pauses to make sure all the envelopes with her house address are out of sight. Tom uses the promise of adding someone on Facebook as a way to avoid sharing his personal mobile number with an acquaintance:

> I'm very private pretty much across the board with social media, Instagram, everything. I only have certain people on it and I only post certain things as well because I'm of the opinion only certain people should be allowed to know more than that, so I'm really private. Again, it's also good for the phone number thing, it's really great to be like, 'Yes, sure, I'm sure I'll call to you on Facebook, yes, we'll keep in touch,' and then it just never happens.

Atiya employs similar tactics to keep unwanted contacts at bay from her personal life:

> [I say] 'Just add me on Snapchat', instead of, 'Give me your number', because you've found that, unless it's someone you actually want to constantly be in contact with, only close friends or family members, so generally you don't give out your number, you say, 'Add me on Snapchat.'

Whilst culturally specific issues did not arise strongly through our focus groups and interviews, one conversation which comprised mostly Asian teens, did highlight the importance of privacy:

> Within the Asian community, people, not people but Asians want to keep, I can't speak for all Asians but for my lot, keep everything within the household, don't speak about anything outside of the household, and if anything needs to be resolved, whether it be

money, family, school, relationships with the elders, they know everything sort of thing…

Further research is needed to understand culturally specific issues related to privacy; however the above insight suggests that young people from different communities may have added layers of complexity in navigating teen practices along with cultural norms of their families and communities.

Whilst parents worry about privacy, it is paradoxically the case that online communication between young people actually gives them a treasured degree of concealment from the supervisory gaze of adults. In her ethnographic research with American teens, Boyd (2014) found it was mostly authority figures that young people wanted to keep at bay from their online lives. When teens aren't able to control the context of their online lives, for example, by parents insisting on being their 'friend' on Facebook, they achieve privacy by encoding their content so it is only meaningful to their desired audience, whilst being in full view of everyone (Marwick and Boyd, 2014). One young person we interviewed had a Facebook account for her family and then a secret account where she connected with her friends. Lucas describes, in detail, complex practices that he and his peers take to achieve an equilibrium between a desire to reach out and connect alongside a desire for privacy:

> I would say about privacy, there's quite a wide range of different types of people in terms of privacy, like some people are open, like obviously there are features of private accounts. For some people the goal on Instagram is to get the most followers. Sometimes I feel like that's my motivation, not always but sometimes if I feel like I want to expand my range of people in my circle, but others are quite reserved, private account, very limited in the posts they share. On Snapchat as well, you can select who can see your story, and people are very picky, like they'll scroll down their friends' list

and they'll say, 'I don't want them to see it.' It's different things like that. Yes, different things because obviously different applications have different options in terms of privacy. Like Facebook, what I did was, it's very difficult to do but if you've got a PC, you go on your Facebook and you can restrict who can see your friends' list. Normally you can restrict who can see a post. Like if you went and posted photos from a 'night out' if someone wanted to do that but they don't their mum to see because it'd be embarrassing, they can restrict their mum from seeing that.

With privacy such a highly valued asset, the importance of trust is strongly associated with it. Whilst blocking family and friends from all her social media profiles, Ruth chooses to share her account passwords, and along with them access to her private messages, with her boyfriend and best friend. This creates complex scenarios whereby even private messages need to be policed to ensure they are acceptable to be viewed by her password confidants. The online social lives of teens is one whereby privacy cannot be conceptualised as an absolute, but is in fact mutually constructed with, and interdependent on friends (Blum-Ross and Livingstone, 2017).

The complexity and nuanced nature of privacy online presents a challenge for practitioners who want to help young people manage vulnerability associated with mental health problems. This is because the very fact that practitioners are authority figures may mean that they are exactly the sort of people that teens want to keep their lives most private from. We believe this paradox requires practitioners to approach conversations with teens in ways which seek to understand and respect their desire for privacy, whilst leaving the door ajar for them to share when they are ready to do so. It also requires that practitioners aim to understand the contextual and complex nature of privacy, which should be conceptualised as a shared and social endeavour that is negotiated between young people rather than as simply a set of individual choices. The refrain of 'don't post that online' or 'take that down' is a common one in many teenage households.

Rose continually discusses what can and can't be posted online with her friends as they take selfies with each other. This negotiation assumes a degree of mutual trust and respect in her social group with serious social sanctions for noncompliance. If a friend posts a picture of you that you don't like, explains Rose: 'you ask them to delete it and, if they don't delete it, you say you'll post a picture of them they don't like, and then they delete it.'

When as adults we discuss issues of privacy with young people, we need to recognise and appreciate the complexity of privacy and and its contingent and collaborative nature. It is not always within the gift of one individual to manage their privacy online, it is rather something that is continually negotiated and managed. An excellent blog post by the charity Young Scot includes a number tips for young people about how to maintain a positive online presence. These include the following five pieces of advice:[1]

1. **Google yourself** – it may sound vain but on this occasion you're excused – you need to know what people see when they look for you.

2. **If you ain't using it – delete it** – find all of your old profiles and any unused accounts that you no longer use and delete them.

3. **Remember, there's more than one page on Google** – make sure to look through as much of Google as you can in case you miss anything.

4. **Spring clean your history** – it will take time but go through your Twitter/Instagram/Facebook and check every post and delete any that paint you in a bad light.

---

1   Reproduced with permission from Young Scot. See https://young.scot/information/lifestyle/creating-a-positive-online-presence

5. **Get rid of the evidence** – take down any pictures which make you look bad and ask friends to do the same.

These very practical tips are the sorts of things that practitioners may want to make use of when helping young people think about online privacy and assert their rights.

Sharenting and the rise of the over-sharing parent

When practitioners are working with teens, they are likely to be also engaging with parents and carers. It is therefore salient for practitioners to consider how they encourage parents and carers to role model good collegiate approaches to online privacy and resilience. The rise of 'sharenting' or in other words when parents share information about themselves and their children online, is increasing in popularity, raising concerns about infringement of young people's rights (Blum-Ross and Livingstone, 2017). Sometimes referred to as *intimate surveillance,* this form of sharing often begins at gestation when a pregnancy is announced by sharing the first foetal ultrasound image on platforms such as Facebook. There is any number of pregnancy apps available on the market which provide opportunities for pregnant women to monitor many aspects of the foetus, including heart rate. Once born, almost every aspect of development can be monitored through wearable devices and sensors which are embedded into everything from changing mats to baby scales. The practice of setting up social media profiles for infants in their own names from birth is commonplace and so children may have their digital footprint displayed from the earliest moment of their lives (Lupton and Williamson, 2017).

Parents who share images, blogs or other media about their children have a dilemma in that that they are on the one hand primarily responsible for their child's privacy, whilst at the same time compromising it themselves through their desire to share information about themselves as a parent. Parents have varied motivations for 'sharenting', from a desire to chronicle their child's life, through to giving and receiving peer support from others in similar circumstances. Parent blogging is popular and Mumsnet even has a blogging network, with some parents making a living from this activity (Blum-Ross and Livingstone, 2017). What is the impact for children of parents sharing information about them online, particularly when they are vulnerable or have mental health problems? What does it mean for parental focus on their children and what are the impacts of constant distraction and curation for those young people?

In Chapter 2 we discussed the notion of context collapse whereby different aspects of our identity may become connected online, sometimes unintentionally, and with possible negative consequences. An adult asking for parenting advice about managing teen confrontation on a social media platform is simultaneously sharing information about the their child's behaviour. The child does not have any control of this. Whilst the intended audience might be the adults' friends and peers, it may be the case that the post might be visible to the child and their friends. What are the moral and ethical issues arising from this scenario and is it reasonable for a young person to have their privacy eroded in this way? These are all issues for practitioners to be aware of when working with families of teenagers with mental health problems.

Quantified teens and passive data sharing

There are aspects of privacy that we can control and those that are less obviously a concern. Issues of privacy should also be considered in respect of the data we generate through our internet searches and interactions online. This personal data that we generate is collected and stored on proprietary platforms that have a commercial motive to exploit these data (Lupton and Williamson, 2017). The 2018 revelations about Cambridge Analytica's use of Facebook data to influence both Donald Trump's election campaign and the Leave EU campaign have brought public concerns about questionable data harvesting practices to the fore. They have similarly focused government attention toward regulation of social media companies and this remains a topical issue as this book is being written. One study found that of over 80,000 health-related websites, 90 per cent of those sites sent information to third parties, with 70 per cent of these including specific information about symptoms, treatments and diseases (Bauer *et al.*, 2017).

In August 2017, Google introduced a new function to their website for Americans putting terms related to depression into their search engine. A knowledge panel provides the option to undertake a clinically validated PHQ-9 checklist to self-assess your level of depression. Whilst Google professes to be providing the tool as a means of raising awareness of depression, it is clearly the case that the end user is providing valuable data to the company and it is unclear how this data is used. In an article for the British Medical Association, Simon Gilbody (2017) argues that data generated by the screening programme may encourage over-diagnosis, supplier-induced demand and could be used to direct market antidepressants. Despite overwhelmingly positive reporting in the press, we argue that such developments are problematic and should be subject to proper scrutiny.

Data is not just being captured and harnessed in respect of health – increasingly, the formal education system is using tracking devices to monitor children and young people, from CCTV cameras to fingerprint or retina scanning to identify children, and monitor movement and purchases in the school canteen (Lupton and Williamson, 2017). It is also the case that both for-profit and government organisations routinely use algorithms based on big data from our digital transactions to predict behaviour and to categorise people and profile them (Bauer *et al.*, 2017). These all raise questions and concerns for our privacy as citizens and for civil society that it is important we engage with as citizens.

In addition to our internet searches and interactions, we are also increasingly generating data through everyday objects that have a 'smart' component to them. Sometimes referred to as the internet of things, objects such as smart TVs, consoles, monitors, and smartwatches can come with an IP address which allows them to receive, process and transmit data on the internet. Some children's toys such as drones and video games, as well as GPS enabled wearables such as smartwatches, can be connected to mobile apps. These devices enable commercial companies to capture valuable marketing data whilst being more appealing to children and young people. However, Davis (2017) argues that manufacturers are often unwilling to pay for security such as encryption and so young people are emitting data that is being harvested, processed and sold without their knowledge, and which is vulnerable to hacking. An increasing number of educational products are being made available to schools which enable physical, educational and emotional monitoring of young people (Lupton and Williamson, 2017).

The increasing data surveillance of young people's lives can be viewed as an extension of existing responsibilities of the state to care for and promote the wellbeing and improvement of young people. It can be argued that by participating in the generation of data and being monitored in the education system, young people are taking responsibility for managing and optimising their lives in positive ways. However, it is the case that neither young people nor many adults fully appreciate or understand the implications of the increasing quantification of every aspect of our lives. Lupton and Williamson argue that:

> People's life chances and access to opportunities are increasingly becoming shaped by the types of social sorting afforded by dataveillance. People have few opportunities to challenge the inferences and predictions that are made by algorithmic calculations. They often have little knowledge about how corporations are exploiting their personal details and using them to construct detailed profiles on people used for decisions about their access to employment, insurance, social welfare, special offers and credit. (2017, p.786)

Whilst at an individual level, many apps are desirable and posting pictures of our children is a normal behaviour for any proud parent, it is worthwhile standing back and considering the broader picture and the wider consequences for the many different facets of active data sharing and passive data surveillance and to consider what this may all mean for the future of children, teens and young adults.

Whilst helping young people tune in to how their data are being used by companies, it may also be helpful for them to understand how they can contribute their data for social good. There are a growing number of charitable and other organisations through which we can opt in to share our data for clinical research and social good. As an example, Open Humans is a non profit that enables participants to share data with projects they care about. The project enables participants to contribute to projects, earn badges to recognise their involvement and to engage with community members and content. Individuals can also start a project hosted with Open Humans.[2]

The ways in which we inadvertently generate data, and how that data is used by companies, is a facet of digital literacy that we should endeavour to equip ourselves with both as practitioners and as citizens. It is only by developing the knowledge ourselves that we can gently guide young people towards making active and responsible choices regarding their data as a component of their connected lives.

Young people as digital citizens – five digital rights

The consideration of children's rights in respect of digital technologies is a new and emergent field. As we have seen, there is a danger that generation of what is perceived to be objective data about young people may be used to make decisions about them without their own voices and agency being at the centre (Lupton and Williamson, 2017).

What do teens think about their rights as digital citizens? An important deliberative process was undertaken in 2016 that

---

2   www.openhumans.org

brought together people under the age of 18 in youth juries to share experiences about being a digital citizen. The aim was to generate a common understanding of digital citizenship, consider the merits of various solutions, and to arrive at proposals to address the challenge (Coleman *et al.*, 2017). This project explicitly aimed to counter adult-driven considerations about use of the internet and to enable young people to talk about what is important to them.

The juries found that, as they distinguish less than adults between on and offline, young people expect the same rules and fairness to apply in all aspects of their day-to-day lives whether they take place in person or via the internet. They see rights and responsibilities applying equally in both spheres (Coleman *et al.*, 2017). The young people were concerned with the opaque power companies have to use and track personal data and control content. The juries showed how, once young people are able to consider their digital rights in depth, they are dissatisfied with and concerned about many aspects of the commercialisation of their data. A number of our interviewees had similar insights to share about responsibilities they believed internet companies should take. For example, Ava had ideas about social media providers:

> I think it would help if social media firms had alerts themselves telling young people – or anyone, really, who was spending too much time on social media. Or an alert or warning if your photos or things like that had been digitally copied, or manipulated, or something like that, because I know for some friends that's been a real problem, like people taking screenshots and things like that.

The work of the jurors was part of, and informed by, the 5 Rights framework which takes the existing rights of children and young people under 18 according to the United Nations Convention on the Rights of the Child, and articulates them for a digital world. 5 Rights encourages organisations to become signatories to the following:

- **The right to remove** – every child and young person should have the right to easily edit or delete all content they have created.

- **The right to know** – children and young people have the right to know who is holding or profiting from their information, what their information is being used for and whether it is being copied, sold or traded.

- **The right to safety and support** – children and young people should be confident that they will be protected from illegal practices and supported if confronted by troubling or upsetting scenarios online.

- **The right to informed and conscious use** – children and young people should be empowered to reach into creative places online, but at the same time have the capacity and support to easily disengage.

- **The right to digital literacy** – to access the knowledge that the internet can deliver, children and young people need to be taught the skills to use, create and critique digital technologies, and given the tools to negotiate changing social norms.

Rights are of course relational, in that one person's rights may impinge upon another's. Some features which impinge on rights are encoded into the architecture of social media platforms so that they cannot be adapted by people who use them. For example, on Facebook a parent can post images of their child and Facebook treats those images as being owned by the parent alone. This is despite the fact that the child may not wish for that image to be shared (Blum-Ross and Livingstone, 2017). This is an issue we explored in more detail earlier in this chapter and is shown here to illustrate the complexity and contingent nature of online rights and responsibilities. We hope that by considering some of these issues as practitioners, you can in turn help young people to consider them for themselves.

Internet service providers (ISPs) have a responsibility to protect children and young people from harm and protect their rights; many are doing so and there are a number of industry bodies that are progressing this agenda. Whilst we do not cover this topic here, more information can be found in *Children's online activities, risks and safety: A literature review by the UKCCIS Evidence Group* (Livingstone *et al.*, 2017).

A framework for mindful use of digital technologies – the Five a Day

In this chapter we have encountered a mire of complexity and obfuscation in respect of young people's rights and related issues such as privacy and control. In this section we offer a simple framework which we hope may provide a counterbalance to some of this complexity by helping you think about promoting the digital resilience of the vulnerable young people that you support.

The UK's Children's Commissioner has produced a *Digital 5 A Day*, which is a simple framework to guide parents in how they support their children in their everyday use of the internet and smart devices. The *Digital 5 A Day* draws on the NHS evidence-based Five Ways to Mental Wellbeing and is designed to be straightforward and easy to understand. The five steps are set out below.

Connect

The internet has enabled everyone to maintain friendships and family relationships no matter where they are in the world and children often say that chatting with friends is the best thing about social media. It is important to acknowledge that this is how children keep in touch but it's also important to have a conversation with them about who they are connecting with and their privacy settings. Remember to keep a dialogue open and talk to your child to understand how they're spending their time and so that they can come to you for help should they need to.

Be active

Activity is important for mental wellbeing and all children should have time to switch off and get moving. Children don't have to be athletes to be active. Find something that they enjoy – be that swimming, walking, dancing or yoga – researching an activity or place online before going out is a good way of combining online and offline and provides an opportunity for you to use the internet together.

Get creative

The internet provides children with unlimited opportunities to learn and to be creative. From learning to code, to building complex structures in Minecraft®, to creating video content, the summer can be a great opportunity for children to build their digital skills. Time spent online doesn't have to be spent passively consuming content. It can be educational, creative and can provide opportunities to build skills for later life.

Give to others

As well as using the internet to learn about how to get involved with local and national charitable schemes, children can give to others through their everyday activities. Remind children that by giving positive feedback and support to friends and family as well as reporting the negative behaviour of others, they can help the web make a positive place for everyone.

Be mindful

We hear that children often feel pressured by the constantly connected nature of the internet. While they might want to do other things, it can be difficult for them to put their phones down when apps are encouraging them to engage. Being mindful about the amount of time that your child is spending online – and encouraging them to be mindful about how this makes them feel – is important. Encourage children to come up with ways of managing this, e.g. keeping a diary as way of logging the amount of time they are spending online or downloading an app that helps them manage their notifications.

Whilst not a panacea to the challenges we have identified in this chapter, we hope this framework is a means of bringing you back to our original proposition of approaching the internet as an asset to be leveraged as much as it is a problem to be solved. Enabling young people to be knowledgeable about the internet, critical in respect of their rights, and to develop a mindful approach to internet use, are important facets of meaningful digital citizenship.

Conclusion

In this chapter we have addressed issues of digital resilience and digital rights. Whilst on the surface this may not appear to be a primary concern to practitioners helping teens with mental health difficulties, a rounded appreciation of all aspects of digital citizenship,will equip practitioners to help young people navigate this complicated territory. We do not suggest that practitioners should necessarily be concerned with teaching teens about digital rights, but an awareness of the issues equips you to help vulnerable teens exercise their rights and mitigate the downsides of their connected lives.

In conclusion, we set out key takeaways from the chapter which we believe are salient for practitioners supporting teens who have mental health problems.

Adult views dominate

Adult points of view have tended to dominate discussion about the internet and a rights-based orientation can help practitioners conceptualise the internet from a young person's perspective.

Terms and Conditions

The building blocks of our interactions with social media platforms and search engines are mired in opaque and often obfuscated Terms and Conditions.

Young people are concerned about privacy

When given the information and space to consider these issues, young people are unhappy about how their rights are compromised by internet companies and how their data are used without them fully appreciating the extent of tracking and commercialisation. As practitioners we should respect young people's desire for privacy, whilst at the same time building trust so that they can ask for help when they need it.

Privacy is contingent

Privacy cannot be conceptualised as an absolute, but is in fact mutually constructed with, and interdependent on, friends. It is important to be aware of the contingent nature of privacy online when helping young people think through what is important to them in terms of privacy.

Sharenting

There is a steady increase in parents sharing information about their children online which has downsides for young people's privacy and autonomy. Practitioners have a valid role in helping parents and carers consider how they they can role model good citizenship online and avoid sharing information about their children without their consent.

Commercialisation of data

Data is harvested and commercialised by companies such as Google, as exemplified by their tentative steps into the sphere of mental health, through their use of PHQ-9 checklist on their US site. Such developments could have unintended consequences for internet users, and we should be alert to the downsides as well as the benefits they could present.

5 Rights Framework

The 5 Rights framework takes the existing rights of children and young people under 18 according to the United Nations Convention on the Rights of the Child, and articulates them for a digital world.

Digital 5 A Day

This is a simple framework for practitioners to consider how we may help young people develop digital resilience in the face of this complexity.

As we have suggested throughout this book, practitioners have an important and valuable role in listening, supporting and guiding young people to think reflectively about their choices as well as arming them with the knowledge to do so.

Useful resources

Better Internet for Kids provides information policy, practice, resources on internet safety, and positive online content – www.betterinternetforkids.eu/web/portal

RErights is a participatory project with young people exploring digital rights – www.rerights.org

Digital 5 A Day – www.childrenscommissioner.gov. uk/2017/08/06/digital-5-a-day

Chapter 8

A three-step framework for supporting teens' digital resilience

Introduction

Sam: Just ask them [young people]: 'Do you use the internet to help?' But at the same time, you shouldn't necessarily ask it specifically about mental health. Maybe a better question would be, 'What do you use the internet for?' Or, 'What do you look at on the internet?' That sort of thing, and not pressuring people into telling them exactly what they want, because obviously some people might be embarrassed about some things that they watch on the internet. So it's like you want to sort of ask them what they look at on the internet without pressuring them into saying anything they don't want to.

In this chapter we consider how practitioners can have helpful conversations with young people that enable them to harness valuable aspects of digital media whilst steering through aspects of online life which may be problematic. The question is not whether we as practitioners should be incorporating the internet into our practice, but rather *how* we go about doing it in ways which are helpful to young people. In one of our focus groups we asked participants to imagine how practitioners might broker a helpful conversation about the internet and their mental health. We include these as examples throughout this chapter.

In our exploration of digital rights in Chapter 7 we illustrated how adult perspectives about the internet can overshadow and obscure young people's lived experience. Adult viewpoints often crowd out young people's points of view and this in turn can have the effect of limiting the participatory potential of social media, digital technologies and the internet. Being self-aware about our own relationship with, experience of and attitudes towards the internet is important, as a lack of reflexivity may lead us to impose our own values and beliefs on the teens we are there to help. We advocate that practitioners are alert to and avoid a judgemental orientation; otherwise we run the risk of our own attitudes jarring with how young people experience their connected realities. Matt describes the inadequate response he got from a teacher when asking for some support relating to his confidence online:

> Because it's like, I've gone to one of the teachers, who I've started to sort of confide in a lot, about these sorts of things, and she's a little bit old-fashioned, and she doesn't understand it, she just sort of says to ignore it, which in theory is good, but is not always the best thing.

In contrast, Matt describes a more positive response from a counsellor, which he puts down to her deeper understanding of social media:

My counsellor is fairly young, so she sort of understands where I'm coming from, like I talked about bitchiness and talked about, I've talked about the stuff that happened in the group chat, and [she] had doubts, and she understands where I'm coming from. I mean, I get to share the self-experience of it as well. And she'll just suggest stuff, like, 'Why don't you go and make a group chat with someone else?' like make group chats with the drama group, which I've actually done, as a way of getting back.

The young people with whom we had conversations did look to practitioners for help navigating their connected lives. Mariam describes who she would go to for help when she experiences downsides of the internet and it is clear that family, friends and practitioners are at the forefront of her mind:

I'd probably approach my older siblings, or my parents, or just a close friend. Or the school nurse, because she helps me with a lot of my problems.

She also bemoans the lack of information that she has been given by practitioners about online information and services:

I've been given leaflets before about… But it's mostly been these helplines, and that doesn't cater to everyone's needs. Like, a lot of people might not like using helplines. But I did, I think it was last week, I found out about the Childline app, but I'd never even heard of it. I'd heard of Childline, but I'd never heard of the app, until I had to watch something. And it was advertised on there, because they were sponsoring it.

The above experiences described by teens suggest that some adults are not sufficiently engaged with digital media to be able to guide young people in helpful ways. Gabriel (2014) identifies three common adult responses to teen participation in online culture:

- **Banning** – reducing or removing risk to a young person by restricting use, filtering content or banning them from accessing the internet.

- **Blaming** – putting a young person down or criticising them for their use of the internet in ways which are not socially acceptable.

- **Educating** – encouraging a young person to behave responsbily online by educating them about the potentially harmful effects of the internet.

We believe that, whilst setting expectations and boundaries is appropriate, blaming and banning as default options are not only unhelpful but may restrict teens' access to the many beneficial aspects of internet use. Whilst education has a valuable role, we have seen throughout this book that parents and practitioners often lack the knowledge to transmit compelling educative messages to teens. Indeed, teen online practices are largely hidden from the adult gaze and so it can be challenging for practitioners to have a credible and knowledgeable voice in this regard. Martha has a simple prescription for adults supporting teens with mental health problems:

> It is important for adults to have involvement in their young adult's online life, but it's also important to respect the young adult's online life.

That adults should balance involvement with a respectful distance is a common theme from the young people we spoke with. That is not to say that adults should not have an authoritative voice when discussing the internet with teens, but it is to say we should be aware of the limitations of our knowledge and avoid a soapbox stance. Sometimes an educative position can be something quite simple, such as pointing young people to useful content:

Martha: I think there needs to be some kind of – whether it's a pamphlet, a leaflet or something, saying, 'Try and avoid these websites.' I've seen a lot on Facebook like, 'Do you have…?' And you've got a lot of younger people who, let's say, 11 to 14 and they're taking these tests and going, 'Oh, I think I've got this now.' And it's kind of over…

Mariam describes a situation when a practitioner helped her find useful information about mental health on the internet:

I was given, obviously, the website for MindMate, and my school nurse encouraged me to go and have a look at it… So I went on it one time, and it was just really helpful.

How can practitioners help parents and carers set the right tone when it comes to digital media? There is substantial evidence which indicates that a consistent *authoritative* parenting is the most effective style of parenting, that is where clear standards and limits are set but reasons and motivations are provided. An authoritative voice is markedly different to an *authoritarian* style of parenting, the latter being characterised by an expectation that rules are to be obeyed without reason or explanation. *Permissive* parents are responsive but not demanding and avoid confrontation; *uninvolved* parents are neither demanding nor responsive (Yardi and Bruckman, 2011).

Evidence indicates that children with authoritative parents tend to be happy, capable, successful, more socially competent, and have higher self-esteem (Yardi and Bruckman, 2011). Young people tend to be more self-regulated in their use of the internet and social media when parents support their autonomy, are involved in their lives and give them unconditional positive regard (Hansen and Holmes, 2014). Practitioners need their own authoritative voice and to help parents and carers develop theirs. But they also need to take into account and leverage the tacit knowledge of young people themselves. As Young Minds identify in their report on digital resilience:

There is a consistent message from the literature that young people are often best placed to offer solutions for how best adults can support them in managing risk and staying emotionally resilient online. We have seen that young people's immersion in the online world and their unique understanding of the social contexts that arise provides a valuable source of know-how when developing solutions. When asked, young people have often provided simple and workable solutions for tackling unhealthy online behaviours, such as tools and timers built into social networking platforms, and have clearly articulated the ways in which these might be designed and implemented. (Young Minds, 2016, p.47)

In our focus groups and interviews we found that young people often had sensible advice to share, such as this from Ruth:

I think kind of education for young people and for adults on where the internet is good and where is not so good. And, actually, let the young people, actually, realise just how intelligent they are without using the internet, because everyone has got something good in them and they're not necessarily going to find it from the internet, they're going to find it from themselves.

Martha similarly promotes reciprocity between adults and teens, advocating an orientation of mutual inquiry which can be beneficial both to adults and to young people:

Also, I am aware of the fact that that is difficult for parents because they're not as aware on social media. But it can be a two-way thing. The child can help the parent with understanding social media and the parent can help the child with posting the right things and saying the right things on social media.

The OECD argues that educators who engage with students through shared inquiry, problem-based and cooperative approaches are most likely to navigate this territory successfully (OECD, 2015). We believe this applies not just to educators, but to any practitioner working with young people who wants to leverage the potential of the internet. Through our conversations with young people, we found they had a range of strategies to manage their mental health and to reduce negative impacts on their emotions. Zoe described how she self-regulates her internet use:

> I think if it makes you feel worse, I definitely switch off Instagram and stuff. As I said before, I'll either dance or listen to music, just do something chilled to zone out and get in my own bubble. I'll definitely switch off from interacting on social media and more just using my phone for music or something, just something that focuses on me rather than what everybody else is doing and looking at everything else in life, what's going on, rather than my own. Sometimes I even switch my Wi-Fi off. So if I'm not on my phone, I'll turn the Wi-Fi thing off so I'm not tempted.

Diagnosed with depression, Mariam deploys similar tactics when she feels her use of social media is influencing her emotions in an unhelpful way:

> Like, sometimes obviously I switch off my phone, sometimes I just log out of social media. Sometimes I distract myself with other things, and just talk to people about it, who will understand.

In contrast, Martha takes steps to actively regulate her use of the internet by setting herself rules:

> It's hard to get a balance between the two [online and offline] when you're given free rein. But if you give yourself rules, then it's a lot easier not to get carried away.

Asset-based and cooperative approaches to supporting young people will already be familiar to many practitioners – the opportunity and the challenge is to leverage these existing skills and apply them to a digital context. We hope the evidence we have provided in the previous chapters has given a grounding in terms of knowledge and critical thinking that equips you to do this well.

A cooperative approach places the practitioner in the role of coach, whereby you hold the skills to facilitate a helpful conversation that enables a young person to develop a reflexive and critical approach to the internet. We propose a simple three-step approach for practitioners to take:

- **Explore** – as practitioners we should seek to inform ourselves about relevant teen online practices whilst being wary of assumptions and tropes found in popular discourse and media.

- **Inquire** – practitioners should adopt an inquiring approach where we seek to understand not only the behaviours but their meanings to young people and associated impacts (both good and bad).

- **Ally** – practitioners should take the role of an ally, helping young people make good choices about online behaviours that promote positive mental health, wellbeing and resilience.

It is imperative that practitioners recognise that young people *will* take risks online and that this is a normal part of child development. Rather than judging them, practitioners should equip young people with the knowledge and resources to minimise possible adverse effects associated with those risks. Thinking of child developmental factors, as discussed in Chapter 4, remember that your approach should be appropriate to the young person's stage of development. It is in this way that we can help young people develop digital resilience, with its positive associations with improved mental health and wellbeing.

Explore

Which apps and sites are you using the most at the moment? Has this changed over time? Why? How does this compare with your friends or others in your school?

What/when are the times you find yourself using social media/doing stuff online the most?

Are there any rules that you or your friends have about using phones or social media at certain times or situations? Perhaps some of these are not said out loud but you know everyone understands them.

Do you play any games online with others? Which ones? Who do you talk to on there?

Are there any things you do to make sure you can keep using social media/stay online?

Inquire

What are the things that you see your friends doing online/on their phone/[on particular social media channel] that worry you the most? What do you see others doing online that might be harmful for them?

There have been lots of concerns about what social media companies/[specific social media channels] do with the information they that get from what people post and share – what are your thoughts on this? Is it something that your friends talk about? Does it change the way they use [social media channel]?

I hear that [name of social media channel] has been criticised in the media for how it uses people's data. Is this something you and your friends are concerned about?

Lots of people are talking about privacy online and I was wondering what it means to you. How do you and your friends feel about privacy and what steps do you take to restrict who sees what you post online?

I'm interested to find out what you enjoy the most about [name of social media channel] and what you find less good about it.

Do you do different things online/on social media depending on your mood?

If you see something on [social media channel] that makes you feel worse, how does that affect what you do the rest of the day?

When you post something, how do you think about what happens next – like if you post something at 2am, who is going to see it first at that time?

I read this post about [someone's experience of] mental health and social media that I thought was interesting, it would be great to get your thoughts on it.

Do you follow any celebrities or really popular people? What do you think about what they post and how they present themselves? Has seeing their stuff changed what you put up on [social media channel]?

What have you noticed your friends do on [social media channel] when they are feeling bad?

Ally

What can we think about that might help you use [social media channel] in a way that feels less scary/upsetting overall?

Are there any other apps or settings on your phone that might help with [social media channel] so it feels more manageable?

When you are feeling down, worried or angry, what can you do on your phone that feels safe? How can we set it up so it's easy to make those choices in the moment?

Is there a conversation with your friends that you would like to have about what you all do online? If we think about it now perhaps that might help us think about whether you feel able to have that conversation or may be just what you could do differently?

What would you like your parents/carers to understand about what you do online and how it helps you or makes things worse at times?

A holistic assessment of the impact of digital on a teens' life

Ella: Finding out what they enjoy about the internet or technology and what they don't enjoy, just to get a gauge, because it is very personal what people – what someone might find helpful and someone might not. It's very personal. So I think, if possible, it's getting a bit of a handle on what they do find beneficial and what isn't so beneficial to them. You know? Just so that you can kind of tailor the approach a bit more, because it is very subjective.

We advocate a holistic approach to digital resilience which places teens connected lives in a wider context that is salient to their mental health and wellbeing. Practitioners may wish to consider how digital technologies are contextualised in a young person's life. A recent report from the American Academy of Pediatrics, suggests that practitioners should aim to:

Understand each family's values and health goals – for example, how good nutrition, an active lifestyle, good sleep hygiene, parent–child emotional connection, and creative play fit into the family's typical day – and identify areas in which good health and wellness can be enhanced. Pediatricians can suggest ways in which media can be used to connect, learn, and create instead of simply consume. (Chassiakos *et al.*, 2016, p.12)

This holistic approach to understanding values, context and meanings of digital technology use is a constant message from a number of authoritative sources on this topic. Professor Livingstone, lead investigator for the Parenting for a Digital Future research project, draws on interviews with over 70 families, to challenge the predilection many adults have for setting blanket time limits for technology use. Rather than focus on restricting time using digital technologies and the internet, Blum-Ross and Livingstone (2017) argue that adults should focus on the following indicators of a balanced young person. Are they:

- eating and sleeping enough

- physically healthy

- connecting socially with friends and family – through technology or otherwise

- engaged in school

- enjoying and pursuing hobbies and interests – through technology or beyond?

This orientation avoids blanket or inconsistent banning and instead pays attention to the context in which digital technology is playing a part in a young person's life. We believe this approach is a good basis for our three-step model of *exploring* to seek out information, an *inquiring* mindset and taking the role of an *ally* to cooperatively problem solve where problems arise. As Matt reminds us:

> People shouldn't exactly assume that the internet is a bad place. There are good points and bad points to the internet and it's not what it is, but how it's used…I guess it depends on what you're doing, is the thing.

Leveraging the power of peers

A cooperative approach can extend beyond working with individuals and families through to group settings. Whilst being more vulnerable to peer pressure from friends, teens can also be particularly receptive to positive guidance from their peer group (Hanson and Holmes, 2014). Mariam is keen that young people take responsibility for supporting each other:

> Yes, also I think it's encouraging young people to speak out, essentially. Because adults can't fix everything, like, young people have to play a part in it as well. And talk about it, and I think talking to someone, it doesn't have to be an adult, it could be a friend. And that friend should know what to do, and that friend should be able to inform an adult, or something.

We advocate that practitioners seek out opportunities to embed critical thinking about digital media into peer education between young people. Zoe suggests that there should be more structured conversations between peer groups that shine a light on normative behaviours on sites such as Instagram and which in turn help interrupt and complicate them:

> I think just generally with your friends or with people your similar age. Just generally discussing what you really think because obviously, as I said, people often fake loads of things. You see

loads of people, they take a picture and they show they're having a good time and then you ask them about it and they're like, 'Didn't really', if you understand what I mean.

In this instance, practitioners create structured spaces where young people are able to discuss, reflect and share knowledge and skills about resilience and positive mental health online. We also advocate that practitioners promote a rights-based approach to digital media and encourage young people to think critically about how their online activities are commercialised and how their data is used by tech companies. A cooperative peer approach mirrors the networked affordances of the internet and can be undertaken both offline as well as online through a variety of media.

Lastly, practitioners working with families should consider how a family-based approach might benefit young people. In their report on digital resilience, Young Minds note that older siblings can play a role in supporting their younger siblings in the family. More so than parents, they may have a more nuanced and relatable understanding of their sibling's online behaviours, and so be a valuable source of knowledge, advice and even protective oversight (Young Minds, 2016). Here are some of the suggestions made by a group of 18-year-olds when we asked them what advice they would give to younger siblings:

- Once things are online they won't go, so be careful what you say and share.

- Once you post something it's always there even if you can't see it/find it, not only is the picture yours but it belongs to the internet.

- Don't say things to people over text that you wouldn't say to their face.

Common sense information and advice, given by someone in a trusted role who is older but yet understands teens' digital landscape, can be a powerful means to engage young people in thinking critically and reflectively about digital media.

Role modelling a mindful approach to the internet

Before we consider the art of helpful conversations, we should first consider how to role model positive behaviours, whether that be as parents, as practitioners, or more broadly as adults able to influence young people (Rheingold, 2012). Rafla and colleagues argue that:

> Parent guidance should include the importance of modeling adaptive behavior from an early age and staying informed about technological developments. By paying attention to and actively participating in children's online activities, openly and honestly discussing concerns and reflected values in such use, and enforcing healthy limits, parents can find ways to share the positive aspects of technology with their children while avoiding some pitfalls. (2014, p.8)

Whatever our personal views are about the exponential growth of digital media, this is the reality that our teens are experiencing today. Howard Rheingold, in his book *Net Smart – How to Thrive Online* (2012) makes the case for developing a *mindful* approach to using the internet. Rheingold (2012) identifies literacies that he argues are characteristics of mindful internet use:

- Becoming aware of how we are deploying our attention and developing good habits.

- Being able to make sense of and filter information online.

- Being aware of filter bubbles and echo chambers.

- Moving from being a passive consumer to an active participant online.

- Using the internet to collaborate with others.

- Developing close and wider networks that help us build social capital and reciprocate with others.

Alongside the *Digital 5 A Day* described in Chapter 6, the literacies set out above offer a frame for conceptualising how we might help young people navigate their connected lives. By helping young people take a mindful and self-aware approach to digital media, we enable them to develop important life skills that foster resilience and build social capital. The first step to assisting teens to take a mindful approach to digital technologies is to role model it ourselves.

Connected learning and creative production

> **Ruth:** For like everybody it's not…everybody's not found it that useful using the internet to support their mental health. And, I guess, it's people have got different… What I was going to say was like asking whether…what…if they have any coping strategies already. And then, I guess, that's where you find out if the internet is one, or if they've another method, because everyone is different.

In Chapter 5 we explored how the digital skills and confidence of teens are influenced by wider factors in their lives, such as sociodemographic factors. We found that young people who experience disadvantage in their everyday lives are more likely to also face digital exclusion. This is not just about access but also about differential ways in which young people make use of the internet, with more affluent teens more likely to engage in civic and creative activities and deprived teens predominantly using it to consume entertainment.

Practitioners may wish to consider how to help young people develop digital skills and confidence by mobilising them to engage in interests and creative or civic activities online. Rather than simply criticising or restricting access to the internet, there is an opportunity to inspire young people to engage online in more creative ways. Interest-driven learning has huge potential via the internet that in the past was less available to teens from deprived backgrounds. It could be argued that with more ready access to digital technologies, the main barrier is lack of awareness, motivation and aspiration on the part of young people themselves.

The role of the practitioner could therefore be to open up the possibilities and the motivation to access avenues and possibilities of online learning and self-expression. This approach is called *connected learning* whereby digital media are deployed to reach, engage and enable young people who otherwise lack access to opportunity. Connected learning provides new entry points to creative and civic life for young people who are less advantaged (Ito *et al.*, 2013). A framework for connected learning is set out in Table 8.1.

Table 8.1 The Connected Learning Framework

Connected learning knits together three crucial contexts for learning:

Peer-supported In their everyday exchanges with peers and friends, young people are contributing, sharing and giving feedback in inclusive social experiences that are fluid and highly engaging.

Interest-powered When a subject is personally interesting and relevant, learners achieve much higher-order learning outcomes.

Academically oriented Learners flourish and realize their potential when they can connect their interests and social engagement to academic studies, civic engagement, and career opportunity.

Core properties of connected learning experiences include:

Production-centered Digital tools provide opportunities for producing and creating a wide variety of media, knowledge, and cultural content in experimental and active ways.

Shared purpose Social media and web-based communities provide unprecedented opportunities for cross-generational and cross-cultural learning and connection to unfold and thrive around common goals and interests.

Openly networked Online platforms and digital tools can make learning resources abundant, accessible, and visible across all learner settings.

---

cont.

Design principles inform the intentional connecting of learning environments:

Everyone can participate Experiences invite participation and provide many different ways for individuals and groups to contribute.

Learning happens by doing Learning is experiential and part of the pursuit of meaningful activities and projects.

Challenge is constant Interest or cultivation of an interest creates both a 'need to know' and a 'need to share'.

Everything is interconnected Young people are provided with multiple learning contexts for engaging in connected learning—contexts in which they receive immediate feedback on progress, have access to tools for planning and reflection, and are given opportunities for mastery of specialist language and practices.

New media amplifies opportunities for connected learning by:

Fostering engagement and self-expression Interactive, immersive, and personalized technologies provide responsive feedback, support a diversity of learning styles and literacy, and pace learning according to individual needs.

Increasing accessibility to knowledge and learning experiences Through online search, educational resources, and communities of expertise and interest, young people can easily access information and find relationships that support self-directed and interest-driven learning.

Expanding social supports for interests Through social media, young people can form relationships with peers and caring adults that are centered on interests, expertise, and future opportunity in areas of interest.

Expanding diversity and building capacity New media networks empower marginalized and non-institutionalized groups and cultures to have voice, mobilize, organize, and build economic capacity.

(Ito *et al.*, 2013, p.12)

As a practitioner helping a young person with a mental health problem, it is likely that you will be working with them to develop facets of their identity that build self-esteem and positive self-regard. They may have interests, skills and talents that you would like to help nurture and develop. We propose that being aware of what might be available online to help young people nurture their talents is as important as what resources may be available to them where they live. For example, a young person passionate about crafting may want to set up an Etsy account to sell their work. One of our focus group participants told us about how he uses Amino to engage in micro communities collaborating on niche projects:

It's not a popular one but there's one called Amino which is a smaller community but if you know what Tumblr is, it's like where groups of people, for example, who have a common interest, or for example if people are interested in a particular band or particular TV show, they can join an Amino which is like a group for dedicated fans to share content within a small space. Obviously you will get the odd people who just want to abuse that kind of thing, but generally it's quite a nice community spirit and it's, like, communities within communities, and it's nice to see people from across the world come together for common interests and a common focus group.

As well as bolstering a young person's sense of identity, creative production online affords the opportunity to collaborate and reciprocate with others who have similar interests. Being productive and making a contribution are important facets of wellbeing and developing resilience.

We would encourage practitioners to consider online as well as offline opportunities available to young people. At a workshop we ran on Minecraft® we encountered a probation officer frustrated that a young man she was supporting was only interested in this online game. She bemoaned the fact that she could not engage Paul in other interests that would involve him leaving his bedroom and she was highly critical of his immersion in this activity. Through participating in the workshop the probation officer developed a more nuanced understanding appreciation of Minecraft® and this enabled her to build empathy with Paul. A group of us then helped her problem solve how she might be able to find another way to support this teenager. We came upon the idea of extending his experience of Minecraft® beyond the bedroom by supporting him to visit places which he could then recreate in this virtual world. We created a bridge between his immersion in Minecraft® and other aspects of his life that would enable him to leave the house, get fresh air and do some exercise. We reflected that this was likely to be a much more fruitful conversation with Paul than one that started with a lack of understanding and implied criticism of his interest which he shares with many other teenagers.

Resilience and self-determination

> **Zahid:** I know it probably sounds quite extreme and controversial, but in some kind of way, I think, at some point it needs to be really brought in and both adults and kids need to understand how much it can affect your mental health. Like you know, you get asked a lot about how much you exercise and your diet and you get asked a hell of a lot questions like that, I feel like it's going to at some point, I feel like it would be so good if it could become like something you are asked about for health reasons.

As we have already suggested, we believe conversations with teens should seek to balance the authoritative voice of the adult with the agency of the child (Yardi and Brookman, 2011). They should orientate towards facilitating *resilience* which is characterised by assets that reside within the individual that can be taught, such as self-efficacy, social skills, reflectiveness and a willingness to try new things; and resilience channelled from resources around the young person such as family, peers and community. Resilience is a process rather than a stable set of factors, and occurs when:

> Promotive factors feed into and enhance one another, setting up positive spirals and pathways. So for example, a willingness to try new things might enable a young person to try mentoring, which then builds their self-confidence and enables them to apply successfully for a work placement (and so on). (Hanson and Holmes, 2014, p.21)

Furthermore, in addition to a supportive family and authoritative parenting, some research suggests that young people's level of digital *optimism* may also boost resilience:

> Young people who believed the internet and digital technology benefit society, as well as those who have built more skills using digital technologies, were more likely to be resilient self-regulators online. This suggests that building the fundamental digital competencies of young people could have unexpected yet positive knock on effects in terms of fostering resilience and positive engagement across a host of online settings. (The Parent Zone, 2014, p.4)

In their research into online resilience, The Parent Zone draw on theories of *self-determination* to conceptualise how young people may develop resilience in respect of their internet use (The Parent Zone, 2014). Self-determination is the extent to which one is able to self-regulate when performing a task. Being able to manage short- and long-term desires enables individuals to be resilient in the face of external pressures and impulsive desires, both of which teenagers are vulnerable to from a developmental perspective. There are four degrees of extrinsic motivation which impact on the degree of self-regulation and how likely an individual is to sustain it:

- **External regulation** – where a young person may respond to a reward or punishment to comply with a parent instruction to turn their phone off at a specified time before bed.

- **Introjection** – where a young person maintains a behaviour because they *should do it* without fully accepting it. They may turn their phone off an hour before bedtime because they know it helps them sleep better even though they would rather not.

- **Identification** – where a young person identifies and accepts a behaviour because they can see the benefit. They turn their phone off an hour before bed because they know it helps them sleep better and they have internalised this as something they should do.

- **Integration** – when a young person recognises the value of a behaviour and they integrate it with their values and identity: *'I'm the sort of person that always turns my phone off an hour before bed'* (The Parent Zone, 2014).

Intrinsic motivation has the highest degree of self-regulation and is characterised by an individual acting of their own volition without a defined benefit in mind. It is argued that for young people to develop online resilience they must learn self-regulation. This can be encouraged by parents, carers and practitioners who should focus on the highest degrees of motivation rather than simply rewards and punishment.

The Parent Zone undertook a survey of over 2000 young people from across the UK to test out the extent to which self-regulation along with positive parental support has a positive impact on online resilience. The survey also tested digital skills and the extent to which caregivers mediate young people's online activities. The results showed the importance of all of these factors combined enabled young people to take risks and develop coping strategies in the online world, just as they would in the offline world.

Practitioners helping vulnerable teens will recognise that the family and social contexts in which young people find themselves may mitigate against them making choices that are likely to have a positive impact on resilience. Sometimes they may have limited choices and on the other end of the spectrum they may have few if any boundaries to help them self-regulate. A practitioner can play a valuable role in helping young people navigate this often tricky and complex terrain.

Practical strategies for promoting resilience and self-determination

In this section we suggest key factors for having useful conversations with teens that help build resilience and which we have found useful in our own practice both as parents, practitioners and through our research and policy work.

Be non-judgemental

Whatever your personal views about the internet, it is important to avoid being judgemental. A judgemental or dismissive approach is likely to prevent young people bringing the problematic as well as the more positive aspects of their online behaviours to you.

Be interested but don't pry

Whilst it is important to show interest, it is also crucial not to snoop or pry into young people's online lives. Teens are already keen to shield their online activities from adults, particularly those in positions of authority, so an overly assertive approach could backfire.

Encourage critical thinking

Whilst it is right to avoid being judgemental, it is absolutely okay to encourage young people to think reflectively and critically about the internet and their engagement with it. An approach to critical thinking that enables young people to feel engaged might be as a shared inquiry into issues such as privacy and use of data. This is an approach which opens up the conversation and supports young people to think their own way through the many complex aspects of their connected lives.

Be honest

If a young person asks you to use technology in a way that makes you feel uncomfortable as a practitioner, then be open and honest about your concerns. There is no one size fits all. A conversation resulting from a young person asking if they can text or email you is an opportunity for you to set a boundary that you feel is appropriate whilst at the same not being disapproving or critical.

Encourage self-regulation

Help young people develop skills and confidence in self-regulation so they are able to balance their online and offline lives in ways that promote resilience. This may entail increasing self-awareness about how long they spend on time and on what activities. This knowledge can be a starting point for cultivating personal boundaries between their on and offline lives, and being selective about using the internet judiciously and in balance with other interests and activities.

There is no one size fits all

Whilst there are some absolute principles related to your duty of care, it is generally the case that applying your professional judgement to each individual situation is important. Be aware of organisational and professional responsibilities whilst feeling confident that you can apply your knowledge as a practitioner to an online context, even if it is less familiar that other contexts.

Learn from mistakes

It is important to allow and acknowledge that young people do and will make mistakes online. Helping them reflect on those mistakes and learn from them is an important aspect of adolescent development. The particular qualities of online communication, particularly the spreadability, searchability and persistence of information we share, may mean that the consequences of mistakes have a bigger effect than those made offline. Helping young people understand this is an important aspect of being digitally savvy and resilient.

Set boundaries but do not take away privileges

One response adults can have to concerns about internet use is to revoke access or to control it. Whilst boundaries are important, an approach which shuts down access to the internet may backfire by putting teens off discussing their internet use with adults concerned. When setting rules, keep them simple, state them positively (what you are going to do rather than what you shouldn't do) and co-produce them as a team. Remember that, as well as communicating with friends, young people use the internet to access information, for creative activities, entertainment and news. As a practitioner you may wish to help parents/carers consider how they set helpful boundaries whilst avoiding acting in a draconian manner which encourages young people to act surreptitiously and to close down conversation.

Help young people search for and appraise health information online

The ability to search for and make sense of online health information is a skilled endeavour. Given that good health literacy can be associated with better health outcomes, we believe that the ability to help young people make sense of health information is an important skill for practitioners.

Be curious

Spend some time finding out about online social networks that teens are using so that you understand the contexts in which young people are going online.

Join in

Sometimes it may be appropriate to join in with the young person so you can enter their world on their terms. This should only ever be done if the young person is enthusiastic to do so. Joining in may entail jointly playing an online gamer or watching YouTubers talk about a particular topic together. This could provide an opportunity for a young person to show you their skill or mastery of a game or to demonstrate their superior knowledge of a subject.

Initiate conversations

Do not wait for young people to bring problems or challenges to you. Make sure you incorporate their online lives into the work you are doing with them and make it a normal part of your conversations with them. Signal to them that you are non-judgemental and that you understand that they are many positive affordances as well as adverse effects to navigate online.

Create opportunities for structured conversations

Bring conversations about the internet into the contexts and activities where you are helping young people. This may be through group work, in schools, during a peer support drop-in session, or in youth work activities to name but a few. Enable young people to discuss their experiences and to cooperatively problem solve adverse effects whilst informing each other about the opportunities and possibilities.

Create visibility

Make resources which promote online resilience and opportunities visible by poster displays in waiting areas, links on websites. Bring these materials into established structures and processes for working with young people.

Encourage intentional internet use

Help young people expand their horizons about the opportunities afforded by the internet for creative and civic participation, to learn new things and have new experiences. Consider how you might model this in your own online behaviours.

The above list is by no means exhaustive, but we hope it provides useful pointers for engaging with young people and their connected realities in ways which promote resilience and positive mental health and wellbeing.

Developing critical skills when searching for health information online

Aliya: It's like if you went to go see your GP and to say: 'This is how I'm feeling.' And you say you're feeling out of the ordinary, you want help with it, they do ask you those questions about your diet and your health. And you could be at the gym, five times a week and eating strictly, you know, very health conscious food, but you're still feeling wrong. And what they haven't uncovered is you're watching some strange YouTube video about how great it is to be a size 4 and that you should have your ribs showing.

A key digital skill is the ability to search for accurate and trustworthy health information online. In Chapter 6 we highlighted the variable digital literacies in this regard so an important role for practitioners is to help young people make sense of internet-based information. When we put the term 'mental health' into the search engine Google we were provided with 249,000,000 results in 0.74 seconds. Despite the plethora of information, many of us will not look beyond the first promoted ads that appear at the top of the page. How do we make sense of what is trustworthy and accurate information online when we have it in such abundance?

A first step is for practitioners to find and recommend trustworthy online information to young people. A deeper way to help them is to assist them in developing skills in appraising information for themselves. Simple steps such as starting searches with well-known organisations (such as the mental health charity Mind), looking at three separate sources of information to check if they triangulate, and checking sources to see if they are accurate do not take long and are good critical habits to develop (Rheingold, 2012). We see stories in the media on a daily basis with health-related news, often sensationalised and potentially worrying. NHS Choices has a 'behind the headlines' section in which news stories are fact checked for their accuracy. Pointing young people to these sorts of trusted sources can be effective as a means of countering scare stories in the press.

Young people who are already producing content online, perhaps as gamers or YouTubers, may well already have excellent critical appraisal skills in this domain of their life. So a useful conversation may entail helping them make the connection between this aspect of their lives and their appraisal of health information.

As well as seeking authoritative information online, young people are likely to turn to their peers for information (Rheingold, 2012). This may be a more challenging behaviour to practitioners who are concerned that young people will come across inaccurate information or information which they believe is unhelpful. However, recognising and accepting that this is likely to happen, it makes sense for practitioners to actively discuss peer sources of information and support with young people. Doing your own searches on YouTube, Facebook and other platforms will enable you to know what is out there and for you to be knowledgeable when helping young people navigate information and stories from people in similar circumstances to themselves.

A simple guide for reviewing digital mental health tools

Atiya: You know, I don't know how that would be or how it would work or how whether you could measure it or whatever, but I just think [the internet] is such a big part of our lives now, you know, just how there was so much education on smoking and people who learned that that was wrong because of this and drinking, you know, there needs to be the education so people know and then people are asked about it as well.

An NHS Apps Library has been established for digital tools which have been certified to be safe, secure and effective for use in the UK. Apps included in the library have been assessed to meet a range of requirements. Given the currently small number of apps included in the library, and the vast array of mental health apps on the commercial app stores, here are some pragmatic pointers when appraising digital technologies for teens with mental health problems.

Who has developed the tool?

Has the digital tool been developed by, or in conjunction with, a trusted source (for example, a mental health charity or NHS Trust)? We would expect this information to be included within the tool itself and/or on the developer website.

Privacy and security

Is there a clear and understandable privacy statement in the app that gives you confidence that data entered into the app is kept private and not sold on to others? The privacy statement should set out how data you put into the app is stored and kept secure.

It is important to consider if the name and appearance of the digital tool also protects the privacy of a young person. Some apps disguise their purpose by using a name and design that means another person looking at it would not know that is has a mental health purpose.

Efficacy

Is the digital tool informed by an evidence-based model that is acceptable to services in the UK (for example, cognitive behaviour therapy or dialectical behaviour therapy) and does it provide reliable information? Has an evaluation of the app been undertaken and what does it tell you?

Usability

Is the digital tool easy to use and appealing to its target audience? Evidence indicates that digital tools are most effective when they incorporate persuasive design features (Wozney *et al.*, 2017). These include: visual appeal; relatable to a young person and their context; tailored content; stepped delivery of therapeutic content which requires engagement through incremental steps (rather than being delivered all in one go); good quality multimedia content; self-monitoring functionality. These components are more likely to increase engagement and adherence in online therapeutic interventions for young people.

Peer and professional reviews

Has the digital tool been reviewed both by professionals with relevant knowledge and/or young people? If so, do those reviewed give you confidence?

Costs

Is there a charge to download the app, or is there an option to purchase additional features once using the app? It may be that the app uses a subscription model. Many digital tools generate revenue by charging the end user and it is worthwhile spending a bit of time working out the revenue model for the app to ensure you are comfortable with it. Apps which are free to use may sell your data to advertisers as a way of making money.

Data and storage

Does the digital tool use a lot of data or storage once on your mobile phone? If so, this may put a young person off downloading it and keeping it on their smart device.

Advertising

Sometimes apps that are free to download include adverts as a means of generating revenue. It is important to consider whether it is appropriate to recommend or suggest a digital tool which includes adverts that may push the user to buy products and services.

It is worth remembering that reviews on a commercial app store are not necessarily a reliable indicator of the quality of a digital tool. Visiting the developer's website can be a good way to get more in depth information about the provenance of the app. You can also ask a group of young people to peer review an app once you have done the initial checks we suggest above.

Lastly, we would encourage practitioners to consider the provenance of the digital tool. Has it been developed collaboratively with young people and practitioners? Taking into account all of the above will help you assess whether a digital tool may be useful and to mitigate risks of it having a negative affect.

Conclusion

In conclusion, we have considered how practitioners can have helpful conversations with young people that enable you to harness valuable aspects of digital media whilst steering through aspects of online life which may be problematic. We have argued that adult viewpoints about digital media dominate public discourse and that we need to find more teen-orientated approaches to understanding social media, digital technologies and the internet.

Here we set out key takeaways from the chapter which we believe are salient for practitioners supporting teens who have mental health problems. They are as follows.

Collaboration and cooperation

We propose a cooperative approach which places the practitioner in the role of coach whereby we hold the skills to facilitate a helpful conversation that enables a young person to develop a reflexive and critical approach to the internet.

Explore, inquire, ally

We set out a simple three-step framework to help practitioners orientate towards helpful conversations with teens:

- **Explore** – practitioners should seek to inform themselves about relevant teen online practices whilst being wary of assumptions and tropes found in popular discourse and media.

- **Inquire** – practitioners should adopt an inquiring approach where they seek to understand not only the behaviours but their meanings to young people and associated impacts (both good and bad).

- **Ally** – practitioners should take the role of an ally, helping young people make good choices about online behaviours that promote positive mental health, wellbeing and resilience.

Achieving balance

Drawing on advice from experts in the field, we promote an holistic perspective that focuses on young people achieving balance in all aspects of their lives, of which digital media is one component. This rounded approach takes into account all facets of a young person's wellbeing and avoids reductive responses such as banning, blaming or lecturing. We also advocate a peer-education and mentoring approach whereby teens are encouraged to collaborate and problem solve together.

Role modelling

Parents and practitioners can role model positive behaviours in respect of our own engagement with digital media.

Connected learning

Connected learning enables teens to exploit the creative and self-directed learning opportunities afforded by the internet. Digital media use is constrained by demographic and social factors – practitioners must take into account disadvantage and help mitigate it where they can.

Self-determination

Intrinsic motivation and self-determination are characterised by assets that reside within the individual that can be taught, such as self-efficacy, social skills, reflectiveness and a willingness to try new things; and resilience channelled from resources around the young person such as family, peers and community. Being able to manage short- and long-term desires enables individuals to be resilient in the face of external pressures and impulsive desires. These are useful concepts for thinking about how practitioners can practice and hone a sense of self-determination and self-regulation in respect of their connected lives.

Finally we have suggested some practical strategies for practitioners to employ when helping young people develop digital resilience as well as to develop their digital health literacy when searching for mental health information online. In the next chapter we go on to consider the implications of teens' connected lives for services supporting vulnerable teens.

Useful resources

Skills for Care digital resources for social care practitioners and services – www.skillsforcare.org.uk/Topics/Digital-skills/Digital-working.aspx

Screenagers guidance for digital youth work – www.youth.ie/sites/youth.ie/files/Screenagers-Guidance.pdf

Community learning and development is a national framework of guiding principles for the use of digital technology and social media in Community Learning and Development – https://issuu.com/dacld2012/docs/digitally_agile_national_principles/2

Personalised Family Media Plan from the American Association of Paediatrics – www.healthychildren.org/english/media/Pages/default.aspx

Chapter 9

Implications of digital technologies for young people's services

Martha: If school, instead of saying, 'Here's the definition of depression off Wikipedia', instead if they said, 'Here's what to do if you feel like you are struggling. Here are some good websites that are helpful. Remember to talk to your parents about things.' Instead of always just being like, 'If you've got a problem, come and talk to us, come and talk to us, come and talk to us', because often it's more helpful for them to give us other ways of helping ourselves instead of trying to help us, if you know what I mean. So I think definitely, for sure, I'm sure there are some great websites out there that are made by people who really know what they're talking about and if they made us aware of those websites then that would help, but they don't do that.

Introduction

In this chapter we consider the implications of social media, digital tools and the internet for services and organisations that help vulnerable young people. We hope this will be as equally relevant to an NHS Child and Adolescent Mental Health Service as it is to a local community group and everything in between. Insights from one of our interviewees, Matt, bring home the importance of services taking teens' online lives seriously:

> I grew up in Cornwall and what services were down there, I felt like it was all very old-fashioned and the people that would talk to you would be like, 'Is it something at home? Is it something at school?' And really it's a YouTube video that – and you don't want to sound stupid by saying it. I don't think I've even now, how aware everyone is of the internet and how reliant most of the population are, I don't feel like people take it as a serious thing that really does affect someone's mental health and wellbeing.

Throughout our interviews and focus groups, young people told us how inadequately services are responding to their connected lives. This is typified by an exchange with Matt:

Interviewer: Thinking back, was the topic of internet or social media ever discussed with you during your time with CAMHS?

Matt: No, I don't think that kind of topic was ever talked about.

Interviewer: So, apart from your experience with your parents, have you had any positive experience of professionals talking to you about social media and the internet?

Matt: Not that I can remember. Don't think so.

Despite frustration about how poorly services engage with teens' connected lives, young people have ideas and suggestions for how services could do things better:

> Yes, I think the NHS should have a list of websites that they or even YouTube have that you could go on to help with your mental health and also have this warning page of what the internet could do to your mental health.

Zoe articulates how schools could produce more embedded learning about the internet beyond a one-off lesson:

> I think what would be more useful is if people [were] kind of more realistic, in a way. With school we did one lesson, just one, on body dysmorphia and they were saying what it relates to. We did just one lesson on the media but it didn't really cover the triggers. We only had one lesson out of the whole year, so it's not really going to stick.

Whilst young people told us they want more substantial education about the internet in a school context, they also shared their worries about the digitisation of mental health services. Perhaps unsurprisingly in an era of funding constraints in the public sector, they expressed concerns that digital services might be a cheaper and second best option to what currently exists. As Zahid explains:

> I think with it being a great learning tool, it is really, really helpful. But as well, with the NHS putting money into developments and projects online, not to take away the focus that face-to-face meetings and things like that are very important. You find lots of services stripped of people and a website to signpost them to, which will make everything feel all better. And sometimes, that's not the case, people still do need that one-on-one care and attention.

Given the strong policy drive towards public services digitising in order to remain relevant to young people, it is striking that many of the teens we spoke with wanted to retain face-to-face services. Aliya echoes Zahid's sentiment:

> I agree massively with that so, so much, because that's something that I worry a bit about having something so digital and it's just – it's not the same level of support.

In this chapter we explore the implications of social media, digital tools and the internet for services and organisations which support young people with mental health problems. Many services are struggling to work out how they can leverage digital technologies to better meet the needs of young people they aim to help. There is no doubt that there is often a substantial disconnect between the connected lives of young people and their mostly analogue contact with services. Whilst this is changing, it is still the case that even texting, the most ubiquitous of technologies, is not routinely used as a communication tool. However, we must ensure the digitisation of services is codesigned with young people to avoid making assumptions and missing the opportunity to improve rather than compromise effective care and support.

Davies *et al.* (2012) identify key ways in which the internet is shaping people's lives and the disconnect this creates with many existing services. Constant connectivity enables young people to engage with their friends, communities and public life both where they live and virtually. In contrast services and practitioners tend to be only available at specific times for discrete periods and often only through face-to-face contact. They argue that innovation is required to bridge this yawning chasm between largely analogue services and the connectivity of young people in many aspects of their lives. But they also rightly assert that we should be engaged in thinking carefully and critically about the use of digital technologies in practice. An orientation towards values and evidence will help practitioners not lose sight of their professional expertise, whilst also drawing on the domain expertise of the young people they want to help.

In a time of cuts to public services, it is not surprising that, like young people, practitioners are concerned about digital technologies being part of a reduction in provision. However, we would argue that in the same way that young people seamlessly blend their on- and offline lives, so might services. This is not a debate about whether face to face is better or worse than online but rather a responsiveness to the preferences of the young person and how their needs can be best met. In our experience, young people desire different ways of interacting with services depending on the context and their circumstances. In a workshop with young people we were surprised by young people's vociferous defense of face-to-face therapy when we had assumed that a tele-consultation might be more accessible and convenient. Instead, young people told us they were worried about snooping parents and noisy siblings. Their home environment typically did not feel a private enough place for them to talk about sensitive issues. These young people did not want online counselling but they did want a way of accessing money for a bus ticket to get to the session. Indeed lack of money turned out to be one of the biggest barriers to attending a counselling session appointment.

In this chapter we consider the implications of the topics we have explored in this book for services. We hope you will find them of interest whether you are a practitioner wanting to improve your services, a manager, a commissioner or a policy maker.

A strategic approach to digital

Taking a strategic approach to digital technologies, social media and the internet ensures that they are embedded within, align to and support organisational purpose, mission and objectives. Where digital is conceptualised as an enabler to an organisation achieving its purpose, rather than an end in itself, we believe it will have the greatest and most sustained impact.

A digital strategy should be codesigned with people accessing services from and staff working within the organisation. In this way you can establish a baseline of current experiences and attitudes towards digital and start from where people are at – finding your advocates and understanding the views of people who may be detractors. In addition to a baseline against which to measure progress, a digital strategy should have a clear set of principles, a set of measurable objectives and associated metrics.

It is important to provide appropriate resources and capacity to enable the objectives in the strategy to be realised. This may include creating either a lead role or dedicated capacity within existing roles to facilitate delivery of the strategy. Every organisation will be different, and the most important thing is for the strategy to be part of the organisation's core business and not an added extra if it is going to be impactful.

The following sections set out the types of themes and topics that we believe should be included in an organisational digital strategy.

Digital inclusion and eHealth literacy

In Chapter 5 we considered the challenges to digital inclusion for young people who are vulnerable and face exclusion. We explored how teens often lack the skills to search for, appraise, and make use of health information online. The normative belief that young people are inherently digitally savvy disguises their variable confidence and can mean that services do not adequately address their needs. We saw in Chapter 2 how young people are engaging with social media to promote their mental health and in Chapter 5 we considered the adverse effects of a range of behaviours online. In Chapter 8 we considered how individual practitioners can leverage the potential of the internet to help young people engage in any number of civic and creative activities.

What is the policy context in terms of young people's digital literacy? A recent report of the House of Lords Select Committee entitled *Growing up with the Internet* (2017) asserts the fundamental importance of children's digital inclusion, along with the responsibility of the Government and other institutions working with young people to promote it:

> Digital literacy, that is, the skills and knowledge to critically understand the internet, is vital for children to navigate the online world. It is also an essential requirement of the future workforce. It is no longer sufficient to teach digital skills in specialist computer science classes to only some pupils. We recommend that digital literacy sit alongside reading, writing and mathematics as the fourth pillar of a child's education; and that no child should leave school without a well-rounded understanding of the digital world. Schools should teach online responsibilities, social norms and risks as part of mandatory, Ofsted-inspected Personal, Social, Health and Economic (PSHE) education, designed to look broadly at the issues that children face online. (House of Lords, 2017, p.4)

Digital skills such as writing and uploading a CV are basic competencies required to progress in the field of employment as well as increasingly to access government and other services. It is for all these reasons that we believe that organisations cannot afford to ignore the importance of digital inclusion and eHealth literacy to young people's mental health.

What can services for vulnerable young teens do to help young people build digital skills and confidence? This will depend on the type of services and the resources available to them. Wherever possible, digital literacy should be built into existing services and programmes, so that they are embedded and more likely to be sustainable. Here are some recommendations for young people's services; commissioners of those services; and policy makers wishing to create a receptive context for digital inclusion for teens affected by mental health problems:

- **Digital inclusion assessment and evaluation** – an assessment of the digital confidence and skills of young people accessing a service enables evidence to be generated in order that interventions are based on quantifiable data rather than conjecture. Evidence provides baseline information that can be used to measure impact of any interventions that are implemented. Measuring impacts against the baseline assessment generates evidence to build a business case for future investment in digital skills development for young people. Ensure digital skills evaluations utilise a range of qualitative measurement tools and softer indicators in progress evaluation. The Tech Partnership's digital skills framework contains a set of competencies and assessment questions that can be downloaded and used by services and organisations.[1]

- **Digital inclusion resources** – there are a wide range of digital inclusion resources that can be made available to young people, parents, carers and other people or organisations that a service partners with. These resources can be made available in a wide variety of ways, from posters on notice boards through to YouTube videos that can be shown in structured group contexts.

- **Digital inclusion activities** – services may wish to generate discussion about digital skills and confidence into existing activities or, where appropriate, by establishing new activities. The Good Things Foundation website has a range of videos and reports which can be used to stimulate conversation.[2] They also have online learning tools under the banner of Learn My Way with over 30 courses. As discussed in Chapter 8, establishing peer-to-peer opportunities for young people to share learning collaboratively can be effective insofar as it

---

1   www.thetechpartnership.com/basic-digital-skills/basic-digital-skills-framework
2   www.goodthingsfoundation.org/about-good-things-foundation

draws on tacit knowledge of teen practices, which may be more elusive for adults.

The above three recommendations are intended as a starting point for building a digital inclusion orientation into services and organisations. However, we suggest that digital inclusion activities which are codesigned with young people are likely to meet their needs most effectively. Commissioners may wish to consider first how they understand the needs of young people, and second, how they build digital inclusion into their commissioning and contracting, along with employing incentives available to them to stimulate this important facet of resilience building for young people.

Practitioner digital capabilities

In our conversations with practitioners, both whilst researching this book and in our day-to-day work, we have encountered variable digital skills and confidence. Even where practitioners use social media, digital tools and the internet in their personal lives, they can struggle to broker that confidence into a professional context. This is in part due to organisational constraints and concerns about risk and information governance; however it is also in part due to the development need for those practitioners not being met. The core capabilities of technically literate mental health practitioners can be described as follows:

- **Awareness** – understanding the role of technology, professionally and personally.

- **Control** – being able to understand, design, use and control technology.

- **Appraise benefits and risks** – value the benefits and assess the risks of technology.

- **Ethics** – respond rationally to technology-related ethical dilemmas.

- **Effectiveness** – assess the effectiveness of technologies.

- **Confidence** – display confidence with learning to use technologies.

- **Keep up to date** – critically evaluate technological progress and innovation (East *et al.*, 2015).

We believe it is critical that organisations take this skill gap seriously and address it as part of their organisational development and training function. A recent House of Lords Select Committee on children and the internet recommends that:

> Specific training modules be developed and made compulsory as part of qualifying in frontline public service roles, including but not limited to, police, social workers, general practitioners, accident and emergency practitioners, mental health care workers and teachers. (House of Lords, 2017, paragraph 217)

Health Education England (HEE) have also recognised this gap and, along with NHS Digital, have a programme of work entitled Building a Digital Ready Workforce. HEE are working with professional health bodies to incorporate digital skills into core competencies of practitioners. They are also funding a range of initiatives to move this agenda forward. Whilst work is being developed at a national level, there are steps that can be taken at a local level to develop the digital skills of the workforce:

- **Training needs assessment (TNA)** – incorporate digital skills and confidence into existing processes to assess the training needs of practitioners, or undertake a specific targeted digital skills TNA. Health Education England have useful resources on their website.[3]

- **Collaborate with young people** – create opportunities to ask young people for their experiences and views about what they want from practitioners in terms of digital capabilities. For example, young people told us that they want their connected lives to be acknowledged and incorporated into their conversations with practitioners. It may be that small measures will make a big difference just by actively discussing the issues with teens who access services.

- **Incorporate digital skills into core training** – review existing training to identify how digital skills can be incorporated and embedded. This might be, for example, considering the impact of social media use on professional identity, through to considering management of risk in safeguarding training. Embedding digital skills into existing training will help it be viewed as an enabler of effective care and support rather than an end in itself.

- **Digital projects** – encourage teams to consider how they can include digital as an enabler in service improvement, redesign or innovation projects. A project focus means that digital becomes an enabler of improving care and innovating in a service or organisation.

- **Digital cafes** – sometimes called *social media cafes* these are volunteer-led meetups that take place around the country for people to share information, advice and help each other. Setting up a cafe-style peer-learning space for your team, service or organisation can reap the benefits of informal peer

---

3   www.hee.nhs.uk/our-work/building-digital-ready-workforce

learning. Involving young people in co-delivering digital cafes can be a fantastic way to enable intergenerational learning and development.

The above are some simple ideas for services and organisations to consider in developing a digitally confident workforce. Organisations should understand the infrastructure required to support a digitally-enabled workforce and aim to remove barriers that get in the way. This may include providing smartphones, making WiFi available and designing permissive policies in respect of social media use. It may also include not banning or blocking sites such as YouTube. Commissioners may wish to consider how they build expectations about digitally confident practitioners into their commissioning and contracting, along with employing incentives available to them to stimulate this important facet of workforce capabilities.

Communicating with young people

As identified in Chapter 2, most young people are avid users of smart devices, digital technologies and social media. However, many services have been set up to communicate by telephone, letter and sometimes email. Fax machines are not yet entirely redundant in the NHS. It is for this reason that a chasm opens up between young people's everyday connected lives and the mostly analogue capabilities of mental health (and other) services.

The excellent LYNC study, led by Warwick University, explored how digital technologies (email, mobile phone calls, text messages, Voice over Internet Protocol) are being used for clinical conversations between health professionals and young people aged 16–24. The study focused on long term conditions, of which CAMHS and Improving Access to Psychological Services (IAPT) were included. The most compelling finding from the study is that use of digital technologies for communication improves patient engagement and experience alongside increased activation (Griffiths *et al.*, 2017). The outputs from the study include a quick reference ebook and series of practical guides for services that comprise the following:

- When is Text and Email Useful? [4]

- Common Concerns among Clinicians[5]

- Confidentiality, Privacy and Consent[6]

- Duty of Care and Equity[7]

- Engaging with the Right Person[8]

- Enhancing Patient Engagement[9]

- Improving Your Patients' Access[10]

- Patient Safety[11]

---

4   https://warwick.ac.uk/fac/med/research/hscience/sssh/research/lyncs/when_is_text_and_email_useful_v6.pdf

5   https://warwick.ac.uk/fac/med/research/hscience/sssh/research/lyncs/common_concerns_among_clinicians_v5.pdf

6   https://warwick.ac.uk/fac/med/research/hscience/sssh/research/lyncs/confidentiality_privacy_and_consent_v3.pdf

7   https://warwick.ac.uk/fac/med/research/hscience/sssh/research/lyncs/duty_of_care_and_equity_v4.pdf

8   https://warwick.ac.uk/fac/med/research/hscience/sssh/research/lyncs/engaging_with_the_right_person_v4.pdf

9   https://warwick.ac.uk/fac/med/research/hscience/sssh/research/lyncs/outputs/enhancing_patient_engagement_v6.pdf

10 https://warwick.ac.uk/fac/med/research/hscience/sssh/research/lyncs/improving_your_patients_access_v7.pdf

11 https://warwick.ac.uk/fac/med/research/hscience/sssh/research/lyncs/patient_safety_v5.pdf

- Using Digital Communication Between Face-to-Face Appointments[12]

- Workload Concerns Going Digital.[13]

The evidence, along with these practical guides, provides a thorough set of resources for services considering how they can incorporate digital communications into their provision. Services introducing digital communications tools should follow organisational and regulatory requirements regarding information governance and clinical risk, as appropriate. They should also employ codesign processes to engage young people in order to ensure digital technologies are acceptable, useful and feasible in practice.

Designing services with digital in mind

We should not necessarily assume that just because young people use digital tools in their day-to-day lives they would prefer to access mental health support through digital media. The evidence suggests that many young people prefer to receive face-to-face support (Hollis *et al.*, 2017) and our experience backs this up. Through our conversations, young people told us that face-to-face support with a trusted professional is important to them. Accessing online support from home, when parents are in the house and a sibling may burst into the room at any moment, is not always welcome or satisfactory. For young people with limited data and memory on their phones, a health app may be disregarded in favour of those which they will use with their peers on a day-to-day basis. As these examples illustrate, it is important to pay attention to the context in which a technology will be used as well as to the technology itself. This is

---

12 https://warwick.ac.uk/fac/med/research/hscience/sssh/research/lyncs/using_digital_communication_between_face_to_face_v4.pdf

13 https://warwick.ac.uk/fac/med/research/hscience/sssh/research/lyncs/workload_concerns_associated_v5.pdf

where the importance of participatory design processes in designing technologies comes to the fore.

When assessing the potential of a digital tool it is worthwhile exploring how it has been developed and if young people were involved in its conceptualisation and design. Participatory design is based on the principle that: 'people who are affected by the introduction of a new technology have the right to participate in the creation of this technology' (Yarosh and Schueller, 2017) in order to develop tools which are useful, effective and meaningful to those who use them. Participatory design in developing digital technologies aims to move beyond the power structures, biases and assumptions between adults and young people and to elicit insights from children who may find it less easy to verbalise their thoughts (Druin, 2002). Yarosh and Schueller argue that to successfully design technologies to promote young people's wellbeing, it is imperative (1) to employ design principles that are developed for children to ensure that the interaction styles are tailored to children's interests and capacities; and (2) that interventions align to young people's mental models and priorities, rather than simply adapting adult language and examples to be age-appropriate (2017).

mHabitat is an NHS hosted organisation which facilitates codesign in digital health. The team has significant experience of codesigning digital tools with young people who have mental health problems. Victoria, co-author of this book, established mHabitat in 2014, and has numerous examples of young people providing insights in design projects that have altered the development of an NHS digital initiative. For example, when developing a outcome measurement app, the developers included games as rewards for completing an outcome measurement tool. To their surprise the children were not impressed. Not only were the games of poor quality compared to those they were used to, they told us that the games detracted from the seriousness they perceived of the digital tool. Games do have a place in digital health but this group of young people rejected adult assumptions about how they might want to engage with them.

Digital technologies can themselves be employed as channels through which to involve young people. Blockanomics is an example of child-orientated civic engagement, in which a bespoke Minecraft® city was developed as part of a Nominet-funded project to engage young people in politics and introduce them to local democracy in a playful way. Such projects endeavour to engage young people through platforms that they feel comfortable with and it is worth considering how similar approaches might be used to engage young people in deliberation about mental health and related services. However, in our experience nothing beats bringing a group of young people together in a room with sticky notes and pizza to codesign ideas for digital technologies as an enabler for their care and support.

Creating a multi-channel presence for your service

Having a strong, clear and relatable web presence is an imperative for mental health services targeted at teens. Reaching out to young people in the spaces that they occupy, rather than expecting them to come to you, is also possible through social media channels. Despite this, our experience is that the quality of websites for young people and use of social media by services is highly variable. The value of a well-designed website is described by Mariam who was introduced to the Leeds MindMate website by her school nurse:

Obviously the MindMate website has a lot of different things to do on it, and things. But there was this one time I went on it. When you get told about it, at first, you're like, 'Oh, it won't help you', or whatever. Like, you kind of brush it away. But I think, in that situation that I was in, I just felt like I should use it, I don't know why. And I went on it, and there was actually, like... It helps, the website did help, because it made me see a different perspective. And it kind of talks you through things slowly. Like, this is just with like an app, as well. It did make me feel better I think, definitely.

Websites and web services should be developed in such a way that they respect the rights of children and young people, as discussed in Chapter 7. The iRights report (5Rights, 2015) provides invaluable information to website developers, including for example:

- If possible, do not collect the data of people under the age of 18.

- If you do collect their data, provide information in simple language informing how you will use their data and give them meaningful choice to agree or disagree, including a willingness to provide services if they disagree.

- Provide, as standard, links to support lines via your company or organisation footers/websites, even if there is nothing potentially disturbing or upsetting on your site, access to information must become a new norm.

- Provide a mechanism whereby young people can easily report or contact you with questions or complaints.

- Put the privacy settings close to any comment box.

Websites and services should be designed collaboratively with young people to ensure the look and feel, as well as the content, are age appropriate. In codesign work with young people we have generated many useful simple and low-cost features that help make websites user friendly. These include features such as: incorporating maps and bus routes into visitor information to make services easier to find; posting pictures of front doors and simple smartphone-made films of the inside of the building so young people know what to expect on a first visit; photographs of staff with biographies so young people know the qualifications and experience of practitioners they are meeting with. None of these components are costly or onerous to produce but can make a big difference to a young person's first impression of a service.

As we saw in Chapter 2, young people are heavy users of YouTube and find vloggers who talk about their experiences of mental distress both aspirational and relatable. There is an opportunity for services to increase trust in their services through the use of stories created with young people who have themselves accessed those services. Contrary to expectations, this doesn't have to entail commissioning expensive video content. We were particularly struck by an example from India of teen survivors of sexual abuse telling their story in person whilst disguised using Snapchat filters

Some services involve young people in generating bite-sized social content and running social media channels collaboratively. For example, a social media account on Twitter can be run in rotation by a group of young people. When embarking on reaching out to young people via social media channels, it is important to have a well thought through plan that takes into account tone of voice, how you will generate content, how often and when you will post, and how you respond to comments. It can be worthwhile bringing in experts to help you set this process up along with young people themselves.

Conclusion

In this final chapter, we have provided some pointers for services and organisations to take a strategic and planned approach to engaging with digital technologies, social media and the internet. The topics covered are not intended to be exhaustive but should provide some inspiration as a starting point. It is imperative that services and organisations develop plans which are commensurate with the capacity they have to deliver them. Commissioners may wish to incentivise services to embrace digital technologies, and policy makers should consider how they can set a receptive context for innovation to flourish.

In conclusion, we set out key takeaways from the chapter which we believe are salient for services and organisations supporting teens who have mental health problems.

An analogue disconnect

The internet is increasingly shaping our everyday lives and interactions; services that are still operating primarily through analogue channels are creating an increasing disconnect with teens' connected lives.

Be strategic

Taking a strategic approach to digital technologies, social media and the internet ensures that they embedded within, align to and support organisational purpose, mission and objectives. Where digital is conceptualised as an enabler to an organisation achieving its purpose, rather than an end in itself, we believe it will have the greatest and most sustained impact.

Digital inclusion and eHealth literacy

Digital skills are basic competencies required to progress in the field of employment as well as, increasingly, to access government and other services. Organisations cannot afford to ignore the importance of digital inclusion and eHealth literacy to young people's mental health.

Practitioner digital capabilities

Even practitioners who use social media, digital tools and the internet in their personal lives can struggle to broker that confidence into a professional context. Organisations should take steps to improve the digital confidence of their staff and remove infrastructure barriers that get in the way.

Communicating with young people

Despite the fact that most young people are using smart devices and digital technologies, many services have been set up to communicate by telephone, letter and sometimes email. Organisations should consider how they can redesign services to take into account digital means of communication, which can often be more acceptable to young people and cost effective.

Designing services with digital in mind

Organisations should consider how they design (or redesign) services with digital in mind and through codesign processes with young people and practitioners. Participatory or codesign processes are based on the principle that people who are affected by the introduction of a new technology have the right to participate in the creation of this technology. As well as ensuring young people's preferences are at the heart of digitally enabled services, codesign means that they fit within the context of their everyday lives and have the most chance of being successful.

Creating a multi-channel presence for your service

Having a strong, clear and relatable web presence is an imperative for mental health services targeted at teens. Reaching out to teens in the spaces that they occupy, rather than expecting them to come to you, is possible through social media channels. Organisations should take a strategic approach to their web presence in collaboration with teens, in order to build trust in services.

Useful resources

LYNC Study Quick Reference e-book and Topic Guides is a quick reference e-book with 10 Topic Guides for patients and professionals who are using or considering the use of digital communication on clinical matters – www2.warwick.ac.uk/fac/med/research/hscience/sssh/research/lyncs/outputs

Innovation Labs is a codesign project that worked with over 100 young people, youth mental health professionals and digital agencies. Together, through two innovation labs and an incubation process, they explored 126 ideas, developed seven of them, and awarded grants to seven partnerships of charities, designers and young people to make them into products. Whilst the Labs finished in 2015, the website contains lots of useful information about codesign with young people in mental health – www.innovationlabs.org.uk/start-here

Freeformers is specifically for companies. Their aim is to enable companies big and small to operate at the speed of digital. They provide hands-on training programmes on a range of topics including Digital Marketing and Cyber Security for individuals, teams and companies and for every person they train, they train a young person for free – www.freeformers.com

Conclusion

We began this book by asking what it would mean if we approached the internet as a resource to be deployed rather than simply a problem to be solved. This question has framed our exploration of the implications of digital technologies for teens with mental health problems. Grounded in the manifest reality that digital technologies are not only here to stay, but are an embedded facet of young people's everyday realities, we have sought to understand how we can help vulnerable teens exploit the benefits and mitigate the downsides.

By seeking to understand teens' connected lives from their points of view, we are better equipped as adults to help them on that journey. Whilst the digital media landscape is constantly changing, we have promoted an approach and orientation which draws on practitioners' existing skills and is not subject to the vagaries of new social media platforms and ever shifting online practices. Drawn from what young people told us they want from parents, carers and practitioners, our simple three-step model to engage with young people's connected realities is as follows:

- **Explore** – as practitioners we should seek to inform ourselves about relevant teen online practices whilst being wary of assumptions and tropes found in popular discourse and media.

- **Inquire** – practitioners should adopt an inquiring approach where they seek to understand not only the behaviours but their meanings to young people and associated impacts (both good and bad).

- **Ally** – practitioners should take the role of an ally, helping young people make good choices about online behaviours that promote positive mental health, wellbeing and resilience.

We recognise that young people will take risks online and that this is a normal part of child development. Our simple framework enables practitioners to help young people in ways which are acceptable and useful to them. By keeping communication channels open, we can minimise the likelihood of teens experiencing adverse effects, and help them deal with them when they do. This balanced approach aims to help young people take advantage of the upsides of social media, digital technologies and the internet; it aims to help them develop digital resilience with positive effects for their mental health and wellbeing. Going forward, we would encourage more teen-focused research on social media and the internet that seeks to understand young people's tacit experiences and which moves from a blunt assessment of time spent online towards more nuanced appreciation of practices, context and meanings. We would particularly welcome further research which focuses on the variations in experience by young people from different cultural, socioeconomic and ethnic backgrounds, as well as those who are vulnerable and experience exclusion.

Understanding social media and digital technologies

In our introduction to social media we introduced the reader to ways in which teens seamlessly blend their on and offline lives – from sharing images with friends on Snapchat through to following their favourite vloggers on YouTube or joining niche communities on Amino and everything else in between. In our conversations with young people we found they are generally positive about their online lives and see many advantages to the internet in respect of their mental health and wellbeing. However, we also found that their always-on connected lives can create pressures and we gained insights into ways in which they endeavour to alleviate them. The teens we spoke with gave us a more nuanced and in depth appreciation of their connected lives than might be apparent to an adult looking over their shoulder at their smartphone screen.

We drew on evidence to understand how social media have particular facets which make them qualitatively different to physical online spaces where young people congregate. These include the persistence of online content, the visibility and spreadability, as well as the ability to search for and find content. Social media dynamics mean that when we post online our audiences can be invisible to us; the contexts we keep separate offline can more easily collide; and the public and private aspects of our lives can converge. These affordances carry downsides and upsides – easy connection to friends can build resilience but the consequences of posting something you regret online can be more far reaching than saying something you wish you hadn't in person.

For young people with mental health problems we found positive effects associated with internet use – these include the ability to search for information anonymously, along with the opportunity to connect with others who have similar experiences through, for example, peer support forums. The internet can be a space where young people build their sense of self-efficacy through engaging in creative production and civic activities, such as making music or signing a petition. We found that vloggers who share their experiences of mental health difficulties are often an important source of relatable information and inspiration for teens. Digital mental health tools, such as mobile apps and online peer support forums, can be useful for young people, although the evidence is limited and we are still learning about their role in mental health support.

Given the current mixed and inconclusive evidence in relation to digital mental health tools, it is likely that a focus on generating good quality evidence will take centre stage in the coming years. Current methods for generating evidence, such as randomised control trials, are not always best suited to digital platforms which iterate regularly due to the pace of technology change. In the context of financial pressures within public services, we believe practitioners will increasingly demand good quality evidence in order to give them confidence that digital tools are effective in improving teens' experience of services and their lives more generally.

Developmental frameworks and perspectives

Appreciating the interaction between the biological, psychological and social changes that happen in adolescence helps us to understand some of the challenges that teens may experience in their connected lives. Social media, digital technologies and the internet are sites where young people experience the well-understood path of child development characterised by conflict, transgression and change. Taking risks, learning from that risky behaviour and having the control to adjust future behaviour based on that experience is an important part of this stage of development on a biological, psychological and social level. The increasing sensitivity of the brain's reward circuitry, particularly to social stimuli, and more specifically to stimuli that reinforces the sense of self, has the psycho-social correlate of teens moving away from family to peers as preferred contacts and greater influencers of their self-esteem.

The quantifiable aspects of social media change how teens can think about their experiences: where previously there might have been some ambiguity or uncertainty that could allow for development of different explanations, the visual concreteness of the numbers of likes is unavoidable, unquestionable. As highlighted by the accounts of the young people we spoke to, the highs and lows of their emotional lives are played out on social media. Furthermore, they recognise this is the case, and routinely comment on the artifice of it, however they are unable to not do it because of how culturally pervasive it is.

Different networks in the brain 'light up' when we are either engaged in purposeful activity or in non-purposeful self-reflection at rest. We know that increased activity in the purposeful network switches off the network involved in self-reflection. It is worth holding this in mind when thinking with young people about what state they are in when approaching online activity – purposeful or self-reflective? How does this change their emotional response to content? We have heard throughout the book from young people taking purposeful decisions to switch on or off their social media, based on their understanding of their needs in the moment. Inquiring with teens about times when they approach social media in moments of distress in a more self-critical state, or simply bored at rest, may help identify more purposeful actions, both on and offline, that help them to manage those moments.

External factors are a change in a young person's circumstances which may be outside their control, such as moving house or school (Ofcom, 2016a). It is therefore important that practitioners pay attention to contextual factors in use of the internet as well as developmental factors. Changes in engagement with the internet will be just one of many factors and external influences affecting children and they should be considered in the round. Research into the combination of biological, psychological and social factors associated with teens' use of the internet is in its infancy. We expect to see more research related to neuroscience and genetics which attempts to understand what happens in the brains of young people as they navigate the web. Big data provide opportunities for us to increasingly understand patterns of social media use which we argue should be combined with qualitative data to elicit the associated contextual factors.

Adverse experiences online

Whilst throughout the book we have advocated an orientation which regards the internet as a resource to be leveraged, it would have been remiss not to address the very real risks, challenges and adverse effects posed by social media, digital technologies and the internet. As practitioners we need to understand those risks so that we can help young people anticipate them, avoid them and respond to them in a resourceful way when they do occur. Rather counterintuitively, we found that exposure to risk is not entirely a bad thing and that encountering adverse effects can help build resilience. Whilst our intuition may lead us to want to protect young people from all risk, a more realistic and proportionate approach may be to help young people minimise the harm associated with taking risks and to learn from those experiences. A helpful way to do this is to avoid blame and keep communication channels open so that young people feel safe to share their experiences with you.

We found that in general young people have a low level of concern about online risk and regard the channels they engage with as simply another media through which everyday dramas are played out, initiated or continued. However, perhaps unsurprisingly, we found that teens who are vulnerable in their everyday lives are more likely to be vulnerable online. This means that practitioners should be alert to how vulnerabilities expressed in the offline lives of young people they support may manifest themselves online.

We found that as well as being a sphere in which adverse effects can be experienced, the internet is replete with resources to help young people inform themselves, understand, and work out how to counter negative experiences. An educative approach that anticipates adverse effects and helps young people become informed and educated is a means of countering adverse impacts and helping young people think critically about encountering material such as pornography online. Information about mental health and peer support are just a couple of valuable assets the online sphere has to offer.

A tendency to focus on the negative implications of social media and digital technologies for young people will no doubt continue to proliferate and it is important that the downsides are understood. However, it is evident that the steady stream of alarmist mainstream media articles can contribute to an atmosphere whereby both parents and practitioners feel helpless to support young people. We hope that our interviews and focus groups with teens have shown a more nuanced and complex connected world than might appear the case when observing a young person absorbed in their mobile phone at the expense of those physically close to them. Adults will likely always be two steps behind the online practices of young people, but an inquiring approach can mitigate this. We anticipate that digital competencies will increasingly be incorporated into professional training and continuing professional development, and will begin to find their way into professional competency frameworks within regulatory bodies.

The importance of digital inclusion

The importance of digital literacy and inclusion may not be an issue at the top of practitioners' minds when considering young people's use of the internet – surely they are much more tech savvy than even the most geeky of adults? However, despite their perpetually connected lives, we should not assume teens necessarily have high levels of digital confidence. In fact, evidence suggests that many teens are more digitally naive rather than digitally wise. Furthermore, it is those teens who are socially excluded that are more likely to lack basic digital skills – socioeconomic status is an important predictor of young people's use of the internet, with those from more disadvantaged backgrounds more likely to use it for entertainment purposes as opposed to those from more affluent backgrounds who are more likely to exploit its creative and civic potential. Digital exclusion is not just about access to digital technologies and broadband, but is also about having the skills, motivation and confidence to use the internet to make the most of what it has to offer.

For practitioners, promoting digital inclusion is associated with helping young people develop confidence to undertake everyday social, civic and participatory activities, such as connecting with friends and family, finding information for homework, and finding high-quality information on the web. All these skills can contribute to a sense of self-efficacy, along with positive mental health and wellbeing. Digital literacy not just about being able to transact and participate online, it is also about being able to engage with the internet critically – understanding its possibilities along with the downsides. Even those teens who are confident in participating in social networks may be less assured when it comes to seeking information about their mental health, and so there is an important role for practitioners in helping them access information, resources and even peer and professional support.

We are concerned that the fast pace of digital change will have unevenly distributed positive effects and it is those who are most vulnerable who are likely to benefit the least. We would argue that practitioners and mental health services must take into account vulnerability and digital exclusion if they are not to inadvertently compound it. The good news is that national bodies are taking this issue seriously as shown by the work of charities such as The Good Things Foundation and inclusion initiatives developed by national bodies such as NHS England. We hope that digital inclusion will be incorporated into NHS and social care commissioning and embedded within the education curriculum over time.

Developing resilience and knowing your rights in a digital world

Given the range of adverse effects that young people can experience online, it is important that practitioners consider how they can help teens develop online resilience. One way to approach this topic is through a rights-based approach which recognises that young people have a right to express views about their connected lives, a right to participate in the online public sphere, and a right for their basic human rights to be respected both online as well as offline.

We have found that even apparently simple things like Terms and Conditions for use of social media platforms can be opaque and give companies that run them the ability to access and use all sorts of personal data. Nurturing a critical and reflective engagement with digital media is an important life skill for teens which enables them to understand how different interests can dominate the internet and how business interests may take precedence over their individual interests.

Through our conversations with young people, we found that given the information and space to consider these issues, they are often unhappy about how their rights are compromised by internet companies and how their data are used without them fully understanding the extent of tracking and commercialisation. We also found a strong desire for privacy which young people will go to great lengths to protect online. Despite the fact that adults often bemoan young people's supposed lack of care for privacy, we found that it is often those adults who contravene young people's privacy by sharing information about them without their knowledge or permission. Practitioners have an important role in helping parents and carers consider how they can role model good citizenship online and avoid sharing information about their children without their consent.

There are a number of frameworks that practitioners can make use of to promote young people's digital rights and help them develop their online resilience. The 5 Rights framework takes the existing rights of children and young people under 18 according to the United Nations Convention on the Rights of the Child, and articulates them for a digital world. The *Digital 5 A Day* is a simple framework for practitioners to consider how we may help young people develop digital resilience in the face of this complexity.

We anticipate that the theme of digital rights will become an increasingly central issue in the public sphere and that legislators will endeavour to counteract the grip of tech giants on our data. We are becoming increasingly aware that, despite the promise of the internet, what we see online is actually controlled by a small number of companies for whom our data are the product. A whole range of innovators are attempting to devise technologies which enable us to keep the data we generate secure and give us control over how and who we share it with. For example, Tim Berners Lee, the inventor of the world wide web, is creating a platform called Solid[1] which aims to improve privacy and enable people to control the data they produce. We predict that these sorts of initiatives will blossom and that governments will attempt to regulate the big tech companies. Irrespective of legislation, there will be increasing pressure on tech companies to increase transparency in terms of data and to take steps to protect young people from harm.

What services and organisations can do to help

Our conversations with young people elicited a common disconnect between their highly connected lives and their mostly analogue interactions with the groups, services and institutions which are there to support them. As social media are providing important public spaces for young people to congregate, it is important that services as well as practitioners are able to engage appropriately with them. There are opportunities for services to support the digital skills of young people and to enhance or adapt services to meet young people in the online spaces that they occupy.

---

1   https://solid.mit.edu

In our consideration of the implications of the internet for services and organisations, we suggest a strategic approach whereby digital tools are considered an enabler to enhance and improve services in pursuit of wider organisational objectives. There is a danger that services think about digital in isolation, beguiled by the promise of a new mobile app but without a deep understanding of how it will add value to the experience of young people or be adopted in practice. We have seen many digital projects fail when they are progressed in an ad hoc fashion without a strategic plan in place.

Developing the challenges of digital literacy which we set out in Chapter 6, we advocate that services and organisations consider how they can support digital inclusion and eHealth literacy of young people they support. Aligned to this, organisations should take the digital capabilities of their workforce into account and put in place measures to improve staff digital confidence whilst removing infrastructure barriers that get in the way. We suggest that organisations should consider how they can redesign services to take into account digital means of communication, which can often be more acceptable to young people as well as cost effective. Lastly, we believe it is important that services should design (or redesign) services with digital in mind through collaboration and codesign with young people themselves. This orientation builds on our proposition in Chapter 7 that young people have valuable insights and experiences that will enable organisations to develop digitally enabled services that meet their needs and expectations. Aligned to this is the importance of having a strong, clear and relatable web presence, which is an imperative for mental health services targeted at teens. Organisations should take a strategic approach to their web presence in collaboration with teens in order to build trust in their services.

We anticipate that the drive to embed digital within mental health services will increase pace as the mismatch between young people's connected presence and largely analogue services becomes increasingly stark. Commissioners of health and care services are more frequently requiring providers to incorporate digital services and we expect this to accelerate. We hope to see a strategic approach to digital technologies in the future which moves beyond developing or licensing a mobile app towards a whole system orientation. An effective strategic approach to use of digital technologies will be codesigned with young people and will address interrelated aspects of infrastructure, digital skills, digital inclusion and service redesign enabled by technology.

Final thoughts

We hope in this book that we have shown how the internet can be deployed as a resource that can have a positive effect in young people's lives and that this asset-based approach has more promise than simply addressing it as a problem to be solved. Social media, digital tools and the internet provide private and public spaces where young people spend significant amounts of time and new contexts in which the everyday dramas of teenage existence are played out. For teens who are vulnerable, including those with mental health problems, the internet affords great opportunities but also potential harms. Adults, practitioners and organisations can play a hugely valuable role in helping teens navigate these choppy waters.

Recent revelations about opaque and problematic use of data by companies such as Facebook, and implications for us at an individual and societal level, are likely to be growing themes over the coming years. Both civil society and legislators are desperately grappling with complex issues of ethics, governance and regulation. These have implications not just for our use of digital technologies as consumers but also for how mental health services make use of digital technologies and data. Growing public disquiet about social media will inevitably have implications for trust in digital mental health services. Against this backdrop, practitioners have an important role in helping young people make sense of their connected lives and taking a thoughtful approach to how they incorporate digital into their practice.

Whilst the sphere of online social networks is ever shifting, and new digital technologies continue to emerge at an inexorable pace, practitioners can leverage their existing professional skills and apply them to this sphere. Practitioners who are willing to explore this landscape so they can deepen their own understanding, who have an inquiring mindset, and who are willing to act as an ally with young people in a process of shared discovery, can provide help, support and guidance that young people want and need.

References

5Rights (2015) iRights Annual Report. *5 Rights.* Accessed on 20/08/2017 at www.5rights framework.com/static/iRights-The-Legal-Framework-Report-Final-July-2015.pdf.

Ahern, N.R. and Mechling, B. (2013) 'Sexting: Serious problems for youth.' *Journal of Psycho-social Nursing and Mental Health Services 51*, 7, 22–30.

Allen, P. (2015) 'Tackling negative thoughts with distraction.' Accessed on 13/06/2018 at www.mind.org.uk/information-support/your-stories/tackling-negative-thoughts-with-distraction/#.WyEgAfZFzIV.

Ali, K., Farrer, L., Gulliver, A. and Griffiths, K.M. (2015) 'Online peer-to-peer support for young people with mental health problems: A systematic review.' *JMIR Mental Health 2*, 2, 1–9.

Alloway, T., Runac, R., Qureshi, M. and Kemp, G. (2014) 'Is Facebook linked to selfishness? Investigating the relationships among social media use, empathy, and narcissim.' *Social Networking 3*, 150–158.

Barth, F.D. (2015) 'Social media and adolescent development: Hazards, pitfalls and opportunities for growth.' *Clinical Social Work Journal 43*, 2, 201–208.

Bauer, M., Glenn, T., Monteith, S., Bauer, R., Whybrow, P.C. and Geddes, J. (2017) 'Ethical perspectives on recommending digital technology for patients with mental illness.' *International Journal of Bipolar Disorders 5*, 1, 6.

Bell, J. (2014) 'Harmful or helpful? The role of the internet in self-harming and suicidal behaviour in young people.' *Mental Health Review Journal 19*, 1, 61–71.

Berry, N., Lobban, F., Belousov, M., Emsley, R., Nenadic, G. and Bucci, S. (2017) '#WhyWeTweetMH: Understanding why people use twitter to discuss mental health problems.' *Journal of Medical Internet Research 19*, 4, e107.

Bert, F., Gualano, M.R., Camussi, E. and Siliquini, R. (2016) 'Risks and Threats of Social Media Websites: Twitter and the Proana Movement.' *Cyberpsychology, Behavior, and Social Networking 19*, 4. Accessed on 28/08/2018 at www.liebertpub.com/doi/abs/10.1089/cyber.2015.0553.

Best, P., Manktelow, R. and Taylor, B. (2014) 'Online communication, social media and adolescent wellbeing: A systematic narrative review.' *Children and Youth Services Review 41*, 27–36.

Birru, M.S., Monaco, V.M., Charles, L., Drew, H. *et al.* (2004) 'Internet usage by low-literacy adults seeking health information: An observational analysis.' *Journal of Medical Internet Research 6*, 3, 1–12.

Blum-Ross, A. and Livingstone, S. (2017) '"Sharenting," parent blogging, and the boundaries of the digital self.' *Popular Communication 15*, 2110–2125.

Boyd, D. (2010) 'Digital Self-Harm and Other Acts of Self-Harassment.' [Blog post]. Accessed on 28/08/2018 at www.zephoria.org/thoughts/archives/2010/12/07/digital-self-harm-and-other-acts-of-self-harassment.html.

Boyd, D. (2014) *It's Complicated: The Social Life of Networked Teens*. New Haven, CT: Yale University Press.

Brewer, J.A., Worhunsky, P.D., Gray, J.R, Tang, Y., Weber, J. and Kober, H. (2011) 'Meditation experience is associated with differences in default mode network activity and connectivity.' *Proceedings of the National Academy of Sciences 108,* 50, 20254–20259.

Bright, C. (2017) 'Defining child vulnerability: Definitions, frameworks and groups.' Children's Commissioner. Accessed on 22/10/2017 at www.childrenscommissioner.gov.uk/wp-content/uploads/2017/07/CCO-TP2-Defining-Vulnerability-Cordis-Bright-2.pdf.

Briones, R. (2015) 'Harnessing the web: How e-health and e-health literacy impact young adults. Perceptions of online health information.' *Medicine 2.0 4*, 2, 1–13.

Buckner, R.L., Andrews-Hanna, J.R. and Schacter, D. (2008) 'The brain's default network.' *Annals of the New York Academy of Sciences 1124,* 1–38.

Burrow, A.L. and Rainone, N. (2017) 'How many likes did I get?: Purpose moderates links between positive social media feedback and self-esteem.' *Journal of Experimental Social Psychology 69*, 232–236.

Campbell, D. (2017) 'Facebook and Twitter "harm young people's mental health".' *The Guardian*, 19 May. Accessed on 20/05/2017 at www.theguardian.com/society/2017/may/19/popular-social-media-sites-harm-young-peoples-mental-health?CMP=share_btn_fb.

Chassiakos, Y.L.R., Radesky, J., Christakis, D., Moreno, M.A. and Cross, C. (2016) 'Children and adolescents and digital media.' *Pediatrics 138*, 5, e20162593.

Childline (2016) 'It turned out someone did care: Childline Annual Review 2015–16.' Accessed on 22/05/2018 at www.nspcc.org.uk/globalassets/documents/annual-reports/childline-annual-review-2015-16.pdf.

Children's Commissioner (2017) 'Growing up digital: A report of the growing up digital taskforce.' Accessed on 19/08/2017 at www.childrenscommissioner.gov.uk/wp-content/uploads/2017/06/Growing-Up-Digital-Taskforce-Report-January-2017_0.pdf.

Clement, S., Schauman, O., Graham, T., Maggioni, F. *et al.* (2015) 'What is the impact of mental health-related stigma on help-seeking? A systematic review of quantitative and qualitative studies.' *Psychological Medicine 45*, 1, 11–27.

Coleman, S., Pothong, K., Perez Vallejos, E. and Koene, A. (2017) 'The Internet on our own terms: How children and young people deliberated about their digital rights.' *5Rights*. Accessed on 20/08/2017 at http://casma.wp.horizon.ac.uk/wp-content/uploads/2016/08/Internet-On-Our-Own-Terms.pdf.

Common Sense (2016) 'Technology addiction: Concern, controversy and finding balance.' *Common Sense Media Inc.* Accessed on 10/09/2017 at www.commonsensemedia.org/sites/default/files/uploads/research/csm_2016_technology_addiction_research_brief_0.pdf.

Cooper, K., Quayle, E., Jonsson, L. and Svedin, C.G. (2016) 'Adolescents and self-taken sexual images: A review of the literature.' *Computers in Human Behavior 55*, 706–716.

Cowie, H. (2013) 'Cyberbullying and its impact on young people's emotional health and well-being.' *The Psychiatrist 37*, 167–170.

Craig, S.L., McInroy, L.B., McCready, L.T., Di Cesare, D.M. and Pettaway, L.D. (2015) 'Connecting without fear: Clinical implications of the consumption of information and communication technologies by sexual minority youth and young adults.' *Clinical Social Work Journal 43*, 2, 159–168.

Davies, C. (2014) 'Hannah Smith wrote "vile" posts to herself before suicide, say police.' *The Guardian*, 6 May. Accessed on 11/06/2017 at www.theguardian.com/uk-news/2014/may/06/hannah-smith-suicide-teenager-cyber-bullying-inquests.

Davies, T., Wilcox, D. and Farrow, A. (2012) 'The Digital Edge: Using digital technology to support young people.' *Nominet Trust.* Accessed on 14/04/2107 at www.nominettrust.org.uk/wp-content/uploads/2017/11/The-Digital-Edge_updated_31.07.pdf.

Davis, H. (2017) 'How and why is children's digital data being harvested?' The policy and internet blog. University of Oxford. Accessed on 12/06/2017 at www.blogs.oii.ox.ac.uk/policy/how-and-why-is-childrens-digital-data-being-harvested.

Ditch the Label (2017) 'In game abuse: The extent and nature of online bullying within digital gaming environments.' Accessed on 19/08/2017 at www.ditchthelabel.org/wp-content/uploads/2017/05/InGameAbuse.pdf.

Diviani, N., Putte, B., Giani, S. and Weert, J.C.M. (2015) 'Low health literacy and evaluation of online health information: A systematic review of the literature.' *Journal of Medical Internet Research 17*, 5.

Druin, A. (2002) 'The role of children in the design of new technology.' *Behaviour and Information Technology 21*, 1, 1–25.

Dyson, M.P., Hartling, L., Shulhan, J., Chisholm, A. *et al.* (2016) 'A systematic review of social media use to discuss and view deliberate self-harm acts.' *PLoS one 11*, 5, e0155813.

East, M.L. and Havard, B.C. (2015) 'Mental health mobile apps: From infusion to diffusion in the mental health social system.' *JMIR Mental Health 2*, 1, 1–14.

Eloise, M. (2017) 'How to do Instagram right according to 15 year olds.' *Dazed*. Accessed on 13/08/2017 at www.dazeddigital.com/artsandculture/article/37029/1/how-to-do-instagram-right-according-to-teenagers.

Ellis, L.A., Collin, P., Davenport, T.A., Hurley, P.J., Burns, J.M. and Hickie, I.B. (2012) 'Young men, mental health, and technology: Implications for service design and delivery in the digital age.' *Journal of Medical Internet Research 14*, 6, e16.

Englander, E. (2012) 'Digital self-harm: Frequency, type, motivations, and outcomes.' Massachusetts Aggression Reduction Center. Accessed on 11/06/2017 at http://webhost.bridgew.edu/marc/DIGITAL%20SELF%20HARM%20report.pdf.

EU Kids Online project (2014) 'EU Kids Online project: Findings. Method. Recommendations.' Accessed on 13/06/2018 at https://lsedesignunit.com/EUKids Online/index.html?r=64.

Farrugia, L., Grehan, S. and O'Neill, B. (2017) Webwise 2017 Parenting Survey. Accessed on 13/06/2018 at www.webwise.ie/news/webwise-2017-parenting-survey.

Firth, J. and Torous, J. (2015) 'Smartphone apps for schizophrenia: A systematic review.' *JMIR Mhealth Uhealth 3*, 4, e102.

Fitzpatrick, K.K., Darcy, A. and Vierhile, M. (2017) 'Delivering cognitive behavior therapy to young adults with symptoms of depression and anxiety using a fully automated conversational agent (woebot): A randomized controlled trial.' *JMIR Mental Health 4*, 2, e19.

Frith, E. (2017) 'Social media and mental health: A review of the evidence.' Education Policy Institute.

Fuchs, C, (2017) *Social Media: A Critical Introduction.* London: Sage.

Gabriel, F. (2014) 'Sexting, selfies and self-harm: Young people, social media and the performance of self-development.' *Media International Australia 151*, 1, 104–112.

Gilbody, S. (2017) 'Should Google offer an online screening test for depression?' *BMJ.* Accessed on 13/06/2018 at www.bmj.com/content/358/bmj.j4144.

Görzig, A. (2016) 'Adolescents' viewing of suicide-related web content and psychological problems: Differentiating the roles of cyberbullying involvement.' *Cyberpsychology, Behavior, and Social Networking 19*, 8, 502–509.

Grant, S. and Lappin, J. (2017) 'Childhood trauma: Psychiatry's greatest public health challenge?' *The Lancet Public Health 2*, 7, e300–e301.

Gray, N.J., Klein, J.D., Noyce, P.R., Sesselberg, T.S. and Cantrill, J.A. (2005) 'Health information-seeking behaviour in adolescence: The place of the internet.' *Social Science and Medicine 60*, 7, 1467–1478.

Griffiths, F., Bryce, C., Cave, J., Dritsaki, M. *et al.* (2017) 'Timely digital patient-clinician communication in specialist clinical services for young people: A mixed-methods study (The LYNC Study).' *Journal of Medical Internet Research 19*, 4, e102.

Griffiths, M. (2009) 'A "components" model of addiction within a biopsycho-social framework.' *Journal of Substance Use 10*, 4, 191–197.

Grist, R., Porter, J. and Stallard, P. (2017) 'Mental health mobile apps for preadolescents and adolescents: A systematic review.' *Journal of Medical Internet Research 19*, 5, e176.

Gulliver, A., Griffiths, K.M. and Christensen, H. (2010) 'Perceived barriers and facilitators to mental health help-seeking in young people: A systematic review.' *BMC Psychiatry 10*, 1, 113.

Hansen, E. and Holmes, D. (2014) 'That difficult age: Developing a more effective response to risks in adolescence. Research in Practice.' Accessed on 22/05/2018 at http://cdn.basw.co.uk/upload/basw_24144-4.pdf.

Hargittai, E. (2010) 'Digital na(t)ives? Variation in internet skills and uses among members of the "net generation".' *Sociological Inquiry 80*, 1, 92–113.

Hargittai, E., Schultz, J. and Palfrey, J. (2011) 'Why parents help their children lie to Facebook about age: Unintended consequences of the "Children's Online Privacy Protection Act".' *First Monday 16*, 11.

Harvey, C. (2016) 'Using ICT, digital and social media in youth work: A review of research findings from Austria, Denmark, Finland, Northern Ireland and the Republic of Ireland.' National Youth Council of Ireland. Accessed on 22/10/2017 at www.youth.ie/sites/youth.ie/files/International%20report%20final.pdf.

Helsper, E.J. and Eynon, R. (2010) 'Digital natives: Where is the evidence?' *British Educational Research Journal 36*, 3, 503–520.

HM Government (2014) 'Personalised health and care 2020.' Accessed on 13/06/2018 at www.gov.uk/government/publications/personalised-health-and-care-2020.

Holland, G. and Tiggemann, M. (2016) 'A systematic review of the impact of the use of social networking sites and body image and disordered eating outcomes.' *Body Image 17*, 100–110.

Hollis, C., Falconer, C.J., Martin, J.L., Whittington, C. *et al.* (2017) 'Annual research review: Digital health interventions for children and young people with mental health problems – a systematic and meta-review.' *Journal of Child Psychology and Psychiatry 58*, 474–503.

House of Lords (2017) 2nd Report of Session 2016–17 HL. 'Growing up with the internet.' Published by the Authority of the House of Lords. Accessed on 22/10/2017 at https://publications.parliament.uk/pa/ld201617/ldselect/ldcomuni/130/130.pdf.

Ito, M., Gutiérrez, K., Livingstone, S., Penuel, B. *et al.* (2013) *Connected Learning: An Agenda for Research and Design. BookBaby.* http://eprints.lse.ac.uk/48114/1/__lse.ac.uk_storage_LIBRARY_Secondary_libfile_shared_repository_Content_Livingstone%2C%20S_Livingstone_Connected_learning_agenda_2010_Livingstone_Connected_learning_agenda_2013.pdf.

Jenkins, H., Ito, M. and Boyd, D. (2017) *Participatory Culture in a Networked Era.* Cambridge: Polity Press.

Jones, R., Sharkey, S., Ford, T., Emmens, T. *et al.* (2011) 'Online discussion forums for young people who self-harm: User views.' *The Psychiatrist Online 35*, 10, 364–368.

Ketting, E. and Winkelmann, C. (2013) 'New approaches to sexuality education and underlying paradigms.' *Bundesgesundheitsblatt-Gesundheitsforschung-Gesundheitsschutz 56*, 2, 250–255.

Klonsky, E.D., Glenn, C.R., Styer, D.M., Olino, T.M. and Washburn, J.J. (2015) 'The functions of nonsuicidal self-injury: Converging evidence for a two-factor structure.' *Child and Adolescent Psychiatry and Mental Health 9*, 1, 44.

Lal, S., Dell'Elce, J., Tucci, N., Fuhrer, R., Tamblyn, R. and Malla, A. (2015) 'Preferences of young adults with first-episode psychosis for receiving specialized mental health services using technology: A survey study.' *JMIR Mental Health 2*, 2.

Lenhart, A., Malato, D., Kantor, L., Benz, J., Tompson, T. and Zeng, W. (2016) 'American Teens Are Taking Breaks from Social Media; Some Step Back Deliberately, but Other Breaks Are Involuntary.' Associated Press NORC Center for Public Affairs Research. Accessed on 30/05/2017 at www.apnorc.org/projects/Pages/HTML%20Reports/american-teens-are-taking-breaks-from-social-media.aspx.

Licoppe, C. (2004) 'Connected presence: The emergence of a new repertoire for managing social relationships in a changing communication technoscape.' *Environment and Planning D: Society and space 22*, 1, 135–156.

Livingstone, S. (2014) 'Children's digital rights: A priority.' *Intermedia 42*, 4/5, 20–24.

Livingstone, S. (2016) 'A day in the digital life of teenagers.' [Blog post.] Accessed on 15/04/2017 at http://blogs.lse.ac.uk/parenting4digitalfuture/2016/06/09/a-day-in-the-digital-life-of-teenagers.

Livingstone, S., Davidson, J., Bryce, J., Batook, S., Haughton, C. and Nandi, A. (2017) 'Children's online activities, risks and safety: A literature review by the UKCCIS Evidence Group.' LSE Consulting London School of Economics and Political Science. Accessed on 22/10/2017 at https://assets.publishing.service.gov.uk/government/uploads/system/uploads/attachment_data/file/650933/Literature_Review_Final_October_2017.pdf.

Livingstone, S. and Mason, J. (2015) 'Sexual rights and sexual risks among youth online.' London: ENASCO. Accessed on 13/08/2017 at http://eprints.lse.ac.uk/64567/1/Livingstone_Review_on_Sexual_rights_and_sexual_risks_among_online_youth_Author_2015.pdf.

Livingstone, S., Ólafsson, K., Helsper, E.J., Lupiáñez-Villanueva, F., Veltri, G.A. and Folkvord, F. (2017) 'Maximizing opportunities and minimizing risks for children online: The role of digital skills in emerging strategies of parental mediation.' *Journal of Communication 67*, 82–105.

Livingstone, T. and Palmer, T. (2012) 'Identifying vulnerable children online and what strategies can help them.' UK Safer Internet Centre, London, UK. Accessed on 23/10/2017 at http://eprints.lse.ac.uk/44222/1/__Libfile_repository_Content_Livingstone%2C%20S_Identifying%20vulnerable%20children%20online%20and%20what%20strategies%20can%20help%20them%20%28LSE%20RO%29.pdf.

Livingstone, S. and Sefton-Green, J. (2016) *The Class: Living and Learning in the Digital Age*. New York: New York University Press. Accessed on 21/08/2017 at http://connectedyouth.nyupress.org/book/9781479824243/.

Livingstone, S. *et al.* (n.d.) 'Children's online activities: Risk and safety.' UK Council for Child Internet Safety. Accessed on 02/04/2017 at https://d1afx9quaogywf.cloudfront.net/cdn/farfuture/MVJMgRIFvDnOXPbrsozW8k_W3a1dXSxExQBQQfQ_TgI/mtime:1484143478/sites/default/files/UKCCIS%20Evidence%20Group/UKCCIS%20Evidence%20Group%20%282012%29%20Review%20of%20the%20Evidence%20Base.pdf.

Lupton, D. and Williamson, B. (2017) 'The datafied child: The dataveillance of children and implications for their rights.' *New Media and Society 19*, 5, 780–794.

Marwick, A.E. and Boyd, D. (2014) 'Networked privacy: How teenagers negotiate context in social media.' *New Media and Society 16*, 7, 1051–1067.

Mascheroni, G. and Ólafsson, K. (2014) *Net Children Go Mobile: Risks and Opportunities*. Milan: Educatt.

Martellozzo, E., Monaghan, A., Adler, J., Davidson, J., Leyva, R. and Horvath, M.A.H. (2017) 'I wasn't sure if it was normal to watch it: A quantitative and qualitative examination of the impact of online pornography on the values, attitudes, beliefs and behaviours of children and young people.' Accessed on 22/05/2-18 at www.nspcc.org.uk/services-and-resources/research-and-resources/2016/i-wasnt-sure-it-was-normal-to-watch-it.

McLean, S.A., Wertheim, E.H., Masters, J. and Paxton, S.J. (2017) 'A pilot evaluation of a social media literacy intervention to reduce risk factors for eating disorders.' *International Journal of Eating Disorders 50*, 7, 847–851.

McLean, S.A., Paxton, S.J., Wertheim, E.H. and Masters, J. (2015) 'Photoshopping the selfie: Self photo editing and photo investment are associated with body dissatisfaction in adolescent girls.' *International Journal of Eating Disorders 48*, 8, 1132–1140.

McDool, E., Powell, P., Roberts, J. and Taylor, K. (2016) 'Social media use and children's wellbeing.' Accessed on 22/05/2018 at www.sheffield.ac.uk/polopoly_fs/1.669622!/file/paper_2016011.pdf.

Mind (2017) 'Cognitive Behavioural Therapy.' Accessed on 13/06/2018 at www.mind.org.uk/information-support/drugs-and-treatments/cognitive-behavioural-therapy-cbt/about-cbt/#.WxuZwzQvzIU.

Miner, A.S., Milstein, A. and Hancock, J.T. (2017) 'Talking to machines about personal mental health problems.' *JAMA.* Accessed on 22/05/2018 at http://jamanetwork.com/journals/jama/fullarticle/2654784?utm_content=buffer9429e&utm_medium=social&utm_source=twitter.com&utm_campaign=buffer.

Mohr, D.C., Zhang, M. and Schueller, S.M. (2017) 'Personal sensing: Understanding mental health using ubiquitous sensors and machine learning.' *Annual Review of Clinical Psychology 13*, 23–47.

Murphy, M. and Fonagy, P. (2012) 'Mental health problems in children and young people.' In *Annual Report of the Chief Medical Officer 2012.* London: Department of Health.

Neter, E. and Brainin, E. (2012) 'eHealth literacy: Extending the digital divide to the realm of health information.' *Journal of Medical Internet Research 14*, 1, 1–10.

NHS England (2015) Future In Mind. Accessed on 03/04/2017 at www.gov.uk/government/uploads/system/uploads/attachment_data/file/414024/Childrens_Mental_Health.pdf.

Nock, M.K. (2010) 'Self injury.' *Annual Review of Clinical Psychology 6, 1*, 339–363.

Nodder, C. (2013) *Evil by Design: Interaction Design to Lead Us into Temptation.* New York: John Wiley and Sons.

Nominet Trust (2017) 'Digital Reach: Digital skills for the hardest-to-reach young people.' *Nominet.* Accessed on 08/07/2017 at https://docs.google.com/document/d/1HBRmt27t4o9XPeOhdnqy2WsM-uYfVi6sYnb5wEuYs_E/edit#.

OECD (2015) *Students, Computers and Learning: Making the Connection.* Paris: OECD Publishing.

OECD (2017) *Pisa 2015 Results (Volume III): Students' well-being.* Paris: OECD Publishing.

Ofcom (2016a) 'Children's media lives – Year 3 findings.' November 2016. Accessed on 03/04/2017 at www.ofcom.org.uk/__data/assets/pdf_file/0015/94002/Childrens-Media-Lives-Year-3-report.pdf.

Ofcom (2016b) 'Children and parents: Media use and attitudes report.' Accessed on 02/04/2017 at www.ofcom.org.uk/__data/assets/pdf_file/0034/93976/Children-Parents-Media-Use-Attitudes-Report-2016.pdf.

Ofcom (2017) 'Children and parents: Media use and attitudes report.' Accessed on 14/04/2018 at www.ofcom.org.uk/__data/assets/pdf_file/0020/108182/children-parents-media-use-attitudes-2017.pdf.

Office for National Statistics (2015) 'Measuring national well-being: Insights into children's mental health and well-being.' Accessed on 22/05/2018 at www.ons. gov.uk/peoplepopulationandcommunity/wellbeing/articles/measuringnational wellbeing/2015-10-20.

Peter, J. and Valkenburg, P.M. (2006) 'Adolescents' exposure to sexually explicit material on the Internet.' *Communication Research 33*, 2, 178–204.

Peter, J. and Valkenburg, P.M. (2006a) 'Adolescents' internet use: Testing the "disappearing digital divide" versus the "emerging digital differentiation" approach.' *Poetics 34*, 4–5, 293–305.

Plummer, L. (2017) 'The best bots you can use on Facebook Messenger.' *Wired Magazine.* Accessed on 12/08/2017 at www.wired.co.uk/article/chatbot-list-2017.

Prensky, M. (2001) 'Digital natives, digital immigrants part 1.' *On the Horizon 9*, 5, 1–6.

Prescott, J., Hanley, T. and Ujhelyi, K. (2017) 'Peer communication in online mental health forums for young people: Directional and nondirectional support.' *JMIR Mental Health 4*, 3, e29.

Przybylski, A.K. and Nash, V. (2017) 'Internet filtering technology and aversive online experiences in adolescents.' *The Journal of Pediatrics 184*, 215–219.

PwC (2015) 'The Price of Eating Disorders: Social, health and economic impacts.' Price Waterhouse Coopers. Accessed on 08/07/2017 at www.pwc.co.uk/services/ economics-policy/insights/the-costs-of-eating-disorders-social-health-and-economic-impacts.html.

Rafla, M., Carson, N.J. and DeJong, S.M. (2014) 'Adolescents and the internet: What mental health clinicians need to know.' *Current Psychiatry Reports 16*, 9, 1–10.

Rheingold, H. (2012) *Net Smart – How to Thrive Online.* Cambridge, MA: The MIT Press.

Rickwood, D., Webb, M., Kennedy, V. and Telford, N. (2016) 'Who are the young people choosing web-based mental health support? Findings from the implementation of Australia's national web-based youth mental health service, eheadspace.' *JMIR Mental Health 3*, 3, 1–11.

Robinson, K.H., Bansel, P., Denson, N., Ovenden, G. and Davies, C. (2014) 'Growing up queer: Issues facing young Australians who are gender variant and sexuality diverse.' Accessed on 20/08/2017 at www.glhv.org.au/report/growing-queer-issues-facing-young-australians-who-are-gender-variant-and-sexuality-diverse.

Seabrook, E.M., Kern, M.L. and Rickard, N.S. (2016) 'Social networking sites, depression, and anxiety: A systematic review.' *JMIR Mental Health 3*, 4, e50.

Seko, Y., Kidd, S.A., Wiljer, D., and McKenzie, K.J. (2015) 'On the creative edge: Exploring motivations for creating non-suicidal self-injury content online.' *Qualitative Health Research 25,* 10.

Schenk, A.M. and Fremouw, W.J. (2012) 'Prevalence, psychological impact, and coping of cyberbully victims among college students.' *Journal of School Violence 11*, 1, 21–37.

Schueller, S.M., Washburn, J.J. and Price, M. (2016) 'Exploring mental health providers' interest in using web and mobile-based tools in their practices.' *Internet Interventions 4*, 145–151.

Schulz, P.J., Fitzpatrick, M.A., Hess, A., Sudbury-Riley, L. and Hartung, U. (2017) 'Effects of eHealth literacy on general practitioner consultations: A mediation analysis.' *Journal of Medical Internet Research 19*, 5,1–12.

Seabrook, E.M., Kern, M.L. and Rickard, N.S. (2016) 'Social networking sites, depression, and anxiety: A systematic review.' *JMIR Mental Health 3*, 4.

Sherman, L.E., Rudie, J.D., Pfeifer, J.H., McNealy, K., Masten, C.L. and Dapretto, M. (2014) 'Development of the default mode and central executive networks across early adolescence: A longitudinal study.' *Developmental Cognitive Neuroscience 10*, 148–159.

Sherman, L.E., Payton, A.A., Hernandez, L.M., Greenfield, P.M. and Dapretto, M. (2016) 'The power of the "like" in adolescence: Effects of peer influence on neural and behavioral responses to social media.' *Psychological Science 27,* 1027–1035.

Sherman, L.E., Greenfield, P.M., Hernandez, L.M., and Dapretto, M. (2018) 'Peer influence via Instagram: Effects on brain and behavior in adolescence and young adulthood.' *Child Development 89, 37–47.*

Smith, L.W., Liu, B., Degenhardt, L., Richters, J. *et al.* (2016) 'Is sexual content in new media linked to sexual risk behaviour in young people? A systematic review and meta-analysis.' *Sexual Health 13*, 6, 501–515.

Taylor, V.A., Daneault, V., Grant, J., Scavone, G. *et al.* (2013) 'Impact of meditation training on the default mode network during a restful state.' *Social Cognitive and Affective Neuroscience 8*, 1, 4–14.

Tech Partnership (2015) 'Get digital basic skills framework. Go ON UK.' Accessed on 17/06/2017 at www.thetechpartnership.com/globalassets/pdfs/basic-digital-skills-standards/basic_digital_skills_framework.pdf.

Teufel, M., Hofer, E., Junne, F., Sauer, H., Zipfel, S. and Giel, K.E. (2013) 'A comparative analysis of anorexia nervosa groups on Facebook.' *Eating and Weight Disorders – Studies on Anorexia, Bulimia and Obesity 18*, 4, 413–420.

The Parent Zone (2014) 'A shared responsibility building children's online resilience.' An independent research paper commissioned and supported by Virgin Media and The Parent Zone. Accessed on 22/08/2017 at https://parentzone.org.uk/sites/default/files/VM%20Resilience%20Report.pdf.

Third, A., Bellerose, D., Dawkins, U., Keltie, E. and Pihl, K. (2014) 'Children's rights in the digital age: A download from children around the world.' Young and Well Cooperative Research Centre, Melbourne. Accessed on 20/08/2017 at www.unicef.org/publications/files/Childrens_Rights_in_the_Digital_Age_A_Download_from_Children_Around_the_World_FINAL.pdf.

Tierney, S. (2007) 'The dangers and draw of online communication: Pro-anorexia websites and their implications for users, practitioners, and researchers.' *Eating Disorders 14*, 3, 181–190.

Tierney, S. (2008) 'Creating communities in cyberspace: Pro-anorexia web sites and social capital.' *Journal of Psychiatric and Mental Health Nursing 15*, 4, 340–343.

Tiggemann, M. and Slater, A. (2013) 'NetGirls: The Internet, Facebook, and body image concern in adolescent girls.' *International Journal of Eating Disorders 46*, 6, 630–633.

Twenge, J. (2017) 'Have smartphones destroyed a generation?' *The Atlantic.* Accessed on 13/06/2018 at www.theatlantic.com/magazine/archive/2017/09/has-the-smartphone-destroyed-a-generation/534198.

UKCCIS (2016) 'Child safety online: A practical guide for providers of social media and interactive services.' Accessed on 23/10/2017 at www.gov.uk/government/uploads/system/uploads/attachment_data/file/517335/UKCCIS_Child_Safety_Online-Mar2016.pdf.

UK Safer Internet Centre (2016) 'Creating a better internet for all: Young people's experiences of online empowerment and online hate.' Accessed on 23/10/2017 at www.saferinternet.org.uk/safer-internet-day/2017/power-of-image-report.

UK Safer Internet Centre (2017) 'Power of image: A report into the influence of images and videos in young people's digital lives.' Accessed on 19/08/2017 at https://d1afx9quaogywf.cloudfront.net/sites/default/files/Safer%20Internet%20Day%202017/Power%20of%20Image%20-%20a%20report%20into%20the%20influence%20of%20images%20and%20videos%20in%20young%20people%27s%20digital%20lives.pdf.

Valkenburg, P.M. and Peter, J. (2007) 'Preadolescents' and adolescents' online communication and their closeness to friends.' *Developmental Psychology 43*, 2, 267–277.

Valkenburg, P.M. and Peter, J. (2008) 'Adolescents' identity experiments on the Internet: Consequences for social competence and self-concept unity.' *Communication Research 35*, 2, 208–231.

Valkenburg, P.M. and Peter, J. (2009) 'Social consequences of the Internet for adolescents: A decade of research.' *Current Directions in Psychological Science 18*, 1, 1–5.

Valkenburg, P.M. and Peter, S. (2011) 'Online communication among adolescents: An integrated model of its attraction, opportunities, and risks.' *Journal of Adolescent Health 48*, 121–127.

van den Eijnden, R.J.J.M., Meerkerk, G.J., Vermulst, A.A., Spijkerman, R.E. and Engels, R.C.M.E. (2008) 'Online communication, compulsive Internet use, and psycho-social wellbeing among adolescents: A longitudinal study.' *Developmental Psychology 44*, 3, 655–665.

Van Doorn, N. (2011) 'Digital spaces, material traces: How matter comes to matter in online performances of gender, sexuality and embodiment.' *Media, Culture and Society 33*, 4, 531–547.

Wentzel, J., van der Vaart, R., Bohlmeijer, E.T. and van Gemert-Pijnen, J.E. (2016) 'Mixing online and face-to-face therapy: How to benefit from blended care in mental health care.' *JMIR Mental Health 3*, 1, 1–7.

Wilson, G. and Grant, A. (2017) '#NotWithoutMe: A digital world for all?' Carnegie UK Trust. Accessed on 22/09/2017 at www.carnegieuktrust.org.uk/publications/digitalworld.

Wood, M.A., Bukowski, W.M. and Lis, E. (2015) 'The digital self: How social media serves as a setting that shapes youth's emotional experiences.' *Adolescent Research Review 1*, 2, 163–173.

World Health Organisation (2018) 'The ICD-11 International Classification of Diseases: The global standard for diagnostic health information.' Geneva: World Health Organization. Draft accessed on 28/08/2018 at https://icd.who.int/browse11/l-m/en.

Wozney, L., Huguet, A., Bennett, K., Radomski, A.D. *et al.*(2017) 'How do eHealth programs for adolescents with depression work? A realist review of persuasive system design components in internet-based psychological therapies.' *Journal of Medical Internet Research 19*, 8, e266.

Yardi, S. and Bruckman, A. (2011) 'Social and technical challenges in parenting teens' social media use.' In *Proceedings of the SIGCHI Conference on Human Factors in Computing Systems* (3237–3246). ACM. Accessed on 13/06/2018 at www. researchgate.net/publication/221516194_Social_and_technical_challenges_in_ parenting_teens%27_social_media_use.

Yarosh, S. and Schueller, S.M. (2017) '"Happiness inventors": Informing positive computing technologies through participatory design with children.' *Journal of Medical Internet Research 19*, 1, e14.

Yates, S. (2017) 'The real digital divide. Understanding the demographics of non-users and limited users of the internet: An analysis of Ofcom data.' The Good Things Foundation. Accessed on 22/05/2018 at www.goodthingsfoundation.org/sites/ default/files/research-publications/ofcom_report_v4_links.pdf.

Ybarra, M.L. and Mitchell, K.J. (2005) 'Exposure to Internet pornography among children and adolescents: A national survey.' *Cyberpsychology and Behavior 8*, 5, 473–486.

Ye, X., Bapuji, S.B., Winters, S.E., Struthers, A. *et al.* (2014) 'Effectiveness of internet-based interventions for children, youth, and young adults with anxiety and/or depression: A systematic review and meta-analysis.' *BMC Health Services Research 14*, 1, 313.

Young Minds (2016) 'Resilience for the digital world.' Accessed on 22/08/2017 at https://youngminds.org.uk/media/1490/resilience_for_the_digital_world.pdf.

Youth Justice Board (2012) 'Preventing religious radicalisation and violent extremism: A systematic review of the research evidence.' Accessed on 23/10/2017 at www. gov.uk/government/uploads/system/uploads/attachment_data/file/396030/ preventing-violent-extremism-systematic-review.pdf.

Further reading

Bert, F., Gualano, M.R., Camussi, E. and Siliquini, R. (2016) 'Risks and threats of social media websites: Twitter and the proana movement.' *Cyberpsychology, Behavior, and Social Networking, 19*, 4, 233–238

Better Internet for Kids (2017) 'The General Data Protection Regulation and children's rights: Questions and answers for legislators, DPAs, industry, education, stakeholders and civil society. Roundtable Report.' Accessed on 22/08/2017at www.betterinternetforkids.eu/documents/167024/2013511/GDPRRoundtable_June2017_FullReport.pdf/e6998eb6-ba3c-4b5d-a2a6-145e2af594f2.

Ebert, D.D., Cuijpers, P., Muñoz, R.F. and Baumeister, H. (2017) 'Prevention of mental health disorders using internet and mobile-based interventions: A narrative review and recommendations for future research.' *Frontiers in Psychiatry 8*, 116.

Hansen, D.L., Derry, H.A., Resnick, P.J. and Richardson, C.R. (2003) 'Adolescents searching for health information on the Internet: An observational study.' *Journal of Medical Internet Research 5*, 4, 1–10.

Harvey, C. (2016) 'Screenagers: Guidance for digital youth work.' National Youth Council of Ireland. Accessed on 22/10/2017 at www.youth.ie/sites/youth.ie/files/Screenagers-Guidance.pdf.

Jones, P. (2013) 'Adult mental health disorders and their age at onset.' *The British Journal of Psychiatry 202*, s54, s5–s10.

Kaplan, A.M. and Haenlein, M. (2010) 'Users of the world, unite! The challenges and opportunities of social media.' *Business Horizons 53*, 1, 59–68.

Libert, T. (2015) 'Privacy implications of health information seeking on the web.' *Communications of the ACM 58*, 3, 68–77.

Livingstone, S. (2015) 'The social network.' *LSE Connect.* Summer, 14–15.

Madden, M., Lenhart, A., Cortesi, S., Gasser, U., Duggan, M., Smith, A. and Beaton, M. (2013) 'Teens, social media, and privacy.' *Pew Research Center 21*, 2–86.

Majeed-Ariss, R., Baildam, E., Campbell, M., Chieng, A. *et al.* (2015) 'Apps and adolescents: A systematic review of adolescents' use of mobile phone and tablet apps that support personal management of their chronic or long-term physical conditions.' *Journal of Medical Internet Research 17*, 12, e287.

Ofcom (2016) 'Children's digital day.' Accessed on 03/04/2017 at www.ofcom.org. uk/__data/assets/pdf_file/0017/94013/Childrens-Digital-Day-report-2016.pdf.

Park, M., Sun, Y. and McLaughlin, M.L. (2017) 'Social media propagation of content promoting risky health behavior.' *Cyberpsychology, Behavior, and Social Networking 20*, 5, 278–285.

Punamäki, R.L., Wallenius, M., Nygård, C.H., Saarni, L. and Rimpelä, A. (2007) 'Use of information and communication technology (ICT) and perceived health in adolescence: The role of sleeping habits and waking-time tiredness.' *Journal of Adolescence 30*, 4, 569–585.

Sabatini, F. and Sarracino, F. (2015) 'Keeping up with the e-Joneses: Do online social networks raise social comparisons?' Munich Personal RePEc Archive 69201.

Seo, H., Houston, J.B., Knight, L.A.T., Kennedy, E.J. and Inglish, A.B. (2014) 'Teens' social media use and collective action.' *New Media and Society 16*, 6, 883–902.

Shaw, J.M., Mitchell, C.A., Welch, A.J. and Williamson, M.J. (2015) 'Social media used as a health intervention in adolescent health: A systematic review of the literature.' *Digital Health*, 1. Accessed on 22/05/2018 at http://journals.sagepub.com/doi/full/10.1177/2055207615588395.

Tiggemann, M. and Slater, A. (2017) 'Facebook and body image concern in adolescent girls: A prospective study.' *International Journal of Eating Disorders 50*, 1, 80–83.

Turner, P.G. and Lefevre, C.E. (2017) 'Instagram use is linked to increased symptoms of orthorexia nervosa.' *Eating and Weight Disorders 22*, 2, 277.

Unicef (2014) *Facts for Life*. 4th Edition. New York: United Nations Children's Fund, New York. Accessed on 06/04/2017 at www.factsforlifeglobal.org/resources/factsforlife-en-full.pdf.

Van Geel, M., Vedder, P. and Tanilon, J. (2014) 'Relationship between peer victimization, cyberbullying, and suicide in children and adolescents: A meta-analysis.' *JAMA Pediatrics 168*, 5, 435–442.

Van Ouytsel, J., Van Gool, E., Walrave, M., Ponnet, K. and Peeters, E. (2016) 'Exploring the role of social networking sites within adolescent romantic relationships and dating experiences.' *Computers in Human Behavior 55*, 76–86.

Wachter, R. (2016) 'Making IT work: Harnessing the power of health information technology to improve care in England.' London, UK: Department of Health. www.gov.uk/government/publications/using-information-technology-to-improve-the-nhs.

Whitlock, J.L., Powers, J.L. and Eckenrode, J. (2006) 'The virtual cutting edge: The internet and adolescent self-injury.' *Developmental Psychology 42*, 3, 407.

About the authors

Victoria is a social worker by training and has worked in the mental health sphere for over 20 years in a variety of delivery, policy and innovation roles. She is a parent to three teenagers and is endlessly fascinated by their use of digital technologies and frequently attempts (and often fails) to have conversations with them about their use of the internet. She is founder and managing director of mHabitat, an NHS hosted organisation specialising in codesign in digital health; and Co>Space North, a collaboration and co-working space in the centre of Leeds. Her PhD research was an online ethnography of the blogosphere in which people accessing and working in mental health services came together to discuss topical issues related to mental health. Victoria and her Pets As Therapy dog Bibi are regular volunteers on mental health inpatient wards in Leeds.

James is a consultant child and adolescent psychiatrist, a specialist in assessing and managing mental health problems in young people. He has been interested in the relationship between technology and the internet with our mental health since writing a paper on the subject as a student in 2004. He continues to see this complex relationship play out in his clinical work: whilst his team develop online interventions to support families, in clinic a 7-year-old shows him a seemingly real video of a man being eaten by a crocodile on their parent's mobile phone. Alongside his clinical work, James is also currently the Senior Fellow for Mental Health Technology at NHS England, the lead commissioner for health services in England. In this role, he works with colleagues across the system to harness the benefits and manage the risks of technology in mental health care.

Between us we bring a bio-psycho-social approach to the topic of this book and draw on a number of different disciplines from the social sciences to neuroscience, and design thinking to appreciative inquiry. In 2014, Victoria and James promoted health care professionals having everyday conversations about technology with people who use their services through a pledge campaign for NHS Change Day using the Twitter hashtag #NHStalktech. We continue to believe that open-minded curiosity about how technology can positively and negatively impact our lives is key.

Index